Meet Me In The Badlands
Exploring Central Oregon with Jim Witty

Introduction by Rick Steber

Outing articles reprinted with permission from *The Bulletin,* Bend, Oregon. All rights reserved. No part of this publication may be reproduced or transmitted in any form or by any means, electronic or mechanical, without written permission from the publisher and *The Bulletin.*

Meet Me In The Badlands: Exploring Central Oregon with Jim Witty
COPYRIGHT©2009 by Family and Friends of Jim Witty

ISBN 978-0-615-32645-0

Privately published in 2009 by Family and Friends of Jim Witty

The Book Team:
Lori Witty
Edna Witty
Joan Witty
John Witty
Deedee (Witty) Sihvonen
Alan Sihvonen
Linda Quon
Mark Quon

Design by Mark Quon
Quon Design + Communications
(541)617-1911
www.quondc.com

Cover photographs of Oregon Badlands Wilderness by Greg Burke
http://www.pbase.com/gb_photo/root
gosolar@bendtel.net

Photos that appear in this book are not necessarily the same photos that were featured at the time of original publication. Special thanks to all photographers who donated their beautiful photos.

Illustrations by Gretchen Lawrence
gcl@atcnet.net

Maps by Greg Cross

For information regarding editorial, marketing sales and distribution, call (541) 617-1911.
All proceeds from book sales go to The Jim Witty Memorial Fund.

Printed in the United States by Maverick Publications
Bend, Oregon

"For those of us who savor sagebrush, juniper and pines, Central Oregon offers a succession of pinch-me-I-must-be-dreaming moments.

These giddy realizations strike when you're standing shin-deep in meadow grass on a cloudless morning or tracing imaginary routes in your mind up a very real South Sister from a lesser ridge top over a trailside lunch.

String enough of these together and you're liable to end up with a life well-spent."

Jim Witty
1958 - 2008

"Jim Witty loved to play and his zest for the outdoors, and for life, is clearly evident in his writing. *Meet Me In The Badlands: Exploring Central Oregon with Jim Witty* is the perfect book for all readers who enjoy a well-told story and have a hankering to get out and discover new territory in and around Central Oregon."

Rick Steber
Award-winning author

"Those who love words and wild places will welcome this collection of 'Wittycisms' from the late Jim Witty. His passion for rugged country connects through the magic of the printed page.

Sometimes a writer comes along who elevates the consciousness of his community and takes the reader along like a trusted guide, a personal friend. Jim Witty's words and adventures are authentic – his prose stands as timeless as the desert and the mountains."

Gary Lewis
Author and host of Gary Lewis' High Desert Outdoorsman

"As a great admirer of Oregon's high desert, Jim provides a voice for the area's intricate and subtle beauty. From gnarled, old-growth juniper to verdant, desert streams, this book will leave you with a greater appreciation of our amazing natural heritage. You would be hard-pressed to find a more eloquent voice for Oregon's wild desert places."

Brent Fenty
Executive Director, Oregon Natural Desert Association (ONDA)

"Jim Witty was many things, including the perfect outdoor companion and loyal friend. Above everything he was a wordsmith. He studied words and understood their power."

Map Guy
Friend & Outing Companion

"Jim was properly regarded as a fine writer, which he was. But his writing, I thought, was more than just a collection of well-chosen words and phrases. It was a glimpse of his soul."

John Costa
Editor-in-Chief, The Bulletin

"Jim was an amazing writer and an amazing person who was as easy with a smile as he was with the turn of a phrase. As journalists, we all envied Jim as the guy who got to go hike on the clock and then write about it. But the truth is that none of us could have done what Jim did — at least not the way he did. But we knew that too. We were writers from 9-5. Jim, he was an artist."

Eric Flowers
Editor, The Source Weekly

"Jim's stories touched readers in a way that reporters dream of, and dream of with envy."

Dave Jasper
Writer, The Bulletin

"Writing about the outdoors was in his blood."

Chris Sabo
Trail Specialist, Deschutes National Forest

Jim was a desert rat…and I will think of him every time the minimalist desert landscape stuns me with its understated beauty. From one desert rat to another, thanks Jim."

Julie Johnson
Writer, The Bulletin

TABLE OF CONTENTS

Dedication	2
Introduction	3
Be Aware... Be Prepared...	6
Central Oregon Map	8
Southeast Region	**11**
Trail to Flatiron Rock	13
Where High Desert, Forest Come Together	15
Footloose on Frederick	18
Juniper: Veterans of the West	21
Bend's Ocean	24
Savoring Solitude	26
Out There, Somewhere	29
Wherever You Go...There You Are	32
Winter is a Good Time for Badlands	34
This Desert Place	36
A Closer Look at the Badlands	38
Oasis of Birds	40
Paulina Creek	43
What Lies Beneath	45
Down to the River	48
Southeastern Oregon's Outback	51
China Hat Butte	53
Found It: Map Guy and a GPS Help Jim Witty Locate an Enormous Juniper	55
A Butte-iful Day: Horse and Lava Buttes	57
An Inspiring Day at Fort Rock	59
History Cast Indelibly in Lava	61
Paulina Lake is Picture Perfect	64
Pay a Visit to Coyote, Horse and Bessie Buttes	67
Newberry National Volcanic Monument	69
On Top of His Game	71
Southwest Region	**75**
Falling for Autumn	77
Get Out While You Still Can	79

TABLE OF CONTENTS

Take a Sip of Nature at Soda Creek 82
Powder Outage 84
Mountain Biking 87
Biking Bend's C.O.D. Trail 89
The Awkward Joy of Ice Skating 91
Lava Lands 93
Broken Top: Trail to Alpine Splendor 96
Enjoy the Quiet of Vista Butte Sno-park 99
Choose Your Adventure 102
Irish and Taylor Lakes 105
Snomobiling at Wanoga Sno-park 108
Revisit an Old Friend: The Upper Deschutes 110
Where's Waldo Lake? 112
An Uncluttered View 114
Tumalo Mountain 116
Lucky Lake 118
Todd Lake Welcomes Fall 120
Calm, Cool and Collected 122
High Desert Museum 125
Big, Beautiful, Blue 128

Northwest Region **133**
Along the Metolius River 135
Discovering Dry Canyon 137
Peaceful Resting Places 140
Fish Lake 143
Don't Pass This Up 146
Hike West, Hike Green 149
There and Back Again 152
Taking the Path Less Traveled 154
Where the River Flows 157
McKenzie River Trail: A Fat Tire Favorite 159
A Good Outlook 161
Shevlin Park 164
Shop Sisters the "Witty" Way 166
Scenes from Autumn 168

TABLE OF CONTENTS

Northwest Region *continued*

Three Creek Lake	171
The Tumalo Creek Trail	173
Devastation and Renewal	176
High Trailing It	178

Northeast Region — **181**

A Sunday Drive through Crooked River Canyon Country	183
Finding Yourself in Sundown	186
A Scenic Edge	189
Haystack's Snow White Look	191
Central Oregon 'Butte-ies'	194
Peter Skene Ogden State Wayside Rich in Vistas	197
Snug and Friendly	199
Steins Pillar	201
On Walton Sno-park	203
'Tis the Season to Ride Skull Hollow	205
Scenery Worth $4.31 a Gallon	208
Leave It All Behind at the Mill Creek Wilderness	211
Riding the River	213
Steelhead Falls	216
Sim ...What ... Stus?	219
Skeleton Rock	221
Golden Opportunity	224
Smith Rock State Park a Mecca for Hard-core Climbers	226
The Deschutes River Canyon is Ruggedly Lonely	229
Floating and Fishing	232
A Taste of 'The Middle D'	235
In Search of Thundereggs	238
Antelope Flat Has It All	241
History Unfolds at John Day Fossil Beds	243
Past Meets Present	246

TABLE OF CONTENTS

Classic Central Oregon	**251**
Central Oregon Favorites	253
"Wow"	256
Going with the Flow	260
In One Day, You Can ...	263
You Are Here	266
Afterword	**271**
About Jim	**272**
Message from Map Guy	**277**
The End of the Roll	**278**
A Special Thanks	**279**
Acknowledgments	**280-282**
Contact Information	**283**
Index	**285**

DEDICATION

Jim loved the outdoors. He believed the beauty and bounty of our natural resources provide a critical foundation for our society and make an important contribution to the quality of our lives. Jim worried that our exploding population growth combined with detachment and disinterest would continue to degrade what he found so fulfilling and inspiring. But he never let any of that dampen his optimism or his genuine interest in the people he encountered. Jim hoped that his adventures and writings would encourage us to get out and discover what he loved, and that our discoveries would strengthen our willingness to care for, to preserve and to protect.

And so we dedicate this book to our wonderful memories of Jim, to the literary legacy he left to all of us, to his friendly optimism, and to his hopes for the future. He would want us all to enjoy each other and our lives, the words he wrote and the wonder of what he wrote about.

The Book Team:

Lori Witty
Edna Witty
John Witty
Joan Witty
Deedee (Witty) Sihvonen
Alan Sihvonen
Linda Quon
Mark Quon

INTRODUCTION

By Rick Steber

The snapshots in Jim Witty's photo album reveal two conclusive truths – Jim had a genuine love of the outdoors, and when he was in the outdoors he was having fun. He might be barreling off Tumalo Peak on a pair of cross-country skis, standing in waders knee-deep in the Deschutes River while gingerly removing an Elk Hair Caddis from the lip of a native rainbow, or standing in a meadow near Cultus Lake with his arms slung around the shoulders of his sons, Danny and Keven. In each photograph Jim is smiling. When he was outdoors that smile came easily.

"Jim's first real outdoor experience occurred when he was maybe three years old," recalled John Witty, Jim's older brother. "We were living in Southern California and Jim wandered away from home. He went over some steep, really dangerous ground, and finally just ran out of trail. I found him in a canyon clinging to the hillside, hanging on for dear life. Thinking back, I suppose that moment was a harbinger of things to come because from then on, Jim was always taking off, hiking somewhere, and more times than not he ended up at a place he hadn't intended to be."

Jim graduated from Hemet High School, attended Cal Poly State University and graduated with a degree in journalism. His career as a newspaper reporter included stops in California, Hawaii and Washington before he moved to Oregon and went to work for *The Bulletin* as an environmental and natural resources reporter. A year later he became the outdoor recreation writer, and for Jim and the newspaper, it was a perfect fit.

Jim made the most of Central Oregon's many and varied outdoor activities. He hiked, biked, fished, rock climbed, canoed and camped. He liked nothing better than to get far away from everyone and everything, pitch a tent in the wide open and revel in solitude. He could spend hours perched on a rock, watching a storm bully over the Cascades: thunderheads building into citadels, lightning flashing and a smattering of rain opening little eyes in the sand. He was an observer of nature. He took note of everything around him. And he wrote wonderful stories about what he saw and his varied outdoor adventures.

But that is not to say Jim did not enjoy people, because he most certainly did. If you, a perfect stranger, happened to meet Jim along the trail he would more than likely stop and want to visit. And, from this chance encounter, what would likely strike you was that you felt privileged to have met this big, friendly, easygoing guy who had such a zest for life. With Jim there was no pretense and no embellishment, but he did have a knack for spicing up a conversation with stories of his personal experiences. Everyone Jim encountered went away with the same impression, that they had just met a man who was absolutely genuine, just a real nice guy.

INTRODUCTION: BY RICK STEBER

While the outdoors defined Jim, it was his passion for music that provided him with an entertaining diversion from his writing. Mark Quon, Jim's friend from high school, recalls, "When we were in high school, we used to grab our guitars, drive out on the desert and play music all night. Jim was constantly working on his guitar skills, and what he lacked in ability, he made up for in enthusiasm. He played the harmonica, too, and sang with a passion. I can picture him in the light of a campfire, head thrown back, eyes closed and looking eerily like Eric Clapton, playing his guitar and singing. More than anything, Jim had a real appreciation for good music and avidly listened to everything: David Bowie, Bob Dylan, Jackson Browne, Willie Nelson, The Jayhawks, John Prine, and on and on. If he was playing, or just kicking back and listening, music always got him pumped."

Jim was serious about his writing and his sister, Deedee Sihvonen, recalls, "Writers are observers. They notice details that other people often miss. Jim was like that. He loved words. Oftentimes he agonized trying to come up with the perfect word or combination of words that would convey exactly what he meant to say. And Jim was a reader. He read all the time because he wanted to see how other writers put words together and how they were able to impart knowledge and wring emotion from a sentence. Jim wanted to paint a picture with his words but more than anything he wanted to touch the reader's soul."

For Jim, the western landscape was more than topography and landforms, dirt and rock, trees and sage. He enjoyed the mountains – the richness of the flora and fauna, the stately fir and pine trees, and the lakes and streams – but he developed an intense love for the Badlands, located only fifteen miles east of Bend. Here, in the rain shadow of the Cascades, he discovered the dry air became more clear and sharp and that it seemed to give all things a special brilliance, softening and sweetening the pigmentation of the raw earth, and that at night it seemed to polish and enlarge the stars. On the Badlands Jim saw forms and colors and light and scale just like a painter does and he developed a new vocabulary, a rich palette of earth colors – tans, ruddy red, burnished copper, pale brown, juniper green, basalt black. He appreciated the taste of sagebrush and the smell of raw soil and alkali flats. He watched puffs of lazy clouds

INTRODUCTION: BY RICK STEBER

traverse the summer sky, slowly marching west to east, and respected the hard-defined edge of black rimrock against deep, blue sky. He marveled at the hardiness of five hundred year old twisted juniper trees, dry river washes, ancient lava flows, desert wildflowers, and he admired the big game hunters who had inhabited this region during the last great Ice Age, leaving behind pictographs on rocky cliffs. But Jim also harbored a fear that the modern world would wipe away the open spaces and that his grandchildren would never be able to see, experience and cherish all those things he had been able to see and do. He said he sometimes felt like a caretaker, merely recording what the world had been like in his lifetime, and he understood what a splendid, spacious, diverse, magnificent and terribly fragile planet we live on. And more than anything, he knew in his heart that though we come to love a particular place, we could love that place to death.

Jim wrote of places and his concern for those places and his stories did touch his readers. Through hard work and determination he had developed an originally distinctive and colorful voice. Lori Witty, Jim's wife, said, "Jim had such a real zest for life. He lived in each moment and always found an element of good even in the worst situation, and beauty in the ordinary. When it came to writing he believed that less is more. He was never one to waste words and I think his readers appreciated that."

The one thing Jim always wanted to do was to incorporate his stories into a book. But he was not able to complete the task. He died suddenly of a heart attack on November 17, 2008. He was only 50 years old. It is a fitting tribute to Jim that his family and friends have worked together to produce Jim's book, *Meet Me In The Badlands: Exploring Central Oregon with Jim Witty*.

The life of Jim Witty – father, devoted family man, outdoorsman, lover of life, musician, communicator, conversationalist, gifted writer – cannot be described in mere words. His legacy will be preserved in his writing and in the way he is able to inspire his readers and instill in them an appreciation for their surroundings and to motivate them to preserve what we do have. One of Jim's favorite authors was Aldo Leopold who wrote in his conservation classic, *A Sand County Almanac*, "There are some who can live without wild things and some who cannot." Jim Witty was one who felt compelled to live with wild things.

BE AWARE ...

Most of the articles, maps and pictures contained in this book are reprints from Jim's work at *The Bulletin,* Bend, Oregon's daily newspaper. All materials from *The Bulletin* were generously made available to us through John and Denise Costa and the staff at *The Bulletin.* We very much appreciate their cooperation in our efforts to turn Jim's intentions to produce this book into a reality.

Articles have been divided up by regions: southeast, southwest, northwest and northeast, in relation to the city of Bend. Each article includes the date it first appeared in print. The text is essentially as it was when published, although articles may have been edited slightly. **It is important that each reader recognize the information contained in these articles was accurate at the time it first appeared, but may not currently reflect the conditions to be found in the area discussed. Such things as fees, access, trails, roads, signs, and even trail and road distances can change over time. Readers should always consider the date of original publication and check current sources for updated conditions.** We have included a list of resources on page 283 that are available to help in that process. *The Bulletin* was not involved in the selection of the material contained in this book nor is it in any way responsible for the accuracy of the information included.

BE PREPARED ...

My brother Jim enjoyed the story he read recounting Daniel Boone's answer to a question about whether or not he had ever been lost during his wanderings in the wilderness. The intrepid frontier hero reportedly contemplated the question for a moment and then replied, "I can't say as ever I was lost, but I was bewildered once for three days." Jim and I found solace in the response because it made us feel a little better about the many times we found ourselves profoundly "bewildered" (lost as far as we could tell). It also points out two very important realities. First, no matter who you are, where you are, and how experienced or inexperienced you are in the outdoors, if you spend much time outside, you will get yourself lost. And most importantly, it reflects that if you are prepared, getting lost is a manageable problem that may result in inconvenience and some discomfort, but need not end in real misery or tragedy.

Jim learned to do three things whenever he went on any kind of an outing:

1. **Always tell a responsible person where you are going and when you expect to be back.** Jim believed in being sensible and therefore, flexible about where he went. If the weather or the road conditions or the hour of the day counseled for a change of destinations, Jim changed his plans and made an effort to update his responsible person as to his new destination and estimated time of return.

2. **Carry the best devises you can afford that might enable you to communicate and get help if that becomes necessary.** Cell phones can be good, but remember that some of the best places begin where dial tone ends. Since they became available a

few years ago, Jim carried a SPOT (described as a "Satellite Personal Tracker"). It allows the user to select from three messages and transmit them from almost anywhere. One option is a message to your choice of recipients (via cell phone text message and e-mail) that says, "All is well, life is good, here's where I am." They get the message and a link to Google Earth where they can actually see your location.

The second SPOT option is a similar message to your choice of recipients that says, "Nothing life threatening, but I could really use some help, here's where I am." (As in, I'm stuck in the mud, the truck broke down or I need some help packing out the elk I just killed.) The third message option is the biggie, and is sent to all available emergency responders saying, "I'm in a serious, life threatening mess, here's where I am, send the cavalry." Depending on your outlook, another attribute of SPOT is that you can virtually always send out a message, but no one can call you to see if you can make it in to work on your day off.

3. **Have enough supplies to safely spend a night (or two) if that becomes necessary.** The third thing Jim learned to do is what Daniel Boone relied on to make him so casual about being lost for three days at a time. It isn't dependent on batteries or satellite access or cell towers. It is tried and true self-reliance. Whenever you venture out into unpopulated areas, be prepared to spend the night, even if that wasn't your intention!

Take a fanny pack or a day pack and equip it with some essentials - matches and/or a lighter and something to start a fire with (even if everything is wet), a compass, a small flashlight, and water to drink. Jim also liked to carry one of those squeeze bottle purifiers that allows you to drink water that might otherwise make you very sick. Even in the summer, throw in a season appropriate coat or other clothing that can keep you warm overnight. If you're unprepared, Central Oregon nights, any time of the year, can be dangerously cold.

Your two most basic overnight survival concerns are warmth and water. Except for the water, the pack can weigh less than 5 pounds and makes it easier to carry a camera, cell phone, snacks, etc. Then take it with you, every time you go out. Daniel Boone was reportedly once captured by the Shawnee and, after proving himself worthy, was eventually adopted into the tribe. His Shawnee given name was "sheltowee," roughly translated as Big Turtle, a reference to his habits of moving slowly and carefully through the woods and always carrying a pack.

Jim knew from experience that if you spend much time in the outdoors you will eventually find yourself "bewildered" by your circumstances or your surroundings. Smart outdoors people like Jim Witty and Daniel Boone knew that it was worth the effort to be prepared and to be safe.

— John Witty

CENTRAL OREGON MAP

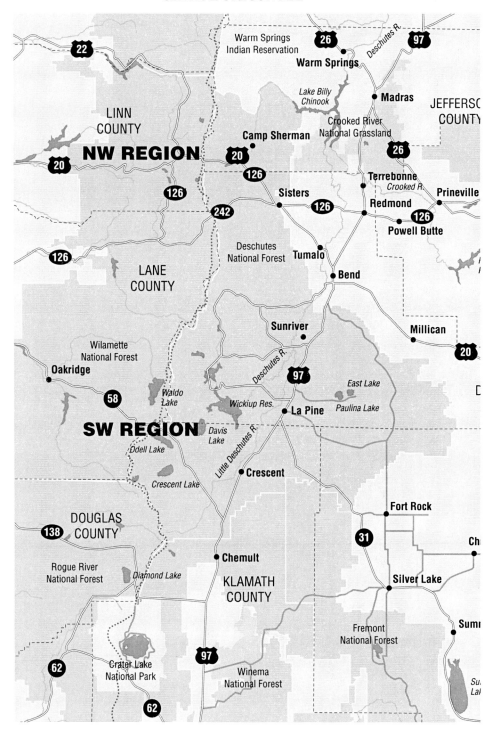

CENTRAL OREGON MAP

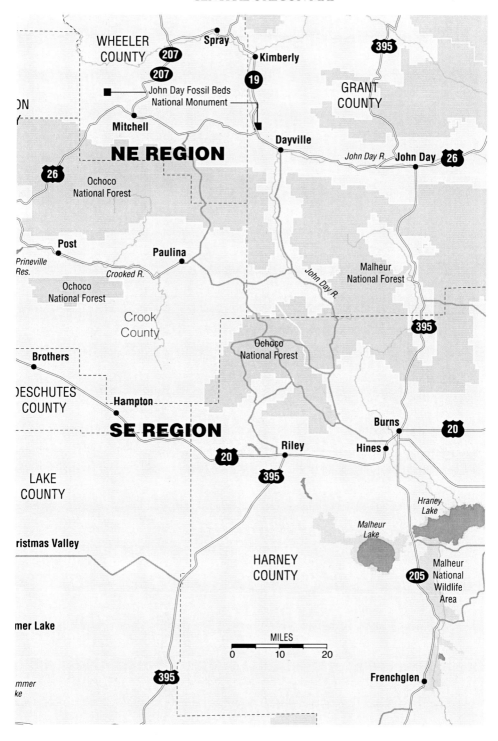

Southeast Region

The Badlands / photo courtesy of Greg Burke

"The country of my affection lies just to the east ... I walk in the desert seeking a semblance of peace and always get that primal recognition that less is more."

The view from atop Flatiron Rock in the Badlands is commanding.
photo by Mark Quon

Trail to Flatiron Rock

A Western state of mind

Published: May 23, 2007

I finally figured out why I like hiking in the Badlands so much.

More than any mixed conifer forest, any sylvan glade or snow-capped peak, the Badlands Wilderness Study Area is a microcosm of this sprawling, rough-edged, big-hearted region we live in.

The West. It's a land of contradictions. It appears flat until you notice the contours. It looks empty until you start seeing all the life. It can be sizzling hot or bitter cold.

Bulletin colleague Andrew Moore pointed out the thing that strikes you when you're out in the midst of all that. There's a lot of land out here.

We were enjoying a day out on the Badlands, hiking to Flatiron Rock. The Badlands is about 37,000 acres of burnt brownie lava flows, rabbitbrush and gnarly old junipers. It's dry and dusty, and once you trek in a ways, the landmark ridges disappear from view and you're left with a cloistered view of things.

The Badlands is small compared to many potential wilderness areas. It's a little piece of wild land on the edge of something so vast that it can be difficult to comprehend. But the concept of the West (and all that topography) is approachable if you break it down, take it five or six miles at a time. And remain open to what you see

Trail to Flatiron Rock *continued*

and experience along the way.

Some things are obvious. We saw a dust devil pick up steam, touch down in a series of little whirling eruptions, and race out over the High Desert toward us only to dissipate before either of us could pluck a camera out of the pack and focus. And, not long after we discussed the conspicuous absence of pronghorn in the area, a pair of "speed goats" trotted by (again, we botched the camera thing).

Some things are more subtle.

Flatiron Rock is a big jumble of volcanic boulders about three miles from the trailhead. From the base, you'd never know there are open trails up top that lead past clumps of Great Basin ryegrass, little caves, portals and other items of biological and geological interest. Climb atop the rock and you have a 360-degree view of the surrounding countryside, including the entire Cascades array.

In late 2005, Bureau of Land Management officials completely closed the Badlands to motorized vehicles. For years, environmentalists have campaigned to include the area just east of Bend in the National Wilderness Preservation System. The BLM recommended the Badlands for wilderness consideration in 1990; approval is contingent upon congressional action.

The result is a hiking experience, close to town, that feels as if you've traveled far and wide.

Hiking back toward the trailhead and car, we marveled at the tenacity of the wildflowers: delicate purple, blue and yellow blooms all enjoying their day in the sun. Everywhere, the sandy soil is dusty and dry; how do they survive?

Friday was a warm one. Henry the dog sprinted from shady spot to shady spot, sprawling briefly at each before resuming his journey. We found ourselves discussing the laid back magnificence of these open spaces and the enormity of the Western sector of the United States. The conversation took us from the dry rolling landscape between Burns and Boise to the bizarre hoodoo beauty of the Four Corners country in the Southwest and back again to this corner of a remarkable region.

We rounded a bend in the trail, the highway came into view and the hike was over. With a slam of the car door, the wide open West was just a state of mind once again.

Editor's Note: On March 30th, 2009, President Obama signed the Omnibus Public Lands Management Act, designating the Oregon Badlands as wilderness.

If You Go:

GETTING THERE: From Bend, drive about 16 miles east on U.S. Highway 20. Turn left at milepost 16 into a dirt parking lot. The trailhead is here.

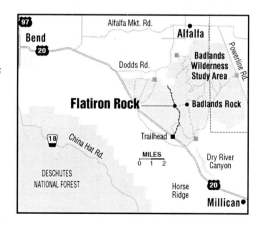

Puffy clouds and blue skies mark another brilliant March day on the Central Oregon High Desert near Pine Mountain.

photo by Jim Witty

Where High Desert, Forest Come Together

Transition zones promote species diversity

Published: *March 12, 2008*

"When we come to the place where the road and the sky collide
Throw me over the edge and let my spirit glide
They told me I was going to have to work for a living
But all I want to do is ride
I don't care where we're going from here
Honey, you decide."

Until the other day, I'd never really understood what (singer-songwriter) Jackson Browne meant by that: "the place where the road and the sky collide." I was traipsing uphill on a little road in the desert south of Millican when a friend of mine burst into song.

The road reared up in front of us and at the highest point seemed to crash headlong into a sky so blue and flecked with clouds so puffy and white that it looked digitally enhanced.

We'd come to that place and it was perfect.

This time of year, the High Desert comes charged with revelations.

Where High Desert, Forest Come Together *continued*

This country, roughly west of Pine Mountain and south and east of Horse Ridge, goes from rolling sage plains to scattered ponderosa to pine forest in the wink of an eye. The place where the High Desert and the mountains collide.

I like transition zones.

Not only are they visually and topographically interesting, they provide habitat for wild animals, large and small. Irregular edges promote species diversity. Borders can be biological hot spots.

A prime example is the Cabin Lake area to the southeast. Just north of the Fort Rock basin, Cabin Lake is no lake at all. Rather, it's a transition zone between the desert and the pines that attracts wildlife and birds from both sectors. There are a couple of viewing blinds there adjacent to some small water basins from which to watch the passing parade. Stay in there long enough, and you'll get to see most of the area's inhabitants.

"Generally speaking, when a variety of habitats come together, that's always a popular place," said Oregon Department of Fish and Wildlife biologist Corey Heath. "They meet a variety of needs without them having to travel so far."

Elk, for instance, gravitate to such zones.

They'll forage in the open with the ability to "dash for cover" if necessary.

"Plant diversity is greater in these areas also," Heath said.

For part of the year, the South Millican region is open to motorcycles and four-

Transition zone between the desert and the pines.

photo by Jim Witty

wheelers. But between Dec. 31 and July 31, the area's trails are quiet and inviting to hikers and other self-mobilizing desert rats, in deference to the sage grouse. The beleaguered birds are known to mate and rear their broods there during the spring and early summer.

According to Andy Kerr, author of *Oregon Desert Guide,* those fortunate enough to observe the sage grouse mating ritual are in for a "Wild Kingdom"-style visual and aural feast.

"In the early spring, the larger and more strikingly marked males congregate each dawn at leks (assembly areas for courtship), where they undertake elaborate rituals of display to entice the females to mate with them," Kerr writes. "All will gather again in the evening and often will pull an all-nighter when the moon is bright."

Kerr goes on to paint a fascinating picture of what goes on out there in the open ground among the sagebrush.

"The males strut among the females with tail feathers fully erect and fanned, and head and neck held high," he writes. "The yellow comb over each eye is expanded, the sagging chest sac partly filled with air, and the wings drooping slightly. The grouse take in, and rapidly exhale, a large volume of air and make a unique and unforgettable sound (one authority has described it as swish-swish-coo-poink) while exposing yellowish skin patches on the chest. Males also do a 'dance' in which they aggressively brush each other."

"There's a fair number of (sage grouse) out there," said Heath.

Because they can't tolerate habitat destruction, Kerr calls the grouse "the spotted owl of the desert."

With comfortable temperatures and a relatively low dust quotient, it's a great time to poke around the sage steppe and ponderosa pine uplands. The trails are there for the walking. The revelations are out there, too, if you're receptive. But you've got to get yourself into the zone.

If You Go:

GETTING THERE: From Bend, drive 23 miles east on U.S. Highway 20 to Forest Rd. 23 (Spencer Wells Rd.). Turn right and follow the road south into the South Millican OHV Trail System. Pine Mountain will be on your left. When snow is present, a high clearance vehicle is essential and caution should be exercised. Spring in the mountains means unpredictable weather. Getting

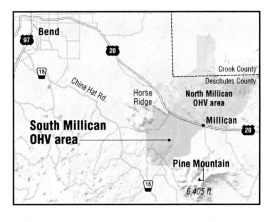

stuck in the snow or mud can bring an otherwise enjoyable outing to a screeching halt (and can be dangerous). Check weather reports. When in doubt, turn around.

CONTACT: Bend-Fort Rock Ranger District of the Deschutes National Forest, 541-383-4000.

Pronghorn antelope, like these east of Millican, form herds in the winter. During the cold months, males forget their breeding season animosities and band together.

photo by Jim Witty

Footloose on Frederick

Eastern Oregon butte is a peaceful place to roam this time of year

Published: January 16, 2008

You can see Frederick Butte from U.S. Highway 20.

Start looking off to the south just past the tiny burg of Brothers and you'll see it looming in the distance, across the sagebrush flats. Turn south just before milepost 50 and you can drive right to it, providing the snow's not too deep to negotiate or the gravel road's not too muddy.

I was out there last Friday scouting a place to pitch a tent for an upcoming cold weather camping story. It's the kind of day trip I'm especially fond of. There's a goal in mind, but not too structured. It's more of a nebulous idea, an opportunity to knock around in the desert, experience some new country and take things as they come. It feels like a mini road trip and I know you know what I mean.

So in keeping with that footloose spirit, I listened to the rumblings in my belly and pulled in to the Brothers Stage Stop on the way east. It's a great place to wind down to desert time, meet some astonishingly nice people, most of whom march to a different metronome, and enjoy a seriously delicious burger. Brothers Stage Stop ranks right up there with perennial favorites the Pilot Butte Drive-In, Dandy's and the Sno-Cap. I'm serious, the double bacon cheeseburger with extra onions is worth the 40-mile drive,

The Frederick Butte area is long on lonesome, especially in winter.
photo by Jim Witty

even if you just turn around and head back home after you eat your fill (just keep in mind, there's temporarily no gas available in Brothers, so fill up on petrol before you head out).

But as long as you're out and about in the High Desert, why not stick around for that mini road trip? The buttes hereabouts can be beautiful this time of year.

At 5,052 feet above sea level, Frederick Butte is a high point. Looking south down Frederick Butte Road, there's Frederick straight ahead, Last Chance Ridge to the west and the aptly named Soldier's Cap next to that.

My dog Hoss and I tromped around near the base of the butte, but soon found the 8-inch deep snowpack a deterrent to further exploration afoot. We cranked the heater and drove.

Other than a whole lot of lonesome out that way, there's not a great deal in terms of developed amenities. Oh, Don and Linda Wallace have a little homestead in the vicinity and the Civilian Conservation Corps had an encampment there in the 1930s. Larger than life rancher Bill Brown used to own a big chunk of the area and reportedly ran thousands of horses there.

"He owned 14,000 horses and he walked everywhere," marveled Linda Wallace, a former schoolteacher and student of the High Desert. "What a character. He walked 50 miles to Burns, no problem at all."

Today, most of the horses are gone and so are many of the hardscrabble homesteaders. This is primarily mule deer, elk, coyote, cougar and pronghorn country.

Footloose on Fredrick *continued*

Don Wallace said he's been seeing a sizeable herd of pronghorn antelope in the flats near his place, northwest of Frederick Butte.

It's one thing hearing about a big herd of these rocket-fast ruminants of the sagebrush steppe, another to see it firsthand. Which is what I did on the way back to Bend at the end of the day.

At first I thought they were domestic sheep, a species that competed with cows on the High Desert in days gone by. Then I realized that this sea of white-rumped animals was a herd of well more than 100 pronghorn. Since I was between Brothers and Mitchell by this time, miles from the Wallace ranch, this must have been a different herd of wintering antelope from the one the Wallaces are familiar with.

I pulled off the road and watched them milling about for a while before they drifted off over a swale and slowly disappeared into the desert. I never saw one run. Which is unfortunate because they can get up and go. According to the North American Pronghorn Foundation, Antilocapra americana can "comfortably cruise" at 30 mph and have been known to reach speeds up to 70 mph. The foundation's Lisa Hutchens writes that the pronghorn is equipped with an oversized trachea, huge lungs and a large heart that allow it to consume massive amounts of oxygen.

She goes on to explain that the pronghorn flares its white-rump hairs to warn the rest of the herd of impending danger, which may or may not explain why these particular animals flowed slowly away from me.

Down to about 20,000 animals in the early 1900s, pronghorn populations in the West have bounced back, according to Animal Diversity Web. Thanks to hunting regulations and habitat protection, there are an estimated 500,000 pronghorn west of the Rockies today.

In Central Oregon, they prefer the great wide open east of Horse Ridge, but I saw a lone animal last year in the Badlands Wilderness Study Area just east of Bend.

Back in the car on the outskirts of Bend, and with my mini road trip coming to a close, I saw a bald eagle soaring out over the juniper.

What a great day.

If You Go:

GETTING THERE: From Bend, drive east on U.S. Highway 20. Turn right, or south, just before milepost 50 on Frederick Butte Rd. The butte is straight out toward the south. The road continues south to the Peters Creek Sink and eventually to the Christmas Valley area.

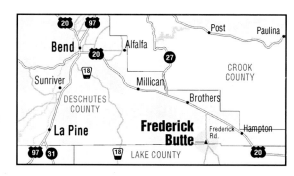

Caution: The road can be impassable, depending on the weather.

CONTACT: Bureau of Land Management, 541-947-2177.

Dead Junipers provide habitat for a variety of critters.
photo by Jim Witty

Juniper: Veterans of the West

The tough hombre of the High Desert West

Published: January 09, 2008

The western juniper is far from statuesque, not even close to colossal when compared with other tree species, and is given to growing in contorted, stunted, twisted, warped, crumpled, distressed and arthritic configurations.

It's mostly at home in areas of scant rainfall (9 to 14 inches a year) and in shallow, volcanic soils that would drive a normal tree to higher ground. It's coyote sturdy, a tough hombre uniquely suited to the tortuous terrain of the High Desert West. Nowhere is it more abundant than in Central Oregon, where it grows on about 3 million acres, in varying densities.

The juniper tree has its detractors, and they have valid arguments. Because natural and native-set fires have dwindled dramatically since livestock grazing and fire suppression began, the juniper has monopolized the landscape. According to the Oregon Department of Forestry, there were 420,000 acres of juniper in the eastern part of the state in the mid-1930s. Since then, its range has increased at least tenfold. The juniper sucks water, lowering local water tables, which irritates landowners who have come to view the relatively young stands as invasive pests.

Juniper: Veterans of the West *continued*

It's those juvenile trees, most stock straight and comparatively spindly, that can water down appreciation for Juniperus occidentalis.

But the old soldiers, the gnarled, disfigured veterans, some of which were saplings when Leif Eriksson led his expedition to North America 1,000 years ago (well before Columbus sailed the ocean blue) are a lifelong study in rugged individualism.

"We're so used to seeing all the little trees out there," said desert advocate Bill Marlett, of Bend. "When you get into the ancient junipers, they rival any (trees) in terms of beauty and elegance. You have to go look for the old ones."

But not that far.

According to Marlett, the oldest juniper in Oregon (estimated at 1,600 years old) is up on Horse Ridge, east of Bend. Just across U.S. Highway 20 to the north, the Badlands is full of ancient trees. There are also big trees in the country between China Hat butte and Fort Rock and out toward Post way east of Prineville.

And none of them look even remotely the same.

I've been shooting photos of interesting old-growth junipers for years. I'm drawn to them, partly because they're the ultimate non-conformists and partly because they're a fitting icon for the Oregon High Desert that I love. Coyotes and birds feast on the juniper's berries. Small animals nest in the crannies and nooks. Big game animals, such as mule deer and elk, use the trees for cover.

The juniper forest provides cover for big game and smaller animals.
photo courtesy of Greg Burke

For me, it's the whole package. During a recent hike from the Obernolte Trailhead, on the northwest border of the Badlands Wilderness Study Area, cross country south into the heart of the old-growth juniper forest, I walked quietly, observed carefully and tried to read the vital signs. Although it was quiet, save for the crunch of my boots in the snow and an occasional gust through the dense juniper boughs, the place buzzed with activity. I flushed a cottontail rabbit and a covey of quail. But the fresh coat of snow revealed the usually unseen, a surprisingly varied and concentrated collection of tracks there beneath the big sagebrush, rabbitbrush and bunchgrass. I'm not sure where the jackrabbits and cottontails sit right now in their fluctuating population cycle, but I've a hunch it could be close to a peak. They'd been out in force earlier in the day. I also saw the tracks of deer, the scat of elk and my find of the day, the tell-tale track of a bobcat (not surprisingly paralleling a rabbit's route). A day in the life: The comings and goings would all be erased with the melting of the snow.

The old, old junipers knit the entire scene together.

I don't believe trees see or feel or speak in the conventional sense, but they can tell us much about a place and something, maybe, about ourselves. Despite an increase in human footprints and a random poacher out for an ill-gotten fireplace mantle, this place feels like it's been around awhile and it's breathing OK on its own.

When we walk among the ancient junipers, do we simply see a swath of sylvan sameness or a higher connection to the primitive, soul-churning essence of wild land?

"(Some people) just don't understand how valuable these old trees are," said Marlett. "They are irreplaceable."

At least for the next millennium or so.

Editor's Note: On March 30th, 2009, President Obama signed the Omnibus Public Lands Management Act, designating the Oregon Badlands as wilderness.

If You Go:

GETTING THERE: To reach the Obernolte Trailhead in the Badlands Wilderness Study Area, drive east from Bend on U.S. Highway 20 and turn left on Dodds Rd. Turn right on Obernolte Rd.; the trailhead and parking area is at the end of the road.

Another good place to explore old-growth juniper habitat is the country east of Prineville. To reach the Nature Conservancy's Juniper Hills Preserve,

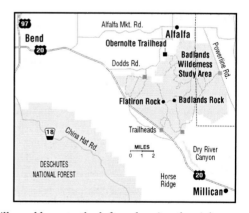

turn right on Paulina Highway in Prineville and keep to the left, eschewing the right fork that leads to Prineville Reservoir. The preserve begins 30 miles out. Turn left on a dirt road just after the milepost 34. The gravel road leads to a barn and Lost Creek Reservoir. Vehicles are not allowed on the preserve. Be aware of the weather. Snow or mud can make gravel roads impassable.

CONTACT: Nature Conservancy, 503-802-8100; Bureau of Land Management, 503-808-6002.

It's easy to blow right by the junipers, sage, shrubs, rocks and sandy soil.
photo by Mark Quon

Bend's Ocean

Diving into the Badlands' Dry Canyon

Published: November 05, 2004

From a distance, the Badlands don't look so bad. Simple, maybe, a little harsh for sure, but not all bad. Drive past them going east out of Bend and you see junipers, some sage and other hardy shrubs, rocks and sandy soil. It's easy to blow right by, subconsciously categorizing this stern country as monotonous, uncomplicated, a wasteland.

Do me a favor. Stop the car. Get out. Walk a little bit. Look around.

The desert's kind of like the ocean. What you see from the back of the boat is a whole lot of water. But dive in and you may be confronted with sensory overload.

You won't find any yellow tang or rainbow wrasse or fields of coral out here on this arid reef, but scratch the surface and your perceptions may begin to change.

I went alone to the Dry Canyon last week and noticed things. Like the way old, dead, gnarly juniper snags morph back into soil over time. Like the way discarded beer cans only temporarily mar the landscape (the desert will outlast Coors and Bud and human stupidity). Like the hundreds of animal tracks in the sand after a healthy rainstorm and the explosive whir of a startled owl frightened into flight. The way wind and water work on the rocks, the way wild, windswept, brutal places work on the mind.

The Badlands isn't a full-fledged wilderness ... yet. Bend's backyard wilderness-in-training is actually a WSA (Wilderness Study Area), but there's a growing movement to preserve the 37,000-acre tract as it is.

If you didn't know it was there, you might stumble and fall right into the Dry Canyon. You're walking across the unbroken plain and, wham, there you are looking down into a ribbon-thin gully fringed with weather-worn basalt.

Looking down into Dry River Canyon.
photo by Chris Egertson

It's only a matter of 15 or 20 feet, but it's a different world inside that little slot.

Clumps of Great Basin ryegrass grow in the old streambed, and water from the last downpours fills the tinajas (eroded holes in the rocks) to nearly brimming.

There are primitive Indian pictographs here, but the work of wind, water and vandals makes finding them a challenge. The rocks down here are burnished smooth by an ancient river that once drained Lake Millican during occasional lulls in the Ice Age.

Editor's Note: On March 30th, 2009, President Obama signed the Omnibus Public Lands Management Act, designating the Oregon Badlands as wilderness.

If You Go:

GETTING THERE: To reach this special slot canyon that's off-limits to motorized vehicles, drive east from Bend on U.S. Highway 20. Turn left a few hundred yards past milepost 17. Drive about a half-mile to Road 4 on the left (there's an old cattle chute here and a Bureau of Land Management information board). Park here. I reached the Dry Canyon by walking north then west (left) along a fenceline fronting a big dirt berm. At the end of the berm, I turned north (right) again and walked across the desert until I came to a wide wash. I walked downstream along the dry bed about a quarter-mile to where the canyon narrows dramatically. For the next half-mile or so, the canyon warrants close exploration.

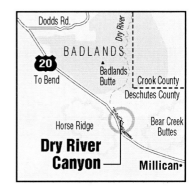

Buttes abound in the High Desert east of Bend. Well-traveled roads, on the other hand, are a rarity. "Hurry and take the road to the roadless area, because it won't be roadless long," Terry and Renny Russell advise in their travel book *On the Loose*.

photo by Jim Witty

Savoring Solitude

Road trip in desert to the east offers respite from civilization

Published: September 04, 2008

I love my vehicle and the roads that get me out and gone.

At the same time, I have a certain disdain for my vehicle and the roads that snake out and up into those rugged places that would be inaccessible to all but the hardiest of hikers if not for, as Ed Abbey would have put it, the infernal combustion engine.

Which makes me a little bit like the person who can't bear the idea of killing an animal, but warms to the thought of a savory New York steak or sautéed chicken breasts stuffed with blue cheese. We can't have it both ways. But we do. I'm not giving up meat or cars anytime soon.

Most of the best outings (including this one) begin and end with the flick of an ignition.

I just reread an old classic, *On the Loose* by Terry and Renny Russell. Published by the Sierra Club in 1967, it's a simple and beautiful paean to the wilderness West. The brothers Russell had this to say about our love-hate relationship with the automobile: "The car has made our cities uninhabitable. It is also the best way to escape them."

Hurry and take the road to the roadless area, because it won't be roadless long. Too much demand.

"The gas pump doesn't know the beauty which it helped to see; and so the gas tax comes pouring in and the pavement comes pouring out.

"And so we push the Big Wheel nearer the edge. The land of the free and the home of the auto dump. But man was born to wander."

And so it was I found myself behind the wheel, headed east, of course, trying to outwit my holiday weekend recreational competitors. Out through the desert I drove, east on U.S. Highway 20, into that marvelously empty country where Labor Day is pretty much like any other.

There are roads out there, to be sure, but none, save for the big east-west strip of blacktop, could be called well-traveled.

Get off on a side road this time of year and you find yourself awash in a yellow sea of blooming rabbitbrush. Because the few trees here are smallish and far between, you can see a long way in the desert.

Flat-top buttes, sailing cumulus, the snow-peaked Cascades back to the west — all many miles distant — are pitched in sharp relief against the brilliant blue of an uncluttered High Desert sky.

I turned off toward Pine Mountain to make a pit stop; my dog Hoss has to get out and run from time to time. A couple of hundred yards up the road, on the far side of a cattle guard, we found ourselves surrounded by milling cows. Another dog and another human, I suppose, might have been a little freaked out when the rangy beasts closed ranks around the rig, but we kept moving (slowly), Hoss feigned nonchalance, and the cows — who seemed put out — wandered away.

Then we were walking (actually, I was walking; the dog was trotting, scuffling, sprinting, moseying and zigzagging, but seldom walking) across a section of desert and I felt how I always feel out here, happy to be here.

As was so often the case, Abbey said it best.

"Strolling on, it seems to me that the strangeness and wonder of existence are emphasized here, in the desert, by the comparative sparsity of the flora and fauna: life not crowded upon life as in other places but scattered abroad in spareness and simplicity, with a generous gift of space for each herb and bush and tree, each stem of grass, so that the living organism stands out bold and brave and vivid against the lifeless sand and barren rock," he writes in *Desert Solitaire*. "The extreme clarity of the desert light is equaled by the extreme individuation of desert life-forms. Love flowers best in openness and freedom."

Back on the highway, we drove east to Brothers, and, after a quick pause at the Stage Stop, headed northeast on Camp Creek Road, a maintained gravel track. The character of the landscape changes along here, with big sage mixing with clots of juniper. Much of the land is given over to private ranches, including Doc and Connie Hatfield's outfit where the couple raises Oregon Country Beef.

At the Bear Creek-Camp Creek intersection, we turned right on Camp Creek and drove through rolling hills, past vintage barns and old outbuildings. This country was homesteaded long ago; the old wooden buildings are living proof.

By this time, we were far from the highway, far from the population centers of Central Oregon and far from the madding crowd.

Savoring Solitude *continued*

So it made perfect sense that I ran into Jason, our Schwan's man, the guy who drives the bright yellow truck and delivers all kinds of handy and delicious flash-frozen delectables to me and my neighbors. He does a good business in this rural precinct, where a trip to the market involves a 100-mile investment.

We traded small talk like long-lost friends who meet unexpectedly in a foreign place, and he told me that the pavement begins again past the "kitty litter plant."

Central Oregon Bentonite Co., on the left not far past Van Lake Road, mines the mineral bentonite and turns it into clumping cat litter. According to owner Lola Weaver, bentonite forms clumps when wet and is easily disposed of. The Weavers sell their product to a Chicago cat litter company. Their bentonite is also used to seal irrigation ditches and ponds.

Camp Creek Road intersects state Highway 380 west of Paulina. A left turn there will take you through Post, the geographic center of Oregon, and into Prineville.

Bentonite, which is mined from the ground east of Bend, is used in cat litter and as a sealant for irrigation ditches and ponds. This plant on Camp Creek Road transforms the mineral into a usable product.

photo by Jim Witty

You can also backtrack a mile or so from the bentonite plant and take Van Lake Road back to U.S. Highway 20, Brothers and Bend.

On the way back home, we followed a side road off of a side road and ended up near the top of a butte before the road petered out all together. We were all alone up there, and I found a good campsite for future reference.

I couldn't help thinking how easy it had been getting up that hill as I followed my tire tracks back down.

If You Go:

Editor's Note: In this particular article Jim had no final destination. His adventure was basically east on U.S. Highway 20 and northeast of the town of Brothers.

The Gerry Mountain Wilderness area is a worthy destination if your tastes run to the wild open.
photo by Mark Quon

Out There, Somewhere

Gerry Mountain WSA quality example of unscathed desert

Published: January 24, 2007

    After visiting the Gerry Mountain Wilderness Study Area, I've decided I use the phrase, "middle of nowhere," a bit too liberally.
    As in, "Where'd you go this weekend?"
    "Well, I found this little trail out in the middle of nowhere."
    The Gerry Mountain WSA makes those nowheres look like the outskirts of so many somewheres.
    You drive 74 miles east of Bend, then about 20 miles to the north (give or take a fence post or two), turn back west on a dirt road and you're getting close. Actually, you're right on the southern boundary of the WSA, a 27,000-acre no-man's land of rolling juniper hills with head-high sagebrush and scattered jumbles of basalt. Snow-covered Gerry Mountain rises 1,100 feet above all that.
    It's a winter range for deer and elk and everything else that comes with that. I saw cougar tracks left in a patch of snow, a golden eagle soaring overhead and piles of spongy elk scat underfoot.

Out There, Somewhere *continued*

I never saw another living soul (of the human persuasion) the entire time I roamed the southeastern portion of the WSA.

Find solitude.

According to the Bureau of Land Management, which administers this 7-square mile tract, a wilderness study area is "an area of public land under consideration for wilderness." It's managed to protect its natural condition until Congress makes a decision. That means cross country vehicle use is prohibited, as is cutting live vegetation. Vehicles are restricted to designated, signed routes.

I parked and left the beaten track, heading north a ways into the heart of this undulating country. It's dry, wind-scoured and lonesome; simple even, if you just consider the big picture. But keep walking and paying attention to your surroundings and you begin seeing the things that you'll remember long after you're warm and snug and safe by the fire. Compact, ground-hugging plants photosynthesizing like mad despite the long, cruel winter. Gnarled bonsai junipers that prove nature's got art completely wired. Tracks and animal dung that confirm the presence of a wild and even risky element that makes wilderness exciting and completely necessary.

Ed Abbey, that cantankerous old grouch who wrote so eloquently of the American West, called it "the only thing worth saving."

Gerry Mountain Wilderness Study Area is a remote, 27,000-acre tract of rolling juniper country. The sagebrush grows to a height of six feet and beyond.

photo by Jim Witty

"We need wilderness whether or not we ever set foot in it," wrote Cactus Ed. "We need a refuge even though we may not ever need to go there."

Even though it takes a couple of hours to get there from Bend, Gerry Mountain is accessible. You can drive the well-maintained dirt road that skirts the south boundary and never leave the confines of your vehicle, if your mobility is limited. If not, the interior beckons.

"That whole area between Bend and Burns, a whole lot of people are intimidated by it or are not inquisitive enough to get off the highway," mused Bill Marlett of the Oregon Natural Desert Association. "Once you do, you find a whole other world out there ... For being just two hours from Bend, it's an area that doesn't get a lot of use. If you're looking for solitude, it's a great place to go."

A ranch mailbox marks G.I. Ranch Road about 74 miles east of Bend off U.S. Highway 20.

photo by Mark Quon

The BLM studied the area 16 years ago and estimated that 20 antelope used the area throughout the year along with 75 mule deer in the summer and 230 in winter. Elk, sage grouse, hawks, bobcat, coyote and other animals also roam the WSA.

Back in 1991, the BLM recommended Gerry Mountain remain a WSA, primarily because of the potential for oil, gas and mineral development there. But Gerry Mountain remains virtually unchanged.

And a worthy destination, if your tastes run to the wild open.

"May your trails be crooked, winding, lonesome, dangerous, leading to the most amazing view," Abbey wrote somewhere along the line. "May your mountains rise into and above the clouds."

As long as they get you into the middle of somewhere you want to be. Or at least on the outskirts.

If You Go:

GETTING THERE: From 27th Street in Bend, drive east on U.S. Highway 20 just past milepost 74 to G.I. Ranch Rd. This unpaved road is unmarked. Turn left at the ranch mail box and drive 20.5 miles to Price-Twelvemile Rd. Turn left, pick up a map from the box, and continue along the southern perimeter of Gerry Mountain Wilderness Study Area. The WSA is on the right.

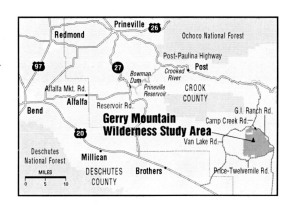

PERMITS: No permits required.

CONTACT: Bureau of Land Management, Prineville District, 541-416-6700.

Want to get the most out of the wide-open desert country? Get thee to the top of a butte.
photo by Jim Witty

Wherever You Go ... There You Are

Answer the siren song of the wild and free High Desert

Published: October 30, 2008

If you can resist a place called Buzzard Rock or Weasel Butte, you are far more disciplined than I.

The siren song of a butte known as Fuzztail, a hat named China or a reservoir called Tired Horse is simply too much; I have to go there or at least get close. If I believed in reincarnation, I'd like to think I was once a coyote rambling east of the Paulina Mountains and west of Stinkingwater Pass. Or maybe clear to the Snake River. But I don't want to get greedy.

A tough life out there on the High Desert, to be sure, but wild and free. And those Central Oregon full-moon nights, what a hoot.

Come to think, being a Homosapien desert rat in Bend or Redmond or Prineville or La Pine isn't such a bad deal. Look left and you're in the green hills, right and there you are, among all those buttes, berms, cones, sumps, springs, dry lakes, abandoned homesteads, lava fields, sage flats, juniper rims, dry washes, one-horse-no-gas towns, tables, plateaus, rimrock canyons, springs, gulches, washboard roads and broken dreams.

It's enough to make a body downright optimistic.

I tend to look at the desert as an attitude, not a specific destination. I approach the mountains differently, but I'm not sure why. I was planning a hike up near Broken Top in the Cascades on Monday but, given the forecast for unsettled weather later this week, decided against recommending a high-elevation outing. It's late October, high time for the other shoe to drop. And when it does, it can get real cold and real nasty, real fast. So I dusted off my desert demeanor, recalling something late author Ed Abbey once said: "What draws us into the desert is the search for something intimate in the remote." Thought provoking.

But this is the same guy who said, "Ah, to be a buzzard now that spring is here." Endearing (if not seasonally appropriate).

The country of my affection lies just to the east, out U.S. Highway 20. Not long and you've got junipers flying by on both sides and you're starting up the Horse Ridge grade. Then you top out and Pine Mountain looms to the south and the great wide open stretches out ahead.

This is where your options begin kicking in. Make a quick right on Forest Road 2015 or Spencer Wells Road and head back toward China Hat country? Continue on to the abandoned store and gas station at Millican and take Pine Mountain Road up to the observatory and beyond? Drive a little farther up the highway and hook in to Fox Butte Road to the south?

Check out Sand Spring, Quartz Mountain and Mahogany Butte? Keep going east past Brothers, Hampton, Glass Buttes, Chickahominy and Sage Hen Valley, stopping whenever and wherever you want? What's out that little road? There's one way to find out.

It's all about the choices out here. And there are many.

I drove out Fox Butte Road, and, on a whim, stayed left where Fox Butte crosses Moffit Road. There are few signs out this way, and the ones you do come across may or may not have something worthwhile to say. Pack plenty of water. There's not much in the way of wet out there.

My pal Hoss, a springer spaniel and certified desert rat (he has papers), and I gamboled up and around several little side roads as the spirit moved us.

Despite a full complement of maps, I found myself half lost most of the time. It was great. I didn't see another soul for four hours.

I did get up to the top of KO Butte, but it might have been Watkins, hard to say. Either way, there's a sketchy road to the top that passes by a big, square cement structure that looks as if it holds water, but I couldn't be sure. At the top, I got out and climbed around the lava boulders and surveyed the 360-degree scene. Open country every which way with a transition to pine and juniper off to the west. Higher ground? More rainfall? An enduring mystery.

I continued west, eventually intersecting with Forest Road 23, a main north-south gravel way that leads back to U.S. Highway 20 and home. The other way (south) gets you to Derrick Cave, The Devils Garden and eventually to the Fort Rock Valley.

It was getting late and I was running low on gas. I did the responsible thing. I turned south to see what was over the next rise, and the next one.

Then I turned around and limped back to the Shell station on the edge of town.

If You Go:

Editor's Note: In this particular article Jim had no final destination. Drive east on U.S. Highway 20 and get gone!

Jim Witty loved the Badlands in all seasons.

photo by Mark Quon

Winter is a Good Time for Badlands

A trusty winter hiking destination

Published: February 25, 2004

     I can't tell you how wonderful it is to be able to get out and hike in February.
Yes, I can. It's good for the sole.
Hiking with boots, not skis, on dirt, not snow.
Remember what that's like?
     The Badlands is a trusty destination this time of year where, barring an unusual blizzard, you can walk out across the desert unencumbered by the vicissitudes of winter.
     Oh, you may get a chilly wind, some cold rain or even a skiff of snow, but a'postholing you almost surely will not go.
     This time of year the Badlands is good. This stern, austere country can get hot and dusty come July, but it's a pleasant place to poke around on a cool day in February.
     Which is what I did.
     There are a couple of convenient ways to enter this 34,000-acre tract of twisty juniper, ubiquitous sagebrush, basalt, coyotes, raw wind, sand, mule deer, water-carved gullies and open views. You can drive east on U.S. Highway 20 to the 17-mile marker, turn left and park near the Bureau of Land Management Wilderness Study Area bulletin board about a half-mile up the road. Or you can do what I did this time, which

was turn left at the 16-mile marker and park at the 16-mile marker trailhead.

The best thing to do is pick up a map at the bulletin board there. There's a well-trod trail from there to Badlands Rock, which is a nice out-and-back trek with the added bonus that you probably won't get lost. Sometimes though, I like to take off across the desert and explore a little. I didn't get lost this time, but I could have. Easily. The seemingly flat, relatively open desert can be deceiving.

Three years ago, I spent a thoroughly engrossing day out here with Bob Speik and a couple of other people participating in a navigation field exercise.

Engrossing, but humbling.

Speik took us out into that flattish expanse of seeming sameness, armed with map, compass and GPS, and got us thoroughly lost. After much consulting and inspecting and calibrating and consulting again, we were still lost. But in the end, Speik gave us a few strategic pointers and Eureka! We found us.

The point (I think) is that those little gullies, gulches and draws make the desert a lot more interesting upon close inspection. The desert's beauty is found in its subtleties.

The Badlands is a Wilderness Study Area, which means it comes with more regulations than all that other BLM territory to the east, but is still open to limited motorized use. Central Oregon environmental advocates are pushing for legislation to make it a full-fledged wilderness. They argue that the elimination of motorized vehicles would also eliminate illegal dumping, vandalism, tree cutting, depositing stolen vehicles and livestock theft (there's a main dirt road that bisects the Badlands and another couple roads open seasonally).

Whatever ends up happening, the trails are off-limits to cars, trucks and motorcycles. It doesn't take long to get away from the highway noise (and if you go cross-country, lost).

This wilderness-in-training, less than 20 miles from Bend, is an excellent place to lose the winter white blues.

And find your hybernating hiker within.

Editor's Note: On March 30th, 2009, President Obama signed the Omnibus Public Lands Management Act, designating the Oregon Badlands as wilderness.

If You Go:

GETTING THERE: From Bend, drive about 16 miles east on U.S. Highway 20. Turn left at milepost 16 into a dirt parking lot. The trailhead is here.

TERRAIN: Some undulations but mostly level.

DIFFICULTY: Easy to moderate.

ACCESS: Hikers.

PERMITS: None required.

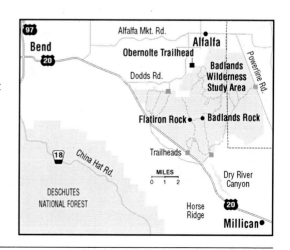

The desert of Central and Eastern Oregon, a land of mind-numbing expanses, is a mix of public and private land. A good Bureau of Land Management map is handy when exploring.

photo by Dean Guernsey

This Desert Place

Much of Central Oregon is desert landscape, but that's not to say it is without beauty

Published: March 15, 2006

When people from other places think of Oregon, they go straight to dripping fir forests and plunging mountain streams. But more than half of the state is desert.

That's one of those nifty and nebulous generalizations I pull out from time to time, usually when I'm raving about how great Central Oregon is. You know, one of those things I heard somebody say one time, liked it and took it for my own.

But this time I looked at a map. And there's definitely a lot of desert over on the right side. OK, maybe more like a quarter of the state when you account for the Wallowas, the Strawberries, the Ochocos and the Blues. But a lot of desert. Much of the country east of the green spine of the Cascades is high desert, 24,000 square miles or so - give or take a few hundred thousand acres - of bitterbrush, sagebrush, treeless scarps and alkali lakes.

Beautiful.

Or not, depending whom you ask.

"Since Man first chipped words on slabs of stone, he has tried to describe the desert," writes E.R. Jackman in the regional classic, *The Oregon Desert*. "He has said it is cruel, brutal, ruthless, ugly, horrible, appalling and fraught with terror."

The desert can be a tough neighborhood, especially if you're part of a lost wagon train in search of green, cool and wet. Thirsty colors perception. So I'll buy cruel, brutal, ruthless. (I prefer stern, austere, stark.) But ugly? Never once.

I walk in the desert seeking a semblance of peace and always get that primal recognition that less is more. Water, or the lack of it, defines this place. So I'm compelled to dial back and appreciate lichens, tumbleweeds and the seductive simplicity of terrain reduced to its mostly horizontal essence. Quaking aspen or incense cedar have it easy. They smack you between the eyes; squat succulentlike plants can only trip you up when you're spending too much time looking at the mountains on the far horizon.

A hike in the desert doesn't have to be a major production, although you'll need to pack the essentials (water, food, extra clothing etc.). Not 25 miles east of Bend, you're in the thick of it, ankle-deep in bunchgrass and bitterbrush.

On my most recent trip out there, I pulled the car over on a side road beneath the flank of Pine Mountain, and we started walking. We headed west, then south in a squall, toward Pine Mountain in the far distance. Snow streamed from a ragged sky, the tiny ice crystals clinging momentarily to the woody branches at our feet, then flaming out like shooting stars. The desert floor is rife with stubby, ground-hugging plants with small leaves, the better to conserve water.

And sagebrush. It's a common shrub of the desert with an uncommon natural history.

According to Ron Halvorson, the Bureau of Land Management botanist who's always good for an eye-popping factoid, the ubiquitous sagebrush has two sets of leaves - perennial and ephemeral. When spring finally arrives on the High Desert, the rain falls and the weather warms, the sagebrush puts out lots of large temporary leaves so it can make hay while the sun shines. Then, when dry, hot summer sets in, those fall off, leaving only the much smaller, drought-resistant leaves to endure the season.

Check out the ground beneath a sagebrush next time you're out that way. Sure enough, fallen leaves. Brutally fascinating.

As we gradually gained elevation, the junipers descended to meet us. First a lone sentinel, then three, and ultimately entire squadrons scattered up the slope. More water up there.

Somewhere inside the juniper zone, we turned around and marched back the way we'd come, noting the same band of evergreen transition on the northern hills far out across the flats. Down the waterless wash with the strewn rocks and deer scat and back to where we began.

Inspired, I took a crack at describing the desert.

Stern. Austere. Stark.

Beautiful. Looks like Oregon.

If You Go:

Editor's Note: In this particular article Jim had no final destination. His adventure took him east on U.S. Highway 20 (about 25 miles east of Bend), then south toward Pine Mountain.

Lichen growing on branches of an old juniper in the Badlands.
photo by Mark Quon

A Closer Look at the Badlands
Naturalist Larry Berrin has an eye for the details
Published: November 01, 2006

Larry Berrin knows birds.

A naturalist at the High Desert Museum, Berrin recently published *Birds of the High Desert: An Introduction to Common Species*, a handy guide to the specific types of birds we're likely to see right here. When he's not out exploring, he spends a lot of time thinking about the flora and fauna of Central Oregon and the nearby Great Basin.

It hasn't always been that way.

Berrin was born and raised in New York City, a perpetually curious boy from the borough of Queens who had memorized the city's subway routes by age 14, with particular emphasis on the museums along the way. He spent much of his childhood poking around natural history exhibits, learning about plants and animals he'd never seen in their natural habitats.

After high school, Berrin headed north to the University of Maine where he earned a degree in natural resources. He received a graduate degree from Antioch University in Ohio and has worked for the national Audubon Society and as a park ranger at Ellis Island in New York. Most recently, Berrin lived on a little farm in Vermont where he produced *Vermont Birds: An Introduction to Familiar Species*.

His travels to the West fueled his curiosity and adventuresome spirit. He and his wife moved here about a year ago. We met up in the Badlands east of Bend Friday to do some birding, some plant identification and lots of general looking around. And we soon found we could help each other out, much like the symbiotic relationship between the algae and fungi (lichens) that adorn so many of the rocks out on the desert. Berrin is adept at discerning this natural environment, from the harsh cry of the pinyon jay, believed to migrate through the region, to the tiny cilia-like fibers that help the sagebrush retain much-needed moisture. And a hundred other things. But he's still learning the lay of the land.

Ancient pictographs can be found in Little Dry Canyon.

photo courtesy of Brent Fenty

I showed him around the Badlands Wilderness Study Area, and he showed me what was going on here from a naturalist's perspective.

The desert is not filled with apex predators, large, dramatic animals that overwhelm the senses with their sinewy beauty or awesome power. You have to look closely, appreciate the subtleties. Like the fine hairs on a great horned owl's wing feathers; they enable the large bird, said to be able to hear a mouse moving beneath a foot of snow, to fly silently. Or the nesting potential of a hollowed-out juniper snag. Or the hind foot of a white-tailed jackrabbit (Lepus townsendii), all that remains of a recent violent encounter between predator and prey.

We walked out across the flats, then along part of the Dry River Trail, stopping often to notice the details: robins in flight, deer scat, the call of a Towsend's solitaire, a Russian thistle tumbling like the brittle weed it is, in the wind.

There are thousands of reasons I get excited about the desert; now I have several more.

The Badlands is an ideal place to get your feet wet. It's a 37,000-acre tract of old juniper, lava outcrops, subtle swales and a slot canyon that transports you into a different ecological niche in a matter of feet.

Maps of the Badlands are available at the major trailheads. Those and Berrin's *Birds of the High Desert* will serve you well.

Editor's Note: On March 30th, 2009, President Obama signed the Omnibus Public Lands Management Act, designating the Oregon Badlands as wilderness.

If You Go:

GETTING THERE: Drive east from Bend on U.S. Highway 20. Turn left a few hundred yards past milepost 17.

CONTACT: Bureau of Land Management, 541-416-6700.

A hairy woodpecker is joined by a chipmunk as it stops in for a drink over the weekend at Cabin Lake, which is southeast of La Pine in Lake County.

photo by Jim Witty

Oasis of Birds

Wildlife blinds at Cabin Lake let you view a variety of characters

Published: October 10, 2007

The birds were there for the water. And I was there for the birds.

Cabin Lake is an old Forest Service guard station at 4,550-feet elevation, situated in a unique spot where the High Desert sagebrush ecosystem brushes up against the ponderosa pine forest. Not far from Fort Rock, Cabin Lake occupies that slender and perceptible border; one moment you're scuffing through rabbitbrush, the next you're walking beneath scroll-barked pines.

And right there along that no-man's land are two rough-hewn wildlife watching blinds, about 100 yards apart, back behind the historical guard station buildings. This ornithological Maginot Line is a birder's dream; species from both worlds mingle here to drink from the small concrete basins that front the blinds. Water is the limiting factor in this bone-dry country.

I settled in on a bench inside and poked my modest 17-85 mm lens through the viewing portal, a square hole cut in the wood, with a plastic veil.

It's a simple set up that truly works. If you're reasonably quiet and don't make any abrupt moves, the birds that swoop in for a drink don't have a clue that anything's amiss. The click of single lens reflex mirrors doesn't bother them. Which means you

This simple blind is one of two at Cabin Lake that provides cover for bird-watchers and photographers.

photo by Jim Witty

can observe the passing parade a la natural — unfazed by the taint of human presence.

The cast of characters is colorful and varied. Going in, I didn't know what to expect, and was pleasantly surprised that so many birds and tiny chipmunks show up for a drink in the middle of the day.

First in were a couple of Clark's nutcrackers, large, gregarious birds that flew down and took immediate ownership of the water hole. I was familiar with these birds from winter encounters at warming shelters in the Cascades. Confident and jaunty, the spike-billed Clark's nutcracker likes to cadge pieces of energy bar from obliging cross-country skiers.

Then came a woodpecker of some kind, which sent me plunging into the Kaufman *Field Guide to Birds of North America*. A white-headed woodpecker, some sort of sapsucker? The learning curve for this bird-watching thing can be steep. I finally concluded it was a hairy woodpecker, although it could have been a downy woodpecker. But the beak was too long.

I know a pinyon jay when I see one. Or two or six. The pastel blue jays descended to the water in a group, which, according to Kaufman, is their preference. Kaufman also shows the central portion of the state as their northernmost range in Oregon.

"In arid pinyon pine and yellow pine woods of the west, this odd, short-tailed jay (more like a small blue crow) wanders in large flocks," Kenn Kaufman writes. "Highly sociable, almost never seen singly. Well named, it feeds very heavily on seeds of pinyon pine."

Meet Me In The Badlands: Exploring Central Oregon with Jim Witty

Oasis of Birds *continued*

I wonder out loud what it feeds heavily on in the land of Pinus ponderosa and they all scatter (I found out later that the pondo is considered a yellow pine).

Throughout the afternoon, at both blinds, I saw a red-winged blackbird, several white-breasted nuthatch, a gaggle of small grey birds I have to admit I could not identify, and a loggerhead shrike.

Of the latter I am reasonably sure, even though they migrate to the southern part of the United States and Mexico in winter. Curious beast, this shrike. According to Stan Tekiela, author of *Birds of Oregon Field Guide*, the loggerhead is a songbird that acts like a bird of prey. "Known for skewering prey on barbed wire fences, thorns and other sharp objects to store or hold still while tearing apart to eat, hence its other name, butcher bird. Feet are too weak to hold prey while eating."

Tekiela says that shrike populations are declining because pesticides are killing grasshoppers, its major food source.

Although I didn't linger until nightfall, this is mule deer, elk, antelope, woodrat, bat, coyote, bobcat, mountain lion, deer mouse and great-horned owl territory. Cabin Lake could be a hoot after hours.

It should go without saying, but I will anyway. This is no place for your family dog (or cat!).

Those in the know recommend bringing a jug of water in case the supply system isn't working. There's an unimproved Forest Service campground nearby, which can be heavily used by deer hunters in season. The nearest water and toilet facilities are in Fort Rock, about 10 miles south.

If You Go:

GETTING THERE: From Bend, drive south on U.S. Highway 97 and then turn left in La Pine on Forest Road 22. Drive 26 miles east, then turn right and drive six miles south on Forest Road 18 (China Hat Rd.). Turn right into the campground and follow the gravel road to the back side of the guard station buildings.

COST: Free.

CONTACT: Bend-Fort Rock Ranger District of the Deschutes National Forest, 541-383-4000.

Paulina Creek below one of many waterfalls.
photo by Mark Quon

Paulina Creek

Waterfalls come in all sizes along the trail to Paulina Falls

Published: August 11, 2004

Paulina Creek is waterfall nirvana. And there's nothing quite like cool, tumbling water to take the edge off a hot, dusty hike.

Last week we visited the mother of all falls on the creek, Paulina Falls, one of the premier attractions inside Newberry National Volcanic Monument. I described Paulina Falls as 80 feet of raw gravitational power, a wide-angle panorama of unbridled hydraulics.

Then we got a taster of the smaller falls downstream, got our hair wet, and vowed we'd get back there to explore.

This week we did. And to top off the fun and sense of adventure, we made the trip with a couple of visitors from Back East who were awed by the scenery and just had to swim in a pool below a waterfall.

It didn't take us long.

We took off from Ten-Mile Sno-park, hiking down the road and turning left onto a singletrack trail. About a half-mile up the windy little path, we came to Road 300, jogged left and then right and began hearing the welcome whoosh of falling water.

Paulina Creek *continued*

The first waterfall we came to was small compared to the big bopper upstream, but we were able to get completely wet, the water cascading over our heads.

But we wanted more. So we walked upstream a little ways and crossed the creek via a wooden footbridge. Then we followed the trail downstream in search of the perfect little waterfall.

That's a completely subjective determination.

Luckily, there are plenty of falls on this steep little creek and we were pretty much all on the same page.

One of the many falls you will encounter while hiking up Paulina Creek.

photo by Mark Quon

It wasn't long before we found what we were looking for - a couple cascading falls with big juicy pools below.

On a hot day, the water's just right. We swam, basked a little in the sun, swam again. We even got behind one of the mini falls for one of those signature photos that remind you of a Hawaii travel brochure.

It's a creek with lots of vertical drop so there are plenty of waterfalls in the eight-mile stretch (there's a trail all the way) between the footbridge and the bottom of the hill.

Explore away. But be sure to use common sense. Sheer cliffs and unsure footing abound off the trail. And some pools are safer for swimming than others, depending on your abilities. If in doubt, just dangle your feet in the water and take a lot of photos.

If you decide to explore the waterfalls, take plenty of water, pack some energy food and a dry change of clothes (very nice to have when you get back to the car). Good footwear is essential. Those functional sandals that aren't afraid to get wet work well but sneakers are fine.

Cowabunga.

If You Go:

GETTING THERE: Drive south on U.S. Highway 97 and turn left on Road 21 toward Newberry National Volcanic Monument. The Ten Mile Sno-Park is located off the north side of the Road 21 leading to Newberry Crater (10 miles east of U.S. Highway 97). The Ponderosa Rim Trail follows along Paulina Creek to the north.

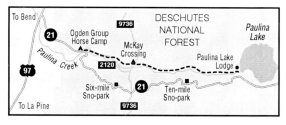

A group of explorers descend into the Lava River Cave.
photo by Mark Quon

What Lies Beneath

Volcanic past gives Central Oregon many great caves

Published: August 31, 2005

If you're into exploring dark, dank, cool grottoes, spelunking may be just the ticket for a late summer's afternoon.

Thanks to its volcanic past, Central Oregon is home to several spelunkable caves.

A hotspot of subterranean intrigue awaits adventurers southeast of Bend, out China Hat Road. The caves - Boyd, Skeleton, Wind and Arnold Ice - were formed about 7,000 years ago when a lava river from Mount Newberry flowed red hot and viscous in a channel. When the eruption ceased, the channel crusted over and drained, leaving a lava tube. The caves were discovered many years later when parts collapsed, creating entrances from above.

If you're heading east on China Hat Road, the first cave you come to is Boyd; it's worth a look. Right before the China Hat pavement ends, take the first road to the left and drive about a quarter-mile to the turnaround. There are no signs here, just a railing and a flight of stairs down into the cave. On a hot day, you'll be struck by the cool as you descend. Boyd Cave is blocked by fallen rocks not too far from the entrance, but rattling around down there gives you a feel for spelunking.

What Lies Beneath *continued*

Back up top, I drove back out to China Hat, turned left (east) and took another left about a half-mile up the gravel road (again, there is no sign). Skeleton Cave is about 1-1/2-miles down the road, next to a spacious turnaround.

Skeleton Cave is a whole lot bigger than Boyd; you can easily stand up and look around in the "lobby." The cavern goes farther than the distance I ventured; caves just aren't my niche.

But they're the perfect niche for the western big-eared bat, which hibernates inside the caves of the region throughout late fall and winter. Bats (almost a dozen species live in the region), an essential insect-eating part of the High Desert ecosystem, are easily disturbed when they're chilling out and are extremely vulnerable, according to the National Speleological Society (speleology is the scientific study and exploration of caves).

According to a section on bat conservation culled from the NSS Web site, it can take bats 30 minutes to raise their metabolism enough to escape their torpor and fly.

"If a passing caver is heard, or flashes a light" toward them, they can go into a "slow panic," according to the Web site. That may cause them to flee into the cold, winter environment in search of safer digs. The caves are closed to exploration from fall until spring to protect the bats. One final note on bats. Despite the spooky stigma attached to them, they're not only harmless, they're beneficial to the environment.

"They eat tons of mosquitoes and other insects," said Kathy Wright, a wildlife specialist with The High Desert Museum.

According to www.batcon.org, a single little brown bat (common to Oregon) can catch and consume 1,200 mosquito-size insects in an hour.

Holy hibernaculum! Bats are our friends. They won't get caught in your hair, are more closely related to primates than mice and rarely contract rabies, according to Bats4kids, an AOL Web site. Bats are wild animals and if we leave them alone, they'll leave us alone.

There are two other caves east of Skeleton - Wind Cave is a tougher trudge and Arnold Ice Cave can't be hiked. The entrance has frozen shut, but it's an interesting place nonetheless. The cave was once used by Central Oregon pioneers as a natural ice storage chamber.

Possibly the best spelunking in Central Oregon can be found inside Lava River Cave, a 5,200 foot-long subterranean passageway about 12 miles south of Bend off U.S. Highway 97. It's a fee site; the day-use fee is $5 and lanterns (a must unless you have your own equipment) are $3. Talk to the helpful staffers at the Lava River Cave entrance office and they'll tell you all about the cave. The other caves out China Hat Road are strictly self-guided.

Before you go caving, make sure you have the proper equipment. Lanterns, big flashlights or lights you wear on your head are best. Each person should carry one. Sturdy boots are a must, given the boulders found inside the caves. And don't forget to dress warmly. It may be 90 degrees where the sun's shining, but it's in the low 40s inside these caves.

As for me, I couldn't wait to get back out in the sunshine.

Deschutes National Forest recreation managers were forced to remove a staircase descending into Skeleton Cave in 2005 due to vandalism.
photo by Jim Witty

If You Go:

GETTING THERE:

Lava River Cave: Drive about 12 miles south of Bend on U.S. Highway 97. Entrance is on the east side of the Highway.

Boyd/Skeleton Caves: From Bend, drive south on U.S. Highway 97 and take the Baker Rd. exit 143, toward Knott Rd., then turn right on China Hat Rd., then...

Boyd Cave: Right before the China Hat pavement ends, take the first road to the left and drive about a quarter-mile to the turnaround. There are no signs here, just a railing and a flight of stairs down into the cave.

Skeleton Cave: Take China Hat Rd. until pavement ends and continue about a half-mile up the gravel road (again, there is no sign). Skeleton Cave is about 1-1/2-miles down the road, next to a spacious turnaround.

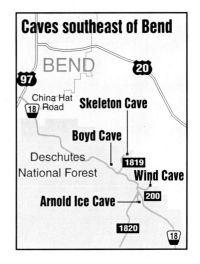

There are ranches, old buildings and lots of wide-open space on the road to the Ana River.
photo by Joan Witty

Down to the River

A little off the beaten path, Ana River provides year-round fishing excellence

Published: February 08, 2006

I might have gone fishin'
But after thinking it over
The road to the river
Is a mighty long way.

    I was humming this old Merle Haggard song, watching the fence posts whir by and the speedometer tick past 80 when the sun came beaming through a cloud break. Rather than following my soaring spirits straight into a speeding ticket or worse, I backed off the accelerator and admired the countryside. Miles of unbroken, sagebrush flat with a stubby, white-flocked mountain range in the far distance. A soaring hawk every .27 miles or so. The prospect of more delicious emptiness over every blip in the blacktop.
    It was a good day to be flying out over the desert. At a little over 100 miles southeast of Bend, the road to this river is far enough to make it interesting but not butt- and brain-numbingly so. I'd like to think Merle would agree.

The Ana River sluices through the desert near Summer Lake. The topography is such that from a short distance, you can't tell there's a stream in the vicinity.

photo by Jim Witty

The Ana River is as improbable as an espresso stand in Fort Rock.

You won't see it until you're right there, gazing down into the steep-sided slot canyon. Just seven miles long, the Ana flows from a series of underwater springs in Ana Reservoir, a 50-acre impoundment, built in the 1940s, that looks more like a big farm pond than a full-fledged lake. The spring water, an optimum 52 degrees the year round, creates a rich crucible of life along its short reach. The Ana makes a series of lazy turns and eventually flows into Summer Lake.

"It's a little spring creek in the desert," said Bill Tinniswood, a biologist with the Klamath office of the Oregon Department of Fish and Wildlife. "It's spring fed. That makes it unique. You have yearlong (insect) hatches. You can fish over rising fish every day of the year."

Which goes a long way in explaining my high spirits this day, but you don't have to be a dry fly fisher to appreciate this oasis in the High Desert.

According to Tinniswood, the soil along the river is highly alkaline, and becomes more so the closer it gets to Summer Lake. Trout don't do well in the lower reaches, but the irrepressible tui chub is said to survive down there.

"The Ana River is different than anything else around Oregon," Tinniswood said.

One reason for the differences is that the Ana lies on the inside edge of the Great Basin, a 190,000 square mile, bone-dry but cool expanse of high-elevation desert land. A major difference between the Great Basin and the desert just to the east of Bend is drainage. All of the rivers, streams, creeks and rivulets in our neck of the woods

Down to the River *continued*

eventually find their way into the Pacific Ocean by way of the Deschutes and Columbia rivers. In contrast, the waters of the Great Basin are inland and isolated.

"The Great Basin is a series of drainages that are closed," Tinniswood noted.

Historically (10,000 years ago), several basins - such as Warner, Goose Lake, Chewaucan and Summer Lake in the southeastern section of Oregon - were connected by a big body of water, Lake Chewaucan, he explained. Today, the basins within the (great) Basin are shut off from one another, with only the shared genetic characteristics of the redband trout and other fish offering a porthole to the past.

If you're looking to see and photograph the Ana River, your best bet is to stay up top, where you can follow the canyon a ways and get a representative sampling of the river below, the desert at your feet and the nearby mountains. If the fishing (go ahead, just try to ignore those swirling trout below) or plain curiosity get the better of you, you'll need to choose your descent (and subsequent ascent) carefully. With an abundance of recent rainfall, the slopes are a muddy mire in some places. Traction is at a premium.

We dropped down to the river several times but did most of our downstream traveling up top.

The river flows roughly southeast to County Road 4-17, where it forms the northeast boundary of the Summer Lake Wildlife Area. Below the county road, the Ana flows inside the wildlife area where the water becomes increasingly alkaline.

If you've got the time and the appetite on the ride back home, stop in at the Cowboy Dinner Tree near the little town of Silver Lake for a cowboy cut 30-ounce top sirloin or whole chicken. They'll make you cry uncle. Call ahead (541-576-2426) or visit www.cowboydinnertree.homestead.com.

Whether you stop or not, it's good traveling country.

Slow down. Plug in a CD. Enjoy the ride.

If You Go:

GETTING THERE: From Bend, drive south on U.S. Highway 97. Just south of La Pine, turn left on State Highway 31. Make a left turn at the sign for Ana Reservoir a few miles north of Summer Lake. Turn right about a half-mile down the road to the reservoir. You can also access the lower reaches of Ana River by turning left off Highway 31 on to County Road 4-17.

For more information on the Great Basin, try *Basin and Range* by John McPhee. For fishing information on the Ana River, try *Guide to Fly Fishing Central and Southeastern Oregon* by Harry Teel or *Fishing Central Oregon* by Geoff Hill, Brooke Snavely and Raven Wing.

View from within Fort Rock, looking down on Oregon's Outback.
photo by Mark Quon

Southeastern Oregon's Outback

Open country at our back door

Published: March 03, 2004

The southeast part of Oregon almost always comes as a surprise to newcomers.

As in, nice sagebrush, but where are the fir trees? But also as in, have you ever seen so much wide open country in your life?

Oregon's Outback is miles and miles of sagebrush, flat-topped buttes and volcanic anomalies. It's also coyotes yipping, pronghorn burning out across the flats, bald eagles soaring and clouds so white, skies so blue and air so pure that your eyes water.

And it's close by.

Oregon's Outback National Scenic Byway, State Route 31, begins just south of La Pine and takes the traveler to Fort Rock, Silver Lake and eventually Summer Lake, Paisley and Lakeview. It's a great starting point for side excursions along the way.

Fort Rock, for instance, is less than 90 minutes from Bend, but seems as if it's 100 years away. It's the hub of historic homesteading activity in the region and still serves a far-flung network of hay ranches and cattle operations. There's a general store and the Waterin' Hole Tavern, a friendly place where locals congregate and strangers don't stay that way very long.

Southeastern Oregon's Outback *continued*

But it's the geology of the place that makes an outing out this way special. Fort Rock State Park, just north of town, is an outsized rock formation that's home to eagles and hawks and a whole lot of history. It used to be the site of a deep inland lake, but now is a crescent-shaped sentinel in the High Desert. Fort Rock formed when red-hot basalt magma boiled up through the water, then cooled. Not far from "the rock" is the cave where 10,000-year-old sagebrush sandals were discovered in 1938, providing scientists with a well-preserved link to the distant past.

Hole in the Ground involves a detour off the highway, which may or may not be covered in snow this time of year. It's a 300-foot indentation that formed when molten lava hit water and caused an explosion.

To the southeast of Fort Rock is the town of Christmas Valley, a jumping-off point for Crack in the Ground (a graphic example of a geologic fault that visitors can actually walk through). It's a 2-mile fissure where winter's ice remains throughout the year. To the east of Christmas Valley are the Shifting Sand Dunes, composed mainly of ash from the eruption of nearby Mount Mazama about 7,000 years ago. And everywhere in between is open space, the kind of landscape that makes the West the West.

Lost Forest, near the dunes, is a remnant stand of an ancient ponderosa pine forest. The road can be iffy; a high clearance vehicle with 4-wheel drive is best.

While the weather can be a little unpredictable, spring is a good time to experience the outback. Soon, wildflowers will start poking through the soil and the desert will be awash in color. Until then though, there's plenty of local color out there where the horizon meets the sky.

Crack in the Ground's winter ice remains year round.

photo by Jim Witty

If You Go:

GETTING THERE: Drive south on U.S. Highway 97. Just south of La Pine, turn left (east) on State Route 31 into Oregon's outback.

The mother of all Beaver State junipers is purportedly somewhere between China Hat Butte and Fort Rock.

photo by Jim Witty

China Hat Butte

In search of Oregon's tallest juniper tree

Published: September 03, 2004

It's not whether you win or lose, it's the journey. In other words, it's not the destination that matters, it's how you play the game.

I spent most of a day trying to get that right.

Don't get me wrong. Good things happened. We enjoyed these perfect oil-browned turkey sandwiches in the shade of some big ponderosa pines, got to see a coyote lope out through the bitterbrush and sage at midday and engaged in some thought-provoking conversation about SUVs and how the Big Bad Wolf got a bad rap.

We even tested our mettle against a broken muffler bracket and came up with a resourceful quick-fix that would have made MacGyver proud.

But we didn't find the state's tallest juniper tree and, quite frankly, that rankled.

It still does a little.

Map Guy didn't make the trip, but he's been there before and gave me a map. It was an official map, not one that he'd cobbled together, so any dissatisfaction aimed at him would be misplaced and morally repugnant. The batteries inside my GPS unit were low, but, since I hadn't replaced them in more than a year, I couldn't very well put that on Eveready. And we all know that blaming Mother Nature is a stupid thing to do.

China Hat Butte *continued*

Even I'm not that stupid.

Which is why I can't help feeling that I got blown out by the home team. Even so, it was kind of fun bouncing to and fro on sketchy, rock-strewn Forest Service roads in the low-slung family sedan.

We sensed that we were close. And we knew that we were thoroughly confused.

The mother of all Beaver State junipers is purportedly somewhere between China Hat Butte and Fort Rock. According to Map Guy, it's a solitary specimen among a legion of pines. You can drive to it. And, to paraphrase my cartographic chum, What's the matter with you? I gave you a map.

Cabin Lake looks like a good place to camp.

photo by Joan Witty

After rattling down a dozen washboard side roads (and reattaching the muffler with the wire from a reporter's steno notebook) all to no avail, we did what no self-respecting football team would ever do. We gave up.

And started saying things like, "It's a beautiful day," and "We sure did see some country," and "What the heck am I going to write about on Monday?"

It really was a beautiful day. And we did see some good country, including the stretch of road between U.S. Highway 97 south of Bend and China Hat, which affords stellar views of the High Desert and takes you into evergreen forests (and even fir trees if you venture around the back side of China Hat). Keep going south on China Hat Road and you'll find yourself in Fort Rock and some serious desert. There's a lightly used campground at the base of China Hat.

Down the road toward Fort Rock, Cabin Lake isn't a lake at all, but it looks like a good place to camp just the same.

As for the writing, I like to look at it this way: It's not the fish, it's the fishing.

Yeah, right. Who am I fooling? I'm going to find that elusive, outsized, water-guzzling codger or die trying.

Maybe then I can slow down and enjoy the picnic.

If You Go:

GETTING THERE: See next article.

The gnarled old codger is found with the help of a GPS.
photo by Jim Witty

Found it: Map Guy and a GPS Help Jim Witty Locate an Enormous Juniper

Ancient juniper is reported to be largest in the state... or is it?

Published: September 09, 2004

Eureka. We found it. And I feel just a little sheepish. It wasn't as if what is arguably Oregon's tallest juniper could remain hidden for very long.

Last week, as you may recall, I went looking for the big tree out past China Hat, and after many a wrong turn and dashed hope, came up empty. This time, we had Map Guy along to show the way. And we might have been skunked again if not for the wonders of modern satellite navigation technology.

A GPS (with working batteries) is a wonderful thing. The functioning GPS does not lie. And sure enough, that gnarled old codger was right there at N 43 33.128, W 120 53.934. An ancient juniper with a massive trunk sharing airspace with a cluster of ponderosa pines.

Here's the deal. The first time around, we made it out Forest Road 22 and 23, but couldn't find Road 700 off to the right. That's because the sign is no longer there. But with the GPS pointing the way this time, we made it down Road 700 to Road 800 and

Found It: Map Guy and a GPS Help Jim Witty Locate an Enormous Juniper *continued*

the big tree. We'd been tantalizingly close the week before.

This juniper is huge. But it may or may not be the biggest in the state. After our wild-goose chase last week, I received several e-mails about the juniper's whereabouts and about other big junipers in the state. There's one out by the Lost Forest, another to the south. Maybe I should look closer to Prineville. Perhaps not reveal the tree's location at all for the tall juniper's sake.

"The juniper you were looking for is labeled 'Oregon's Largest Juniper' on Forest Service firemen's maps," wrote Mark Corbet, who spent several years working on the off-highway vehicle trail system in the Fort Rock Ranger District of the Deschutes National Forest. "Like so many things, the title of largest is always changing. In the mid-'80s, Oregon's largest Western juniper was one located in a fellow's yard in southwest Redmond. I measured the juniper you were looking for and it was bigger than the Redmond tree. A few years later I nominated a Western juniper near the Lost Forest, east of Fort Rock. The last I heard it is still the state's biggest."

This juniper is huge but it may not be the largest.
photo by Jim Witty

Biggest means combined circumference in inches, height in feet and a formula involving the average crown spread, Corbet explained.

Finding the juniper was far from anticlimactic. None in our party had ever seen such a tree. We oohed and aahed for a while and took some photos. Then we hunted up a nearby geocache near and dear to Map Guy's heart.

After taking a wire-art scorpion from the hidden ammo box and replacing it with a suitable trinket, we sat on a log and enjoyed the late summer afternoon.

And I confirmed right then and there that the journey is much sweeter if you reach your destination.

If You Go:

GETTING THERE: GPS coordinates: N 43 33.128, W 120 53.934.

There's nothing highbrow about Horse Butte.
photo by Jim Witty

A Butte-iful Day: Horse and Lava Buttes

Butte-hopping in the high desert

Published: March 24, 2004

Sometimes it's like this.
Why climb a mountain when a butte will do?
Go ahead, take two. They're small.

Last weekend, Dave Jasper, *The Bulletin* arts and entertainment writer, and I decided we were going to do something fun and outdoorsy. His wife and three, count them, three small children were out of town and Dave was just itching to get outside and - climb a butte. I'm guessing he didn't have any plays to attend or recitals to take in. I'm guessing he was a wee bit bored. I'm guessing the Metropolitan Opera hadn't picked last weekend for a live remote.

Because there's nothing highbrow about Horse Butte.

But there's something appealing about this isolated hill or mountain with steep or precipitous sides (thanks Merriam-Webster). Actually, one of the appealing things about Horse Butte is that it's not all that steep or precipitous. And we were feeling a wee bit lazy; Dave's got screaming-twins-at-three-in-the-morning issues, and me, I'm just that way.

We were going to go canoeing but the thought of hefting that big boy on and off

A Butte-iful Day: Horse and Lava Buttes *continued*

the racks left us both worn out.

Plan B looked butte-iful. Sorry Merriam.

Horse Butte is out China Hat Road not far from town. That's a mixed blessing.

Fortunately, it's close and it's pretty in a high-deserty sort of way and there's a commanding view of the countryside from up top.

Unfortunately, it's close. And there's a certain subset of yahoos dead set on marring the prettiness with their empty beer cans, plastic Fred Meyer bags and coyote carcasses. I'm serious. There was a dead coyote at the base of the butte and I'm pretty sure it didn't keel over from old age right there among the carpet remnants.

Lava Butte can be seen right off U.S. Highway 97 south of Bend.

photo by Jim Witty

That said, this short hike is definitely worthwhile, if just for the new perspective it affords. To the west and the north there's suburban sprawl. To the east and south there's a whole lot of Oregon stretching away to the horizon. It's good to get up high and see what you can see.

One butte is rarely enough.

So we saddled up and headed over to Lava Butte off U.S. Highway 97 just south of Bend. The visitor center at the National Monument is closed for another month but the lava's still there and the butte still looms. Besides, the paved trails don't get the heavy traffic during the off-season.

We had big plans and high hopes, Dave and I did, when we parked the car outside the gate and headed out over the cold magma.

I think we lost the fight during the trudge across the asphalt trail that leads to the base of the butte. Dave's got three very little girls. Me, I'm lazy. And that big old butte is every bit as precipitous as it is steep. I've reconsidered; they aren't that small.

If You Go:

GETTING THERE:

Lava Butte: Drive south on U.S. Highway 97 to Lava Lands National Monument entrance.

Horse Butte: From Bend take OR-20/US-20 east to 27th St. and turn right. Turn left at Rickard Rd. Turn right at Arnold Market Rd. and slight left to stay on Arnold Market Rd. Turn right at Horse Butte Rd. Horse Butte is on your right.

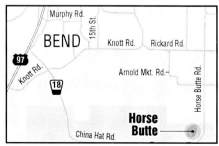

Fort Rock looms on the horizon just before the storm.
photo by Jim Witty

An Inspiring Day at Fort Rock

Dramatic thunderstorm in the eastern desert

Published: August 18, 2004

Last time we were in Fort Rock the wind blew frigid from the north and the snow clotted on the sage.

It was good to hunker down inside our friend Bob Goodrich's cabin with a steaming cup of coffee and keep warm.

This time, we got a taste of something a whole lot spicier from Mother Nature's cookbook.

They tell me there was a thunderstorm in Bend last Saturday evening. If so, there was a THUNDERSTORM out over the eastern desert.

Even Leta Edwards and the locals at the Waterin' Hole Tavern stood up, opened the shades and took notice of the booming, crackling, electrodynamic spectacle to the south.

The sky was ablaze with strobing bolts and zigzag flashes, great interconnecting chains of forked lightning.

Then the rain came in torrents, slanting against the building, churning the desert dust into a muddy gruel. When the brunt of it had passed, we gobbled our chicken dinners (a worthy recipe in its own right) and went walking.

An Inspiring Day at Fort Rock *continued*

The desert is a powerful place.

It can present an unassuming face to the world, but don't believe for a second that it's bland or barren or sterile. There's magnificence in its simplicity, something bold and beguiling in its waffle-iron buttes and vast pancake-flat vistas.

And when there's meteorological magic afoot, the desert becomes the life of the party, a hopped-up wallflower with a gaudy hat and an endless stream of clever one-liners.

The desert is a powerful place. Here, the entrance to Fort Rock beckons.
photo by Mark Quon

This was one fine fandango at the Fort.

As we strolled up Cabin Lake Road toward the big fortress of a rock, the storm was raging off to the south and the north, with occasional outbursts to the east and west. It was dusk, and a full-spectrum double rainbow splashed across the horizon.

I thought of an Indian sometime in the dim past, huddled in Cow Cave weaving a sandal of sagebrush and watching the fire in the sky. Not hard to see why they came to believe that this was the birthplace of Man.

Then the coyotes started up, yipping and yammering and howling from conflicting compass points in a spine-shivering chorus of primitive ecstasy. Are they happy or mournful? Do they celebrate the freedom of the night and communicate with one another in an ancient language only they can fully understand?

Don't know. Don't particularly care. Just felt like howling myself.

The party blazed into the night and we retreated back to the cabin's porch.

Map Guy and I played guitar and the four of us sang songs about love and war and hope and places like this where time stands on end and once-frozen moments pass too quickly.

The night was cool and the coffee hot.

It smelled like rain.

If You Go:

GETTING THERE: Drive south on U.S. Highway 97 past La Pine and turn left (east) on Fremont Highway/OR-31 for approximately 29 miles. Turn left at Cabin Lake Rd. and left on Cow Cave Rd.

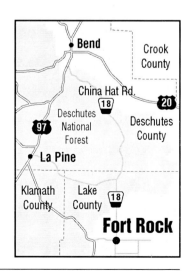

Manzanita are in bloom along the Hoffman Island Trail.

photo by Jim Witty

History Cast Indelibly in Lava

Hoffman Island Trail offers tour of Newberry flow

Published: June 12, 2008

The Hoffman Island trailhead is far from the most prominent in Newberry National Volcanic Monument.

But it's the beginning of one of the most fascinating lava/forest/butte hikes in the region. And, chances are, you'll have the place to yourself. The nearby Lava Cast Forest generates far more visitor interest.

From the trailhead on Forest Road 9720, the trail follows an old railroad logging berm into the same lava flow that created the Lava Cast Forest just up the hill. According to Newberry naturalist Larry Berrin, the lava was red hot and viscous a mere 7,000 years ago. Which means, in a geologic sense, it's hardly had a chance to cool down. There are two other flows in the immediate vicinity, both of which occurred less than 7,000 years ago.

About a quarter mile or so up the trail, you're walking the logging grade between a'a' lava on the upslope side and more of the same down below. A'a' is a Hawaiian term for the jagged lava often formed by a slow-moving flow. As long as we're going Hawaiian, pahoehoe is lava with a smooth, ropy surface that's laid down in large sheets when the molten magma is traveling rapidly across the landscape. Apparently, the lava

History Cast Indelibly in Lava *continued*

of this particular flow boogied down hill at the beginning and slowed down to a sedate crawl as it advanced.

Out on the lava, there are a few remarkably tenacious trees, ponderosa pines that have somehow managed to scratch out a living where there's been just enough erosion to form a scant pocket of soil and just enough water to keep them alive.

Just enough.

These amazing specimens make the word gnarly sound impotent. They're stunted, contorted, arthritic, twisted, tortured, warped and grossly misshapen. In a word (well two) bonsai beautiful.

The trees stay short, partly because of their sketchy foundation and partly as an adaptation to the harsh, windy conditions, said Berrin. The trees can live up to 200 years, but eventually die prematurely out there on the a'a'.

At the far end of the lava field is a stand of aspen, their leaves constantly jitterbugging in the breeze, and farther on, a mixed forest of fir and ponderosa pine. While you can see the lava extending out to your right, there's a lava flow to your left as well, past a dense forest of live and fallen trees. A person standing on one of the nearby buttes would clearly see that you're completely surrounded by lava, even if your perspective doesn't allow for that realization.

"It's a classic kipuka," Berrin explained. Kipuka, another one of those Hawaiian words, is an island of vegetation surrounded by lava.

The trail continues on up the hill, offering solitary views of the western rampart of Newberry Crater and the country downslope to the west. Scan the lava to the right and you'll see several miniature lava tubes, small cave-like openings through which molten magma once pulsed.

Look closely at the trunk of a ponderosa pine. The bark looks like interlocking puzzle pieces.

photo by Jim Witty

After about a mile-and-a-half, the trail fizzles out into a snarl of flowering manzanita and snowbrush.

It's a pleasant and fascinating out-and-back hike.

And, depending on how long you allow for scoping out the little lava tubes and bonsai ponderosa, you should have time to walk through the Lava Cast Forest, a mile up the road. It'll take you about 45 minutes to take the self-guided tour on a paved path. The signature highlight of a hike through the Lava Cast Forest is the tree mold,

Lava flowed through this area, forming the Hoffman Island kipuka, about 7,000 years ago.
photo by Jim Witty

found all along the way. According to the Forest Service, tree molds were formed as lava spilled through the pine forest, flowing against the upstream side of tree trunks. A mold formed around the original tree.

It's an informative jaunt and one that every Central Oregonian (and visitor) should experience at least once. But, if you're looking for a walk on the wilder side, I'd recommend Hoffman Island.

Kowabunga.

If You Go:

GETTING THERE: From Bend, drive south on U.S. Highway 97 to the Sunriver/Lava Cast Forest offramp. Drive eight miles east. The Hoffman Island trailhead is on the right, a small, unmarked parking area is on the left. Lava Cast Forest is another mile up the road.

BEFORE YOU GO: Stop by Lava Lands Visitor Center on south U.S. Highway 97 for information on Central Oregon's volcanic past.

CONTACT: 541-593-2421.

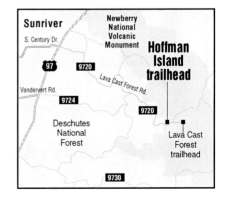

Meet Me In The Badlands: Exploring Central Oregon with Jim Witty

There's a photograph around every bend at Paulina Lake.
photo by Jim Witty

Paulina Lake is Picture Perfect

Hiking, biking trails abound in scenic Newberry Crater area

Published: July 17, 2008

Everyone wants a room with a view.

About a decade ago, archaeologists from the University of Oregon found the structural remains of the oldest house in the West, strategically located on the south shore of Paulina Lake. It's not difficult to see the attraction.

If the scene was even close to similar 10,000 years ago, these early inhabitants had it made. Can you imagine? Achingly blue water lapping at your doorstep. Hillsides teeming with big game. No kiosk down the road collecting your day use fees.

According to a 1998 *Los Angeles Times* report, the UO team also discovered tools, food remnants and artifacts, suggesting the site was once a summer encampment.

The more things change, the more they remain the same.

Head up that way today and what do you find? Summer camp. There's the resort - a store, boat rentals, bar and cabins - and a Forest Service campground. Which was where I was standing, straddling my mountain bike, when I came across the sign that told me I was within 300 feet of the aforementioned historic lakefront property.

There's a 7-mile loop trail around Paulina Lake. If you have trouble blocking out the motorboats and 21st-century lakeside development (I didn't), you can stroll (or

The Loop Trail skirts Paulina Lake and offers many nice rest stops.
photo by Jim Witty

roll) counterclockwise on the trail around the lake and be in the primeval forest in no time. Unless you're prepared for rock-strewn singletrack of the most technical kind, hiking is probably the best bet.

I made a game of seeing how long I could stay in the saddle, picking my way among the boulders and stumps, eventually succumbing to a loss of momentum or balance.

There were clear sections, uphill and down, but the Newberry Crater is, after all, inherently volcanic. Rocks are a major part of the show.

Save for the buzzing cloud of ravenous mosquitoes that didn't seem to share my athletic limitations, I enjoyed myself to no end. Away from the motorized bustle of the campground, I was thousands of years away, watching a small family group of Windust Indians spearing trout over the shoals below, chattering about the weather and those damnable mosquitoes.

Since it was my reverie, it took place more than 7,500 years ago, when nearby Mount Mazama erupted and buried the immediate area in at least a couple of feet of volcanic ash (which preserved the oldest house for scientists to discover).

As the name implies, the loop trail follows the lakeshore back to square one, passing a couple of campgrounds and beaches in the first half of the long, irregular circle.

At 6,300 feet, temperatures were in the comfortable range Monday, which made for a pleasant ride. Along the trail, I saw numerous chipmunks and an osprey hunting fish.

Allow four hours for the hike all the way around the lake, a little less (perhaps) if

Paulina Lake is Picture Perfect *continued*

you're biking (depending on your skill level).

If you're looking for an aerobic challenge, mountain bikes are allowed, in the uphill direction only, on the Peter Skene Ogden Trail, which runs along Paulina Creek from just east of U.S. Highway 97 upstream to Paulina Falls. It's a burn, but there's a series of picture-perfect waterfalls all along the way that invite exploration.

Newberry National Volcanic Monument offers something for every hiker. At 21 miles, the Crater Rim Trail is an arduous path that circumnavigates the entire caldera.

View of Paulina Lake from Paulina Peak.
photo courtesy of Scott Johnson

Other hiking/biking options include Lost Lake trail (3.9 miles), Obsidian Flow trail (.5 mile), Little Crater Trail (1.5 miles) and Silica Trail (.7 mile). It's a rigorous 4-mile hike to the top of Paulina Peak, which offers a commanding view of Paulina and East lakes and the entire caldera (there's also a road to the top).

According to the late Deschutes National Forest geologist Larry Chitwood, adjacent East and Paulina lakes may have been one big body of water (like nearby Crater Lake) at one time.

By about 12,000 years ago, the two lakes had separated, with just a small stream connecting them. The stream was buried by subsequent lava flows, he said.

Both lakes are nutrient rich, which bodes well for anglers seeking big browns, rainbows and kokanee. And both lakes are deep. Paulina goes down 250 feet, East Lake 185 feet.

If You Go:

GETTING THERE: From Bend, drive 22 miles south on U.S. Highway 97. Turn left at the turnoff to Paulina and East lakes. It's about 13 miles to Paulina Lake.

COST: A day pass is $5, available at the gate.

AMENITIES: Hiking and biking trails, visitor center, boat rentals, food.

CONTACT: Paulina Lake Lodge, 541-536-2240; East Lake Resort & RV Park, 541-536-2230; Bend-Fort Rock Ranger District of the Deschutes National Forest, 541-383-4000.

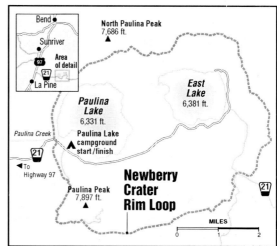

Trail distances from Swamp Wells are more suited to horses than casual hikers. But who says you have to go all the way out and back?
photo by Jim Witty

Pay a Visit to Coyote, Horse and Bessie Buttes

Stomping around Swampy Wells and the country surrounding Newberry National Volcanic Monument

Published: May 09, 2007

The east side of the Deschutes National Forest has a character all its own.

It's the desert rat in a Jeep to the west side's nordic buff in a Subaru (with racks).

You can tell just by the names. Fuzztail Butte, Bessie Butte, Coyote Butte and Teepee Draw are all in the Bend-Fort Rock Ranger District east of U.S. Highway 97. The Three Sisters, Little Fawn Campground, Dutchman Flat Sno-park and a whole lot of other stuff are west of the highway.

Pop quiz: Moraine Lake - which side? Correct, even if you didn't already know. Hooligan Hill - same question. Right again. And I bet you've never heard of the place. See?

To me, the Central Oregon Cascades to the west carry an alpine air about them, not haughty exactly, but refined in a Douglas fir, north-facing slope, buckle up your bindings, adequate snowpack kind of way. The eastern sector is more Western, if you will, with rough edges abounding. Juniper gives way to ponderosa pine over much of the eastern zone; it's hard to imagine Weasel Butte containing a huge stand of old-

Pay a Visit to Coyote, Horse and Bessie Buttes *continued*

growth grand fir and a consistent snow cover, even though (according to the map) it weighs in at 6,388 feet above sea level. But I've never been there.

I have stomped around a bit in the country surrounding the lofty Newberry National Volcanic Monument and I can tell you it's arid and volcanic and very cool. As in sweet, not chilly, although it can get that way, too.

My mascot for the east side of our forest would have to be a coyote; the west might be a wolverine, but with a latte in hand.

I tried to make it in to Swamp Wells a couple of months ago but had to turn back because melting snow mired the road. But it was a smooth sail Thursday for photographer Dean Guernsey and me.

Swamp Wells. If you're thinking it has an east-side ring, you're dead on.

Swamp Wells is a horse camp with corrals, tables, fire rings and bins for manure. But you don't need a horse and trailer to enjoy this cluster of off-the-beaten-track trailheads. Thursday, we had the place all to ourselves. It began snowing when we got there, and kept at it long enough for everything to get that wispy, white, winter-in-the-desert look.

The trails, which take off in all directions, lead to places such as Arnold Ice Cave, Horse Butte and Paulina Lake. Ten, 12, 14 miles and more. Horse distances. But why not go out there and explore at will, hiking as far out and back as you feel like it. Or take the mountain bike.

We hiked out on a couple of the trails to get a feel for the country and spent quite a bit of time photographing a couple of ponds that we figured account for the name of the place. We heard a hawk squealing nearby, but never saw it winging against the leaden sky. This is the kind of place, with a big-country feel, you just know won't reveal everything the first time out. It leaves you wondering what's over the next ridge, around the next fork in the trail.

When we finally left, snow had erased our tire tracks on the gravel way that leads north to China Hat Road. Our path was a blank slate again and the burnt-tree butte out the driver's side window made me think of coyotes and roads that peter out into nothing.

Where would we be without rough edges?

If You Go:

GETTING THERE: From Bend, drive south on U.S. Highway 97 and take the Baker Rd. exit 143, toward Knott Rd., then turn right on China Hat Rd. Turn right (south) on Road 1816 at Bessie Butte and drive 5.8 miles. Turn left on Forest Road 1816. Swamp Wells is about three miles down the road.

COST: There is no fee to park or camp here.

CONTACT: 541-383-4000.

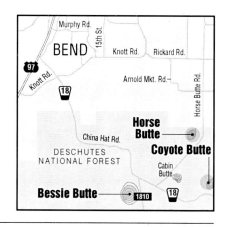

Paulina Falls impresses even in lower-flow mid-summer mode.
photo courtesy of John Gottberg Anderson

Newberry National Volcanic Monument

Volcanic grandeur, lakes and falls galore make Newberry National Volcanic Monument a popular destination

Published: August 04, 2004

    I love my job. One day each week I get to head out into the big open and do something fun.
    Then I get to sit down at my desk in front of a computer terminal Monday morning and think about it all over again.
    No offense, but it beats working in a tallow factory.
    Right now, I'm enjoying myself to no end. I'm thinking about our trip to the caldera at Newberry National Volcanic Monument - reconstructing the day.
    First, we stopped at Paulina Falls. It's tourist-friendly with its big parking lot, restrooms and expansive viewpoint. But all those cushy amenities don't take much away from the rugged good looks of the star attraction.
    Paulina Falls is 80 feet of raw gravitational power, a wide-angle panorama of unbridled hydraulics. Paulina Creek flows meekly out of Paulina Lake before it unloads over a volcanic cliff a few hundred yards to the west. The creek, according to the Forest Service, has qualified for designation as a federal Wild and Scenic River.
    Next stop was Paulina Lake, where there's a restaurant, store, rental cabins and some of the largest brown trout in the Western United States (20-pounders aren't all

Newberry National Volcanic Monument *continued*

that uncommon). A stroll out on the dock reveals a remarkably productive lake; trout, from fingerlings to a couple pounds, were clearly visible finning among the near-shore vegetation.

With 7,985-foot Paulina Peak looming above, the shores of Paulina and nearby East lakes are ideal spots from which to drink in the volcanic grandeur.

It made us want to get up high and see Central Oregon from a different perspective. It's a few miles from the caldera floor to the summit up a well-traveled gravel road. Word is that on a clear day you can see all the way up to Washington and down to California. Our view was a little restricted because of the haze. But the picture of the two lakes way down below is worth the slow drive up, no matter what the atmospheric conditions.

At that point we should have taken in the one-mile interpretive trail at Big Obsidian Flow, but the rumor of more waterfalls below Paulina Lake drove us back west instead.

7,985-foot Paulina Peak is an ideal spot to drink in the volcanic grandeur of Newberry National Volcanic Monument.
photo courtesy of Scott Johnson

We'd heard about them but had never been. We set out on foot from 10-Mile Sno-park on an exploration. After about a mile or so, we found what we were looking for: a lush, tree-lined streambed and cool, plunging water.

I stood under the small falls, water cascading over my head, and grinned, knowing that thinking about clear, running water on Monday was going to be fun.

But not this Monday.

There's a series of waterfalls along Paulina Creek and I'm going back another day.

I love my job.

If You Go:

GETTING THERE: From Bend, drive 22 miles south on U.S. Highway 97. Turn left at the turnoff to Paulina and East lakes. It's about 13 miles to Paulina Lake.

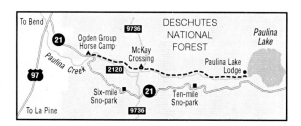

ACCESS: Motorists, hikers, bikers, boaters, horses.

PERMITS: You'll need a Northwest Forest Pass, or you can purchase a $5 day pass, one per vehicle, at the gate.

It's apparent that Howdy's main goals in life are to hunt and please his human, John Witty, not necessarily in that order.

photo by Jim Witty

On Top of His Game

Howdy the chukar hunting dog guarantees a meal for his best friend

Published: November 28, 2007

Bon appetit.

I ate chukar for the first time Sunday evening and it was delectable. Yes, it tasted a lot like chicken, but then, there's a reason that particular fowl is so popular.

I marinated the chukar (an Asian native successfully introduced in the West) in a red wine/garlic mixture, braised it with sliced onions and baked it with a cornmeal stuffing. I suppose those seasonings might have made even my leather hiking boots taste better than average, but these tender little game birds (somewhere between a quail and a pheasant in size) were way better than boot. They were delicious.

Thank you, Howdy.

During the Thanksgiving holiday four years ago, I ambled over hill and dale with my brother, John, and his 6-month-old, wet-behind-the-ears springer spaniel. At that stage of his development, Howdy reminded me of "a gawky middle schooler, full of adrenaline and promise and field-bred joie de vivre."

That day, we experienced the Crooked River Grassland near Grizzly Mountain through the nose of an exuberant, half-grown pup.

Last weekend, we experienced the High Desert southeast of Brothers through the

On Top of His Game *continued*

nose of a mature hunting dog, well tuned to the nuances of the field. Now 4-1/2 years old, Howdy is still every bit as gleeful to be out, as fueled by instinct-driven energy as he was as a pup. No doubt, that wag that starts at his nose, ripples down through his torso and finishes with a staccato wave of his little tail, is a full body smile.

What's changed is his focus. Training has taught Howdy to discriminate between a songbird and a chukar, a jackrabbit and a pheasant.

It's quite amazing, really.

He works the sagebrush and rabbitbrush steppe out ahead like a four-legged windshield wiper ardently looking for birds holding in the cover. But a big difference now is that he's under control; one well-placed whistle and he's back within the range of a 20-gauge shotgun.

It occurs to me that this symbiotic relationship between human and dog is the basis for the everyman's bond with his canine friend. Avid hunter or toy companion, the dog part of the equation aims to please. With a modicum of focused training, it balances out quite nicely.

It helps if you can meet part way.

As author Edward Hoagland said, "In order to really enjoy a dog, one doesn't merely try to train him to be semi-human. The point of it is to open oneself to the possibility of becoming partly a dog."

No offense John (or perhaps, no offense Howdy).

Anyway, Howdy's grown up and reordered his priorities. Kind of like we do.

"When he was a pup, he had unbridled enthusiasm about everything, and his passion to hunt reigned supreme," my brother remembered. "As an adult, his desire to behave and please me now comes in first."

That "he's a well-mannered, gentle, devoted companion every minute of every day" is a bonus. Or vice versa.

Over the course of the day, John, Mark Quon, guide Lonnie Wallace and I covered what seemed like every square inch of Don and Linda Wallace's 640-acre Juniper Rim Ranch near Frederick Butte. If we walked five or six miles, Howdy ran 20 or 30. Chukar, especially, are known for their terrestrial mobility.

We ended up with several quail and chukar, provided by the Wallaces and highly appreciated first by Howdy, and then by those fortunate enough to savor a plateful.

By day's end, Howdy was tuckered, but in no way chukared out. No doubt, he'd have kept on going into the night.

By day's end, having watched Howdy dexterously flush the birds and then retrieve them when his handler's aim was true, I was pretty certain Howdy was semi-human. And we had all become a little more dog.

If You Go:

DESTINATION: Don and Linda Wallace offer upland bird hunting packages at their remote Juniper Rim Ranch off Frederick Rd. east of Brothers. Costs vary. The ranch is not a game preserve; hunters must abide by seasons and bag limits.

CONTACT: 541-419-3923.

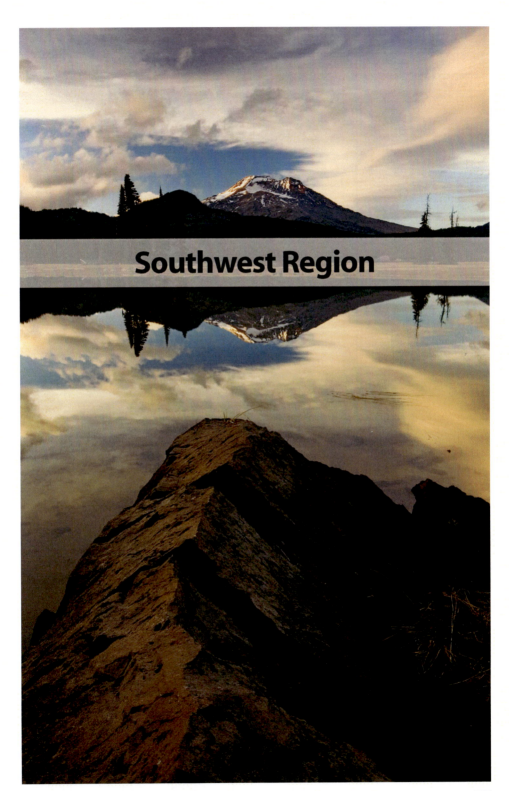

Southwest Region

Sparks Lake / photo courtesy of Tim Gallivan

"The key to a happy hike with Map Guy is to make sure the payoff is bigger than the expenditure of blood, sweat and boot leather. I suspect there's a little of that in most of us."

The Fall River is one of the West's most scenic spring creeks. It's clear and cold with relatively constant year-round flows.

photo by Jim Witty

Falling for Autumn

Colors at Fall River seem brighter on a typical gray, rainy fall day

Published: November 06, 2008

It happens a lot this time of year.

It's Monday. It's raining (or snowing). I look out the extravagant bank of windows in *The Bulletin* newsroom at all that gray and wet, and my mind goes to a recliner, a crackling fire and a good book, preferably one about somebody being battered unmercifully by the elements.

As it happens, easy chairs and fireplaces are conspicuously nonexistent anywhere on these premises. So I drag myself out from in front of a warmly glowing computer monitor and head for the door.

"Nice day for an outing," someone invariably says. It's the one time a colleague can say that with a degree of sarcasm and a better-you-than-me tone. And (kind of) mean it.

But a funny thing happens when the door swings closed behind me. I start having fun.

This past Monday was no exception. It was drizzling, a little on the cool side and my inclination was to stay in the car and drive around with the heater blaring. As it turns out, I conquered my inner sofa spud, donned rain gear and headed out on the

Falling for Autumn *continued*

trail from Fall River Campground.

Everything looks different on a rainy day. Fall River takes on a dreamlike persona; the greens get greener and the gray closes in, shrinking your drippy world to the river flowing past, the trail behind and the trail up ahead.

I half expected to see a wood nymph dart by.

What I did see were big, thick-trunked ponderosa pines alongside spindly lodgepoles, caddis flies buzzing and dipping out over the crystalline stream and golden-mantled ground squirrels, scurrying over downed logs, laying in their final stockpiles before winter sets in for real.

I noticed several piles of fresh elk scat on the trail; the big animals prefer the path of least resistance.

I saw a water ouzel, also known as the American dipper, cruise by, flying low over the water. The ouzel is a fascinating critter. It possesses a protective inner eyelid and an extra layer of downy feathers, the better to swim underwater with. According to *Birds of the Inland Northwest and Northern Rockies,* the ouzel "flies rapidly up and down streams patrolling for food or defending its territory." It spends a lot of time below the surface, "striding along stream bottoms by rowing with its powerful wings."

Fall River is a short (eight miles long) spring creek. Like the Metolius River, the Fall emerges full-size from springs at its headwaters and flows into the Deschutes River.

The river is known for its excellent but challenging fly-fishing for rainbow, brown and brook trout. It's open year-round, above the falls, to fly-fishing only.

Spring creeks, like the Fall, are known for cold, clear water, even year-round flows and temperatures.

The best place to initiate a hike along the Fall River is from the Fall River Campground, operated by the Forest Service. Cross over the bridge and you can follow the trail upstream or down.

Another longer trail follows the north bank of the Fall River, roughly paralleling Forest Road 42.

After a couple hours of exploring the Fall, I returned to the campground trailhead, a little damp around the edges but glad, as usual, that I'd gone hiking.

I rewarded myself with a nice long drive in the soggy Cascades, the heater cranked up high.

If You Go:

GETTING THERE: From Bend, drive south on U.S. Highway 97 and turn right on Vandevert Rd. At the stop sign, turn left and drive one mile to the intersection with South Century Dr., Forest Road 42. Turn right. The Fall River Campground is 10 miles from the intersection, on the left.

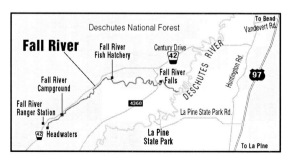

A sailboat floats calmly on Elk Lake with Mount Bachelor in the background.
photo by Mark Quon

Get Out While You Still Can

There's still time to enjoy some more of Central Oregon's outdoors

Published: September 28, 2005

What's the best season to sample Central Oregon's myriad outdoor charms?

It's open to debate, but fall gets my vote. The vacationing hordes are gone, there's a crisp, hint-of-what's-to-come tang to the air, and the autumn colors signal the change. And this year, recent rains have stifled the dust, at least for a short while.

It's only natural to feel the pull of the mountains on a cloudless fall day, to revel in the crunch of the trail beneath your boots, the cackling conversation between flowing water and river rocks. There's an urgency afoot, a vague pang in your soul telling you in a variety of ways that nothing lasts forever. That it's going to get dark and Mom's going to call you in for dinner.

Sooner or later, the snow's going to fly and all of this will change. Until next season.

But there's still time. Pick and choose. Get in your car. Etch these special spots in that part of your brain where you can call upon them when the sun's sinking low at 4 p.m. and Cascade Lakes Highway is 12 feet under.

Todd Lake offers a taste of the high country and it's not far from Cascade Lakes Highway. This mountain lake, about 27 miles west of Bend off Cascade Lakes Highway, offers picnicking, fishing and a wilderness-like setting. At 6,150 feet, Todd Lake will be a

Get Out While You Still Can *continued*

ski or snowshoe destination soon enough. Go now.

The Ray Atkeson Trail at Sparks Lake is more proof that you don't have to pull off a tortuous hike to find stunning outdoor beauty. A family-friendly stroll on a paved, barrier-free path gets you to the good views pronto. And they are sublime. Oregon's photographer laureate knew photogenic when he saw it. And this is it. Lava flows, Sparks Lake, South Sister, Broken Top, gnarly, snow-twisted pines and, oh, that cool Alpine air. Check this out. It's about 30 miles west of Bend on Cascade Lakes Highway.

Not far past the turnoff to Sparks Lake is the **Green Lakes Trailhead** on the other side of Cascade Lakes Highway. While the trail to Green Lakes is a perpetually popular path, why not try the Soda Creek Trail, which takes off not far from the parking area entrance. You'll find yourself in high mountain bliss before you know it. Peak views, a stream crossing, a big meadow. This is the real deal. If you're doing a motor tour, this trailhead is a destination unto itself. **Fall Creek** burbles right by the parking lot. While it's a little late for wildflowers, the creek and the meadow and the mountains looming behind should not be missed. Drink it in.

Heading farther out Highway 46 (Cascade Lakes Highway) from the Green Lakes Trailhead, you have your choice of water-dominated destinations. Past **Devils Lake** (the one with the turquoise cast), there's **Elk Lake, Hosmer, Lava, Little Lava, Big and Little Cultus, Crane Prairie Reservoir, Wickiup and Davis**, all right off the highway. All are scenic and worthy of a stop. There's a cafe at Elk, a store at Lava. Take your pick.

The Deschutes River up here has a different character from, say, downstream near Maupin. It's more like a mountain stream. Accessible at several points along Cascade

Devils Lake is known for its unique turquoise water.

photo by Mark Quon

Lakes Highway, the Deschutes serves up both pretty and pretty good fishing for rainbow trout. Drop a line before your guides freeze up and your hands get numb.

We usually loop back toward **Sunriver** on Highway 42 and visit the **Fall River Fish Hatchery.** You can do this in the winter, but I try to get there as often as possible.

Again, the dry fly fishing can be fast and furious on the Fall, and the hatchery itself is fascinating. You can make them boil by grabbing a handful of pelletized fish food from a gum ball machine on premises and tossing it into one of the hatchery pools. It makes for a suitable exclamation point on a day well spent.

So does dinner in Sunriver, but that's another story.

If You Go:

GETTING THERE: From Bend, drive about 28 miles west on Cascades Lakes Highway. Todd Lake Trailhead will be the first lake option on the right. A little further is Sparks Lake on the left; the Green Lakes Trailhead parking lot is on the right. Further south on Cascade Lakes Highway is Elk Lake on the left.

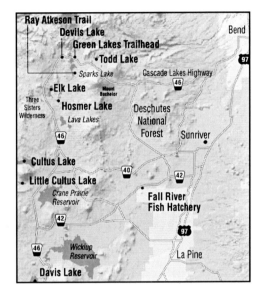

Broken Top is a scenic backdrop at Green Lakes.

photo courtesy of Ellen Jones

Soda Creek meanders through an expanse of open green wilderness.
photo by Jim Witty

Take a Sip of Nature at Soda Creek

Another option from the hugely popular Green Lakes Trailhead, this scenic hike is eye candy

Published: June 27, 2001

Each hike has a flavor of its own.

One's heavy on the arduous. Another is weighted toward the utilitarian, i.e.: there's a little beaver pond with big caddis-sipping brook trout at the end of the line.

The Soda Creek trail is just plain gorgeous. Eye candy for the terminally office-bound. And the trailhead is just a hop, skip and a jump - 28 miles - from Bend.

You begin the hike at the hugely popular Green Lakes Trailhead parking lot.

But instead of looping around the lot to the Green Lakes Trailhead and following the herds of humanity, you can pull in and hang a quick left to park. This trail begins on the right, close to the entrance off Cascade Lakes Highway.

There's a kiosk where you can pay your $6 daily trail fee (on the honor system) if you forgot your annual Northwest Forest Pass. There's also a permit to fill out (free) for the Three Sisters Wilderness.

Scribble quickly. You came here to get away from paperwork, remember?

Soda Creek Trail quickly leads you away from the drone of internal combustion and into the wilderness.

While the trail to Green Lakes, which starts from the same parking lot, is well-pounded by tens of thousands of boots every season, this path is different; it's trodden, but you'll find solitude here, too.

A mile or so through the woods, the trail tops a modest rise and opens out onto the kind of high mountain meadow someone might try to reproduce at a theme park, but couldn't. With Soda Creek meandering through this broad, green park, it's a good place to picnic, or at least linger a spell and take it all in. Wilderness Land: pay one admission at the gate and take in all the attractions free.

You can turn around here and feel like you've had a fine brush with nature. Or, better yet, you can continue on up the trail, searching for scenics. Within 10 minutes you'll come to Soda Creek again.

This time, though, it's got a head of steam up after tumbling down a falls.

Ford it carefully (you'll get your feet wet) and on the other side you'll be sloshing through a dark forest of mixed conifers and switchbacking up the side of a mountain.

Soon you'll be crossing another beautiful open green space, this one a steep sidehill that should be awash in wildflowers very soon. Just around the corner, you'll start hiking across intermittent patches of snow.

Keep going, you've come this far.

A close-up glimpse of Broken Top, all jagged and snow-capped, is just ahead.

The Soda Creek Trail meets Todd Lake Trail a bit farther on.

You can hook around to the lake, hang a left and loop around past Cayuse Crater and on to Green Lakes or go back the way you came.

The third option is better than it usually sounds, especially if you don't have all day; those meadows and the commanding view from the sidehill are worth a second look.

Kind of like riding Splash Mountain a second time just to get your money's worth.

But this is not Disneyland, it's wilderness. And as such, it commands a respect and reverence no theme park could duplicate.

The Wilderness Act defines wilderness as an area "untrammeled by man, where man himself is a visitor who does not remain ... with the imprint of man substantially unnoticeable ... having outstanding opportunities for solitude and primitive types of recreation."

Tread lightly.

If You Go:

GETTING THERE: From Bend, drive about 28 miles west on Cascades Lakes Highway. Sparks Lake is on the left, the Green Lakes Trailhead parking lot is on the right.

ROUND-TRIP DISTANCE: Two miles if you turn around at the first meadow. About nine miles out to Todd Lake and back. The loop back to the trailhead via Green Lakes is almost 12 miles.

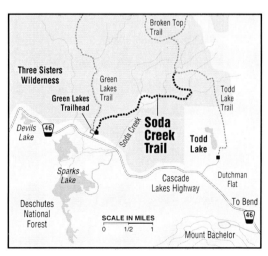

(left to right) Bob Speik, Jim Witty, Karen Cross and Linda Quon snowshoe to Todd Lake.
photo courtesy of Greg Cross

Powder Outage

Snowshoeing is a simple, brisk mode of frosty transportation that can bring out the shrieking snow-lover in anyone

Published: December 20, 2000

There's something primal about powder. Crunching through it, scattering a dusty white wake behind, is nearly irresistible. It's liberating, a playful return to a simpler time of life.

Running, jumping, kicking, squealing. The layers of stern formality separating grown-up from tail-wagging pup peel away, revealing your inner child.

Or not.

Maybe snow's just fun because there's a bunch of it every winter and if we didn't play in it, we'd end up spending all day every day inside in front of a 15-inch computer screen scarfing Twinkies and growing arm wattles.

No, better to blast over fields of virgin fluff. You don't need much more than the kid inside and a pair of snowshoes.

Snowshoes get you on top of the snow where you can cover some ground. Up there, you can get from point A to B without bogging down. You can shuffle slowly, trudge briskly or run like the wind, kicking up a feathery blast with every stride.

Kyle Will likes it best when he's chugging hard and there are miles to go before he

A group of snowshoers gather for a birthday hike at Virginia Meissner Sno-park.
photo courtesy of Kirsten Goldstein

rests. Will, 31, is a talented distance runner. The Bend-based athlete recently won a marathon in Cozumel, Mexico, and is a frequent front-runner in road races throughout this region. But his biggest contribution to Central Oregon sport may still be ahead of him.

Will wants to take snowshoeing to the next level in the Oregon Cascades. While the sport is slowly catching on as a democratic alternative to downhill and cross-country skiing here, it's been a quiet revolution. Will figures the sport here is lagging a half-dozen years behind snowshoe-crazy Colorado and New England.

But Will's gaining converts, two feet at a time.

For the second year, he's organizing two races at Virginia Meissner Sno-park, a 5K and an 8K. Both benefit Big Brothers and Big Sisters and are co-sponsored by the Athletic Club of Bend.

If you've never tried snowshoeing, you ought to. Throw away those images of bearded, bowlegged trappers with oversized wooden tennis rackets strapped on their feet. Today's shoes are hot rods compared to yesterday's clunkers. The new techno-shoes combine high-grade aluminum frames, indestructible synthetic decks and engineered bindings.

At the trailhead at Virginia Meissner Sno-park, Will hooks into a pair of trick teardrop-shaped Crescent Moon Permagrin running snowshoes that are small enough not to clank together on every stride but big enough to float him atop the snow. I get into a pair of Atlas shoes, also suitable for snow running.

Powder Outage *continued*

We start out walking, run a little way because we can, walk again because I must.

It's a wonderful morning, with 6 inches of new snow and a major break in the cloud cover directly overhead. My whippet-thin partner talks on about snowshoe racing, his sponsor Crescent Moon and the tiny animal tracks that cross our trail at intervals. I respond in clipped sentences, keeping the conversation going. I'm a little winded; he's not.

Our route takes us up Wednesdays (named for a group that local nordic legend Virginia Meissner used to ski with on Wednesdays), over Lupine to the Meissner Shelter and down Tangent Loop to our starting point. About four miles.

The ubiquitous blue diamonds mark the trails and make it fairly easy to navigate. But exercise common sense. Dress for the weather, carry a pack with some minimal winter survival essentials and don't let children wander off the trail and get swallowed up in the snow in the wells under trees.

And have fun. The PC will be there when you get back.

If You Go:

GETTING THERE: From Bend, drive about 13 miles west on Century Dr. toward Mount Bachelor. Meissner Sno-park is the first one on the north side of the road.

ROUND-TRIP DISTANCE: The Wednesdays to Lupine to Tangent Loop route is about four miles. Many variations - shorter and longer - are available depending on fitness level.

ACCESS: Snowshoes, cross-country skis.

DIFFICULTY: Moderate.

PERMITS: Required. Permits may be purchased at DMV offices and myriad retail outlets at $3 a day, $7 for three days and $15 for a season pass.

CAUTIONS: No dogs or motorized vehicles allowed. Stay on trails marked by diamonds. Don't snowshoe over a ski track. It ruins the trail for skiers.

MAPS: Available at the trailhead and at the Bend/Fort Rock Ranger District.

Jim Witty introduces Linda Quon to the Zen of Phil's Trail.
photo by Mark Quon

Mountain Biking

Kind of Zen and kind of not

Published: May 18, 2007

If pursuits such as mountain biking, hiking, skiing and fishing weren't so enjoyable, we probably wouldn't go so nuts over them.

Most people I know don't rearrange their work schedules or risk spousal harmony to go get an oil change, or pore over glossy catalogs dreaming of the day they'll be able to afford a super-lightweight, ultra-strong, state-of-the-art lawn rake.

But show them a new Scott fly rod, a vintage Gary Fisher Tassajara mountain bike (that would be Map Guy) or the latest Montrail hiking boots, and they go directly into that thousand-mile stare.

What's even more fun to me than drooling over gear or cooking up another adventure is letting someone in on our little secret.

As popular as mountain biking has become in Central Oregon, it's only On The Map among people who ride the trails. Chum Bob Speik says a lot of things, but one thing he says that I remember goes something like, "He who knows naught, knows naught that he knows naught."

Which never made any sense until this very moment.

When we met at the Phil's Trail trailhead one spring morning, our friend Linda Quon was clueless (which is not a word usually used to describe this high-power, high-

Mountain Biking *continued*

energy PTA president). She'd ridden bikes since she was a tyke, but never like this.

After a tentative "breaking in" period (these trails are skinny), she found the rhythm and was slithering along the winding singletrack as if she were to the fat tire born.

Mountain biking takes cycling to another dimension.

It's not a fancy adjective sort of thing. It's just plain fun. There are rocks and hills and bumps and grinds and trees that loom and trails that snake. It's kind of Zen and kind of not. It's most definitely the here and now; you can't think about the daily battle when the twists and turns keep coming, forcing you to roll with the punches.

There are more than 300 miles of trails in the Phil's system alone (bounded by Century Drive to the south, Skyliners Road to the north, Bend to the east and the dirt helipad to the west). Then there are the sno-parks up higher, with miles of ski tracks that turn into bike trails this time of year. And there's the Deschutes River Trail, Horse Ridge to the east and many other biking trails in the Cascades to the west.

And there are lots of people who know lots about mountain biking in Central Oregon. The Central Oregon Trails Alliance (COTA) is a group of like-minded cyclists dedicated to mountain biking and the preservation of trails.

COTA plans to put grant money toward new trails in the area between Benham Falls and Wanoga and Edison sno-parks. When completed, the new trail system "should rival the Phil's Trail complex in size and scope," COTA spokesman Kent Howes said.

Wait. Read that last paragraph again. This mountain biking thing is big. It's On The Map.

But only among people who ride the trails.

Which brings us once again to Quon. Last time I saw her, she had a big grin on her face and that faraway look in her eyes.

She had helmet hair, and she didn't seem to care.

She's hooked.

If You Go:

GETTING THERE: From Bend, drive or ride about 2.5 miles west on Galveston Ave. (turns into Skyliners Rd.) from the roundabout at Galveston and 14th St., to a paved road on the left that's marked with a biker icon sign. Turn left in the parking lot at the junction where the elaborate system of singletrack begins.

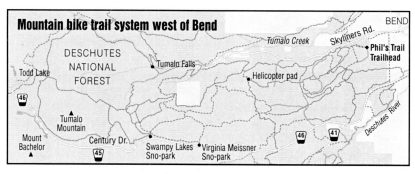

Fred Saporito of Bend navigates the single path C.O.D. trail.
photo by Jim Witty

Biking Bend's C.O.D. Trail

A do-able ride for the weekend warrior

Published: June 17, 2004

Don a helmet and climb astride a mountain bike and it's not hard at all to revert to childhood's happy hour.

As in endless wheelies, rooster tail skids and massive air (if only in your mind). And if you have the superb fortune to share the trail with your teenage son and a fellow named Map Guy, who eagerly embraced his inner child a long time ago, you're in for some fun.

We had some Friday. And, luckily, we had well more than an hour to have it.

Number one son, Map Guy and I took off from the trailhead across Century Drive from the Entrada Lodge and pedaled west on a trail referred to affectionately by locals as C.O.D.

This singletrack path delivered the requisite ponderosa pine-manzanita-bitterbrush Central Oregon gestalt as well as a few tricky rock-strewn sections that had each of us enthralled and frustrated in turns.

But most of what we rode was eminently do-able for a trio of intermediate riders more enthused with down than up, more comfortable with high-tech than highly technical.

Biking Bend's C.O.D. Trail *continued*

What is it with us weekend warriors? Is it somehow shameful when we take a run at a steep section, encounter a poorly placed boulder or two and then slow to a painful putter, teeter and fall?

Yeah, pretty much.

"What you see here, stays here."

"I won't tell if you don't."

Kids.

From the small dirt parking area across from the Entrada, the possibilities are (almost) endless.

You can cross the highway and access the Deschutes River Trail and enjoy the kind of scenic beauty we all expect from Central Oregon. You can ride for miles past rapids and breath-grabbing peaceful reaches for an unforgettable out-and-back experience. Since this is a popular hiking trail as well, use your brakes and appropriate caution.

The C.O.D. trail has some challenging sections near Century Drive.

photo by Mark Quon

Or you can use C.O.D. to hook into the Phil's Trail system on the north side of the highway. Here, singletrack intersects with doubletrack and an ambitious mountain biker could ride all the way to Todd Lake and back on different trails. God willing and the creek don't rise.

We turned around short of Todd Lake. A whole lot short.

But the lupine and paintbrush were in bloom and the trails were (and are) in magnificent condition (even if we weren't).

At various times during our ride we were on C.O.D., Grand Slam and several Forest Service dirt roads.

The wonderful thing about riding mountain bikes on Central Oregon trails is that it's nearly impossible to bring everyday life with you.

Because it's really hard to think about much else when you're riding the infinite wheelie.

If You Go:

GETTING THERE:
Take Century Dr. 1.8 miles south of Reed Mkt./Century Dr. roundabout and park in the small dirt lot. Pick up the trail here.

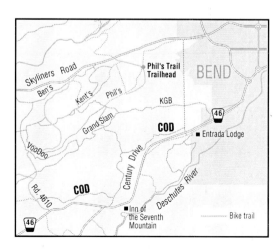

Ice skaters enjoying the ice rink in Sunriver Village.
photo by Jim Witty

The Awkward Joy of Ice Skating

Tumbling fun on ice in Sunriver Village

Published: December 23, 2004

    For me, ice skating is winter's equivalent to bowling.
    Although the two sports couldn't be more different, they do share a few commonalities when I'm involved: I participate once or twice a year, I have lots of fun, and I pretty much stink up alley and rink.
    I'm completely fine with low expectations (as long as I beat Map Guy best two out of three).
    Which is why I had my sights set blissfully low when I recently accompanied my 8-year-old son to the ice rink at Sunriver Village. It was his first time on skates and, given our shared genetics, I figured we'd be gorging on nonpareils at Goody's faster than he could say, "I'm freezing my Zamboni off."
    I figured wrong.
    Daniel was bound and determined to figure this thing out. He clung to the outer rail for a short while, and I led him around for a short while longer. Then he ventured out on his own, took several ungraceful tumbles, but came up smiling every time. I'd like to say he was cracking off flawless triple Lutzes by the end of the session, but that

The Awkward Joy of Ice Skating *continued*

would be less than truthful. Let's just say you don't have to be Brian Boitano to have a splendid time out on the frozen pond.

And if you're skating at Sunriver, the fun factor is multiplied by several features that make this ice-skating experience downright cushy. The rink is covered (and open on the sides), which allows for all-weather skating. The ice is groomed to a buffy smooth perfection with a Zamboni resurfacing machine, which makes for consistent skating conditions. And there's music to fuel the (counterclockwise) flow of little kids and big kids and old-timers and 40-something bowlers. Which makes skating an enjoyable outing, regardless of your skill level.

An ice-skating excursion to Sunriver is also a decent excuse to stroll around the shops in the Village Mall and Country Mall 2 across Mall Drive. The shopping's good and so is the food.

We (finally) opted for the candy store. Warming up inside Goody's over popcorn and vanilla-bean ice cream, young Dan put the day into perspective.

"That was fun," he said, as the ice cream slowly melted down the sugar cone to his hand. "Let's do it again."

I nodded, looked down at my two left feet and thought about bowling.

Jim with his son Danny Witty.
photo by Mark Quon

If You Go:

GETTING THERE: To reach Sunriver Village Mall, drive approximately 13 miles south on U.S. Highway 97 towards Klammath Falls. Take the Century Dr. exit 153 toward Sunriver. Keep right at the fork to go on NF 40/S Century Dr. Enter next roundabout and take first exit onto Abbott Dr. Turn right onto Beaver Dr.

CONTACT: For more information on skate and rental fees and hours of operation, call 541-593-5948.

A plumeria plant grows from a recent lava flow near Kalapana on the Big Island of Hawaii.
photo by Jim Witty

Lava Lands

Whether in Central Oregon or in Hawaii, lava reminds us of the past

Published: May 02, 2007

Lucky we live Central Oregon, eh?

That's a familiar pidgin-flavored refrain among locals on the Big Island (just substitute Hawaii for Bend).

I used to live there and say that. Now I live here and say much the same thing.

I had the opportunity to revisit some old Big Island haunts last week and came away with a renewed appreciation for both places.

Hula, plate lunches and reefs teeming with colorful fish and lumbering sea turtles notwithstanding, there are numerous similarities. In both places, residents and visitors alike focus on doing fun things outside. Population growth presents problems in Central Oregon's cities as well as Hilo and Kailua, Kona on the Big Isle. Perhaps the most striking similarity is the volcanic underpinnings of each place.

You don't have to travel 2,500 miles to see the fiery fruits of Vulcan's labors. Central Oregon is built on basalt. A day trip to Newberry National Volcanic Monument (or a workday lunch on the banks of the Upper Deschutes River) brings us face to face with lava, long cooled.

Lava Lands *continued*

A journey to Hawaii, however, brings the impossibly long view of geologic time hurtling into the here and now. Kilauea Volcano has been erupting since 1983, pumping massive amounts of molten lava down the eastern slope of Kilauea Volcano. It's forming new land right this moment.

It has also destroyed 189 structures, most of them houses in the now-defunct town of Kalapana. I watched that happen 17 years ago as a reporter for the *Hawaii Tribune Herald*. Time after time, a lobe of molten lava would inch its way up to a house only to stop its advance for a few days or weeks while the attention shifted elsewhere. But, inexorably, the viscous focus would return and the house would succumb to a magma-torched fire as reporters, tourists and family members stood nearby and witnessed the slow-motion devastation of this "drive-in" eruption.

Last week, I stood on that very same flow that devastated an entire community and

The outlook offers an impressive view of the lava flow.

photo by Jim Witty

The Trail of the Molten Land in Newberry National Volcanic Monument south of Bend is an ideal place to get in touch with the region's volcanic underpinnings.

photo by Dean Guernsey

saw palm and ohia trees, ferns and one large flowering plumeria emerging from the big field of ropy pahoehoe lava that covered Kalapana and nearby Kaimu Black Sand Beach in 1990. The people have been persistent as well; a handful of houses have been rebuilt atop the new flow, even as Kilauea continues to spew a few miles south and upslope. From my vantage, a couple hundred yards east of the parking lot at what was once the northern edge of town, I could see the current eruption from afar. The leading edge was quite a ways upslope, where the lava was cutting a swath through the ohia forest. I could see the smoke and volcanic plume, remember what it was like to be up close.

I was with G. Brad Lewis, the extraordinary Hawaii photographer who specializes in intimate portraits of the eruption, red rivers of lava pouring into the ocean and expanding the island's shore. I had followed him over a steaming field of black, laced with a network of cracks where lava coursed like blood not far beneath. The soles of my boots had melted in places; my adrenal gland was on high alert. All the while, Lewis casually snapped photos of the lava's fiery entrance into the ocean, perhaps inured by familiarity with this front-row seat on creation. Then I saw the dorsal fin of a tiger shark, a 6- or 7-footer taking in this scene from a completely different perspective.

It was the closest I've ever been to an epiphany in the outdoors. I knew this was powerful stuff; I just didn't know exactly what it meant.

Except that I was seeing what many haven't and won't, and that one bad step could be my last. I rely on that memory whenever I'm out in the Badlands or Lava Lands and start wondering what it was like 7,000 years ago when this lava popped and burbled and eventually solidified.

If you can get to Hawaii, by all means do. The eruption is a world-class natural phenomenon. If you can't, Lava Lands Visitor Center inside the Newberry National Volcanic Monument is a wonderful place to see what makes a volcano tick.

There are several trails and exhibits explaining what went on here.

And keep this in mind as you see all that burnt-brownie lava shimmering lifelessly in the spring sunshine: South Sister could be the next one to blow.

If You Go:

GETTING THERE: To reach the Lava Lands Visitor Center, drive 13 miles south of Bend on U.S. Highway 97, then right into the Visitor Center. Lava Butte, which erupted 7,000 years ago, looms over Lava Lands.

COST: Admission to Newberry National Volcanic Monument is $5 per car, per day.

CONTACT: Bend-Fort Rock Ranger District, Deschutes National Forest, 541-383-4000, Hawaii Volcanoes National Park, 808-985-6000.

A close up view of Broken Top is a much different experience than viewing from afar.
photo by Jim Witty

Broken Top: Trail to Alpine Splendor

Highland spring is a sight worth hiking the two miles to see

Published: August 17, 2005

It's easy to find an excuse not to go.

I'm too busy. I'm too tired. I'll wait until it cools off.

It's a slippery slope. You start making excuses and you just might never get around to traipsing over that next hill to see what's there.

I'm sure glad I went hiking Friday.

The Broken Top trailhead is about four miles past Todd Lake up Forest Road 370, a rutted track that's snow-free and open just a few months of the year.

If it's Alpine you want, this trail is a good place to get it. Though the trail isn't overly long (less than two miles in to the glacial tarn on the north side of Broken Top), you gain about 1,000 feet in elevation; you're in the good stuff right off the bat.

Not far from the trailhead, Bob Speik, who had cobbled this day trip together, showed us a geocache he'd stashed under a log on the mountainside. Then it was up a side trail to the right (off the trail that goes to the Green Lakes area), four happy wanderers with new and improved vistas around every turn. Joining Speik and me this day were Paul Curley, a wilderness-savvy history buff, and Marge Kocher.

Marge Kocher, front, Bob Speik and Paul Curley, crossing the creek, head toward Broken Top.
photo by Jim Witty

It's spring in the high country and the slopes are alive with compact little wildflowers such as aster, paintbrush and sedges, especially along the streams that plummet from way up. Listen and you can hear the breeze that's almost always blowing, the water burbling, the dry snap of grasshoppers caroming from rock to rock. You feel the sun's rarefied intensity. You see boulders and mangled pines and the stunning symmetry of mountains forged by fire. Life, pure and simple, abounds briefly in this harsh place where the narrowest of seasons is bracketed by winter.

As you climb, the trees thin out and so does the air. You huff and puff getting where you're going and find when you finally get there that sometimes the journey does pale in comparison. Because the destination is sublime.

After scrambling up a short-but-precarious, rock-strewn path to reach our destination, we ate lunch inside a sheltered glacial tarn on the north side of Broken Top. At intervals, the old volcano before us unleashed a volley of rocks that spattered into the lake like a blast of shrapnel. Speik recalled an event that occurred in a similar glacial lake on the other side of Broken Top some years ago when a big chunk came off the mountain and created a mini-tsunami.

Jim Witty takes a break on the trail to Broken Top.
photo courtesy of Bob Speik

Meet Me In The Badlands: Exploring Central Oregon with Jim Witty

Broken Top: Trail To Alpine Splendor *continued*

According to Speik, the big wave broke through its outlet, roared down the mountain and flooded a section of Cascade Lakes Highway.

As it is with mountains, Broken Top looks far different up close than it does from afar, say from downtown Bend. Viewed from the tarn, the mountain blazes with striations of yellow, green, ochre and more. In his book *The Wilderness Concept and the Three Sisters Wilderness,* Les Joslin explains that Broken Top began erupting about 150,000 years ago and continued doing so for well more than 10,000 years.

"Repeated glaciation during and after this eruptive period, which has eroded away the mountain's former summit - it stood much higher than the jagged summit's current 9,175 feet - as well as its entire southwestern slope and much of its interior, has exposed the core of this composite volcano," Joslin writes.

That's what we were seeing, the innards of a volcano.

After lunch, we skirted the tarn and two of us made the trek up to the ridge to see what we could see from that vertigo-inducing vantage.

Again, the destination.

From the ridge, Broken Top towers above, and the Three Sisters - North, Middle and South - loom tantalizingly close. Far below are the Bend Glacier and a little lake.

Curley and I caught our breath and caught up with the rest of our party on the way down and I asked Kocher, who's almost 80, how she does it. She said she watches her diet and loves to hike. She led hikes for Central Oregon Community College and the Bend Metro Park and Recreation District for many years and has walked most of the trails in Central Oregon at one time or another.

Perhaps most important, though, she keeps showing up. She's there at the trailhead with her boots on.

No excuses.

If You Go:

GETTING THERE: Take Century Dr. SW towards Mount Bachelor. When approaching the ski resort, veer right onto Cascade Lakes Highway. Turn right at Todd Lake turnoff. The Broken Top Trailhead is about four miles past Todd Lake up Forest Road 370.

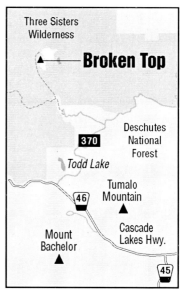

The trail at Vista Butte Sno-park leads you through a white-flocked forest of mixed conifers - firs, lodgepoles and, of course, ponderosa pines.

photo by Jim Witty

Enjoy the Quiet of Vista Butte Sno-park

Challenging routes and smaller crowds await

Published: December 18, 2002

We had what we thought were all the essentials for a fine cross country ski outing Friday.

We had the time, and after weeks of unseasonably warm weather, God knows we had the inclination. Most importantly, we had the snow. Several inches had blanketed the higher elevation sno-parks overnight and we were itching to get out and play in it.

We didn't discover what we didn't have until we were almost 20 miles up the road.

'It's going to be kind of difficult for me to ski today …,' Map Guy drawled as we pulled over at Vista Butte Sno-park.

'What's new?' I replied, feeling rather quick on my feet.

' … without my skis or boots.'

An understandable oversight, I thought. Skis, boots and yes, poles, can be easy to overlook in all the confusion surrounding going skiing. He did remember the sandwiches.

Good things come to those who wait, I told myself as we whipped a U-ey on Cascade Lakes Highway. All's well that end's well, I spat under my breath. Minds are like televisions; they work best when they're plugged in, I muttered, reaching for the

Enjoy the Quiet of Vista Butte Sno-park *continued*

peanut butter and honey on wheat.

In the end, of course, the good things came, everything ended well and Map Guy found a clear channel despite all the snow.

Vista Butte Sno-park is really just a wide spot in the road between Swampy Lakes Sno-park and Dutchman Flat.

The trail takes off west along the highway and about a half-mile out turns east up a steep side hill. After negotiating that, you turn right on to a fairly wide and flat snowmobile track that leads you through a white-flocked forest of mixed conifers - firs, lodgepoles and, of course, ponderosa pines.

The Butte Trail skirts Vista Butte and ends up intersecting the Ridge Loop

Our friend Jim Witty hits the trail.

photo by Map Guy

trail - a good turnaround point. An option is to ski to the top of 6,619-foot Vista Butte for the panorama.

Either route is challenging. Skiing back down the aforementioned side hill along the trail we had broken, I fell a couple of times while Map Guy managed to keep his skis pretty much underneath him on the steeps (one way to keep track of them).

The most unobtrusive sno-park in Cascade Lakes Highway, Vista Butte rarely attracts the crowds that can congest Meissner, Swampy or Dutchman Flat.

From the Vista Butte trailhead, skiers and snowshoers can tie into the Flagline Trail and thus west to Dutchman or east to the Swampy Lakes and Swede Ridge shelters. There are maps at the trailhead or you can pick up the Forest Service's free Winter Ski Trail Guide at the Bend-Fort Rock Ranger District office in Bend's Red Oak Square or at the Deschutes National Forest headquarters on U.S. Highway 20.

Dogs are prohibited on this trail system. Permits, however, are available through the Forest Service for working dogs in harness. And they're limited to groomed snowmobile trails only.

If you're just getting started and looking for a fun and more forgiving place to ski, try Meissner Sno-park, 13 miles west of Bend on Cascade Lakes Highway. With a series of storms forecast to dump more snow in the region, Meissner, at 5,350 feet, will soon be ski-able. The Tumalo Langlauf Club grooms six to nine miles of easy to moderate trail here when snow conditions permit.

No matter where or how far your cross country sticks carry you this winter, there are at least 10 items you should always carry. They are extra clothes, extra food, sunglasses, a pocket knife, a fire starter, a basic first-aid kit, matches in waterproof container, a flashlight, a map and compass (adjusted to 17 degrees declination in Central Oregon).

And don't forget your skis.

If You Go:

GETTING THERE: From Bend, drive approximately 19 miles SW on Century Dr. towards Mount Bachelor. Vista Butte Sno-park will be on your right.

PERMITS: Required. Permits may be purchased at DMV offices and myriad retail outlets at $3 a day, $7 for three days and $15 for a season pass.

CAUTIONS: No dogs allowed. Stay on trails marked by diamonds. Don't snowshoe over a ski track. It ruins the trail for skiers.

MAPS: Available at the trailhead and at the Bend/Fort Rock Ranger District.

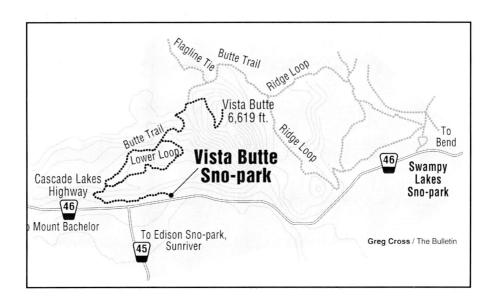

The 252-mile Deschutes River flows south to north. The corridor north of Sunriver and upriver from Benham Falls is known for its lazy stretches.

photo by Anders Ramberg

Choose Your Adventure

Find calm, chaos on the Deschutes River

Published: June 13, 2007

      The Deschutes River means different things to different people.

      Die-hard fly fisher? Mention of the word Deschutes - the river of the falls - probably conjures up visions of an impossibly rugged rimrock canyon lording over a wide and swift Western river. That would be the Lower Deschutes, which has a personality all its own.

      Bend camper? Redmond day user? The Deschutes of Tumalo and Cline Falls state parks is a calmer reach, a river of cattail pockets and skinny water. During the summer months, this section of the Deschutes has lost much of its oomph, thanks mainly to irrigation withdrawals upstream.

      Slack water kayaker, canoer or brown trout angler? The Upper Deschutes, with its sections of big-drop falls and long lazy stretches of mixed conifer splendor, is likely where your mind goes.

      Hiker? Take your pick. We donned our boots and headed south, bound for the lower part of the upper river. The trail from upstream of Benham Falls to the Sunriver area takes you along a postcard-pretty river corridor, when you're not bushwacking over a latticework of downed trees or steering away from the water in search of the

Benham Falls can be reached by hiking downstream from the Benham Falls East trailhead.
photo courtesy of Gary Calicott

double-track path that pushes cleanly south (upriver). The Deschutes River Trail from Sunriver to Meadow Camp near Bend has been cleared of downed trees; as usual, we chose the hard road.

Walt Sullins, my son-in-law-to-be, and I started out on the water's edge, at a river viewpoint and parking area not far upstream from the Benham Falls South trailhead. It's the place where the shuttle bus driver from Sunriver Resort parks to wait for paddlers to take out at the tail end of a 6-mile float from the marina upstream. Time and again, we'd follow the promising fisherman's path upriver only to see it peter out in a welter of crisscrossed timber and deep thicket. So we'd head away from the river, find the path of least resistance and cover some ground until the next opening led back to the water. Always back to the water.

Choose Your Adventure *continued*

That kind of trekking carries with it a sense of adventure that unimpeded trail cruising can't possibly. Or it's a pain in the butt. You choose.

What makes the bushwhacking worth the while is the stuff you see along the way. It's not the destination, it's the journey. Live in the moment. Don't wish your life away. Sit back, enjoy the ride. Find a way to admire your surroundings without tripping over an exposed root wad and planting your face in the muck.

Stop and watch the osprey hunting for trout from overhead. Consider the woodpecker jaunting from one pine to the next and the mallard pair that seem little fazed by your presence (but you just know will be relieved by your passing just the same). At foot level, the toads are out and so are the snakes (although we didn't see any of the latter). This is a dry place. The riparian zone along the river's edge draws kingfisher, otter, beaver, mule deer, elk, black bear and heron. Always the water.

The river itself is home to brown and rainbow trout as well as whitefish and a fly box representation of insects, including several iterations of caddis, mayflies and hulking stoneflies.

This is a stretch of river that doesn't see as much trail use as those reaches closer to Bend. Not that it's far. A 25-minute drive got us to where we wanted to be.

And a 3-hour walk got us out and back again.

This is the Deschutes River of big trees, deep green meadows, of swamp and slowly rotting log jams. For the newcomer, it's easy to love. It's even easier if you're a returnee.

The river boosters are right. The more time you spend along and on and near the Deschutes, the more you'll own it. Walt, my son-in-law in training, is just a year on from a lifetime spent in the big city East. When he stooped and deposited an empty beer can in his pack, I had to smile. Some people get it.

And of course, some people never do.

If You Go:

GETTING THERE: From Bend, drive south on U.S. Highway 97, then right at the sign for Lava Lands Visitor Center. Jog left on Forest Road 9702 toward the river. Just past the railroad tracks, turn left on to Forest Road 600. Turn right toward the river at the first river viewpoint sign. You also can begin your upriver hike at the Benham Falls East trailhead, at the terminus of Forest Road 9702.

ALTERNATIVE: Hike downstream from the Benham Falls East trailhead to the falls. It's about 1/2-mile to the falls.

Permits: A Northwest Forest Pass is required to park at the trailhead.

CONTACT: The Bend-Fort Rock Ranger District of the Deschutes National Forest, 541-383-4000.

Irish Lake's island conjures up Tom Sawyer adventures.
photo by Mark Quon

Irish and Taylor Lakes

A rough road to unspoiled beauty

Published: August 10, 2005

    We were six miles up the dustiest, ruttiest, rockiest, and, for the last mile, thinnest, gravel road I could remember, when the blasted thing petered out to nothing. One second sketchy road, the next a dense wall of fir trees with no lake in sight.
    That's when 8-year-old Danny looked over at me from the passenger side, smiled, and brightly said, "Where's Map Guy when you need him?"
    "Good thing he stayed home or we'd probably be lost," I spat, not quite so brightly. Kids.
    After consulting the proper charts, it didn't take a Map Guy to tell me that I'd made a wrong turn in our quest for Irish and Taylor lakes, and ended up a half-mile (through impenetrable forest primeval) from Lemish Lake.
    We turned around, bumped, bounced and ground back over that brutal dirt road and eventually found the error of our ways down around Little Cultus Lake. The fun had just begun.
    Because the road to Irish and Taylor lakes is worse.

Irish and Taylor Lakes *continued*

Taylor Lake is fishable and studded with conifer along its shores.
photo by Mark Quon

You'll need a high-clearance vehicle to negotiate the 4636 Road. But it's all worth it when you reach these two gorgeous lakes up by the ridge of the Cascades and the Pacific Crest Trail. Taylor Lake is the first one you come to, on the south side of the road; Irish Lake is on the north, and the PCT skirts its west shore.

Both lakes have the requisite conifer-studded shores and gin-clear water. Irish boasts a big island that got our Tom Sawyer blood boiling. "Wouldn't it be cool to canoe out there and camp?" "Wonder if there's any wildlife out there?" We planned a trip right then and there that involves a boat, lounge chairs, steaks and a big cooler full of beverages.

If it's hiking you want, hop on the PCT heading north and you'll be in mountain lake heaven. Look at the Forest Service map and you'll discover that the area is thick with little lakes, most with at least some sort of population of scrappy little mountain trout.

Both Irish and Taylor are fishable and good for a cooling soak.

We admired both lakes, cooled off in Irish Lake, ate a snack while admiring some more, but left the fishing rods sheathed in the back of the Jeep. Nothing much doing in the mid-day heat.

If you get in the water, don't mind the leeches too much. The small, greenish-black, wormlike creatures are found in just about every body of water hereabouts. We adults got into a conversation about the little blood-sucking creatures and the kids got a little freaked out.

I promised I'd check it out. Here's the story. Yes, they are nature's little vampires. And yes, a few may attach to your skin if you swim in a lake in the Central Oregon Cascades (you can pick them off). But, no, leeches don't normally pose a health problem.

Presley Quon and Danny Witty (demonstrating his Ninja skills) take a break on the way to Irish and Taylor lakes.

photo by Mark Quon

"They are relatively harmless," said Ted Wise, a fisheries biologist with the Oregon Department of Fish and Wildlife. "They're very prevalent around most of our lakes. We're not aware of any health risks."

Leeches are, however, a rich food source for the trout in these high lakes, Wise said.

Wise and his ODFW colleagues planted 3,000 cutthroat trout fingerlings in Irish Lake and 3,000 brook trout in Taylor Lake earlier this year [2005]. The little trout are up to the challenge of a harsh high-mountain winter, said Wise, so the recent stocking bodes well for future summers.

A drive to Irish and Taylor lakes (without the unnecessary detour) is a good way to wile away a summer day. It's all the more pleasing when you stop to think that in a couple short months, snow will block your passage for another season.

If You Go:

GETTING THERE: From Bend, drive about 46.0 miles west and south on Cascade Lakes Highway (46), then 0.8 miles west on Forest Service Rd. 4635, then 1.7 miles south on Forest Service Rd. 4630, and then 6.4 miles west on Forest Service Rd. 4636, need high clearance vehicle for last four miles.*

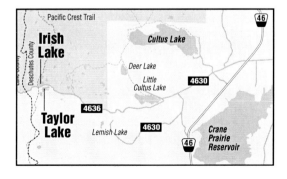

*Source: www.fs.fed.us

Out and back to Elk Lake Resort is a good 30 miles on groomed snowmobile trails and on Cascade Lakes Highway beyond the snow gate.

photo by Jim Witty

Snomobiling at Wanoga Sno-park

A new experience gives new meaning to the permagrin

Published: January 01, 2003

Up until two weeks ago, I'd never ridden a snowmobile.

I'd seen them jamming across Dutchman Flat and, while skiing, definitely heard them whining up the trail, but in 40-plus years, I'd never straddled one and hit the gas.

It was high time.

So when Bob Speik (who had ridden on the back of one once) called and invited me to go snowmobiling with him and Andrew Mallory, there was little hesitation.

The chance to catch these two colorful characters together and have a little adventure at the same time was an opportunity not to be missed. For those who don't know them, Speik is a seasoned mountaineer and survival skills instructor who never met a quip he didn't like. The British-born Mallory is a television host for the Discovery Channel, the BBC and currently the Fox Network. A descendant of George Mallory of Mount Everest fame, he ran safaris in Africa for several years.

We convened at Wanoga Sno-park where Mallory was setting up camp for his Safari Adventures snowmobile tours. Headquarters is a big wall tent with a stove and chairs and most importantly, carafes full of steaming hot chocolate and coffee.

Just outside was a row of state-of-the-art sleds all shiny and sporty and intriguing with their sleek profiles and racing stripes.

Inside the tent, Mallory and guide Mike Lapat spoke of the trail to Elk Lake and how much fun it is to show newbies what snowmobiling is all about. Someone smiled and said that the permagrin is a common side effect of riding snowmobiles.

After picking out a helmet that fit and learning the basics of the machine (throttle, kill switch and the all important brakes), we were good to go. Out and back to Elk Lake Resort is a good 30 miles on groomed snowmobile trails and on Cascade Lakes Highway beyond the snow gate.

With thumbs up all around, we zoomed off up the trail in single file, leaping headlong into the realm of motorized winter recreation and getting used to these powerful contraptions beneath us.

It didn't take long.

By the second mile or so we were accelerating into the moguls and leaning into the turns.

After a little more practice time at Dutchman Flat, we got out on the (snowed-in Cascade Lakes) highway and opened it up a bit.

Familiar territory in the summer, the highway in winter is transformed. Devils Lake for instance, clear as gin in August, is covered in snow in December save for a winding channel in the middle.

When we reached Elk Lake, I was surprised to see more than 40 snowmobiles parked outside and a full-house lunch crowd inside. Nordic skiers often ski into the resort, spend the night and ski back out the next day. The only other way in and out is via the resort's sno-cat, a half-van-half-tank that rumbles back and forth to civilization.

Over lunch I learned that there are about 1.64 million registered snowmobiles in the United States, almost 17,000 in Oregon. The snowmobilers in the lodge that day ran the gamut from young families to older couples.

After burgers and fries and chili dogs, we returned the way we'd come, growing more confident by the mile.

When it was all said and done, a couple things struck me about the new experience. I was more fatigued than I thought I'd be. And it was more fun than I'd imagined.

Then Speik noted the ease with which the sleds negotiated hills, adding that elevation gain is one of the downsides of mountaineering.

I started to grin and realized I already was.

If You Go:

GETTING THERE: Drive west on SW Century Dr. for approximately 12 miles towards Mt. Bachelor. Wanoga Sno-park will be on the left side of the road.

PERMITS: A sno-park pass is required to park.

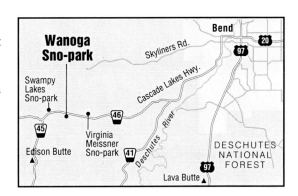

Bend's Upper Deschutes is easy to access and larded with juicy whitewater rapids.
photo by Mark Quon

Revisit an Old Friend: The Upper Deschutes

It's easy to forget about some of the most accessible parts of the Deschutes River

Published: May 08, 2002

The Deschutes River rolls through Bend, as dependable as an old friend.

I pass over it on the Colorado Street Bridge every morning and then again after work. I see it on the way to the post office, the mall and the library.

It's an integral part of Bend and Central Oregon, a constant contributor to the quality and flavor of the region. But with Bend's Upper Deschutes virtually underfoot, it's easy to give it short shrift in favor of more distant riverine destinations. That would be a mistake.

Because the Deschutes River Trail is a treasure, a delightfully scenic path that wends through town and on up the river past serene runs, frothing rapids and a couple of full-fledged waterfalls.

A great hike that will get you acquainted (or reacquainted) with the beauty right out the back door begins at Meadow Picnic Area and takes you a mile or four miles or even eight miles upriver. It doesn't take long to leave urban growth boundaries, traffic circles and crosstown traffic backups far behind.

The Upper Deschutes River is larded with juicy whitewater sections punctuated by wide, tranquil stretches suitable for canoeing or cooling off in the summer. The day-use areas aren't very far apart. There are Lava Island Falls (1.2 miles from the Meadow Picnic Area trailhead), Dillon (4.5 miles) and Benham falls (8.5 miles). Other points of interest include Big Eddy - a sprightly set of rapids, and Aspen day-use area where the river rests after plunging through a constricted unraftable bottleneck upstream at Dillon Falls.

It's a 17-mile hike from Meadow Picnic Area to Benham Falls and back - quite a trek in anyone's book.

Hikers often walk just a portion of the trail from Meadow to Benham Falls, choosing to turn around at one of the day-use areas. Or they park a shuttle car at the Benham Falls Picnic Area and drive back.

To get to the picnic area, drive 10 miles south of Bend on U.S. Highway 97 and turn right at the Lava Lands Visitor Center exit. Make a quick left on to Road 9702 and proceed four miles to the parking lot.

The one-day three-falls round-trip tour is prime for mountain bikers. Here and there along the way, the bike trail, which officially begins at Lava Island Falls, diverges from the hiking trail and later joins it again.

It's all good as long as bikers and hikers use courtesy and common sense (this is no secret spot; the trails can get congested on weekends during the warm months). The Forest Service advises mountain bikers to slow down and alert others as they approach. Horses are restricted to a separate trail.

When you're not keeping watch over the many moods of the Deschutes or doing your bit to promote harmony among multiple users, there are plenty of birds, trees and flowers to draw your attention.

Willow, chokecherry, birch, aspen and of course, ponderosa pine can all be seen along the trail. Also watch for osprey and kingfisher hunting for rainbow and brown trout, as well as great blue heron lurking in the shallows. Canada geese and all manner of ducks also use the Deschutes corridor as a flyway.

All this nature along the Deschutes River Trail is a bracing reminder for the return visitor, a surprise to the uninitiated.

I know I'll never look at Mirror Pond quite the same way again.

If You Go:

GETTING THERE: From Bend, drive about six miles SW on Cascade Lakes Highway. Turn left on to a gravel road just before the Widgi Creek Golf Course. The turn-off is marked with a small sign leading to the Meadow Picnic Area.

ACCESS: Bikers, hikers.

PERMITS: No permit is required at Meadow Picnic Area. A Northwest Forest Pass is required to park at the other day-use areas.

Waldo Lake, Oregon's second-largest natural lake, contains many small islands covered with timber.

photo by Jim Witty

Where's Waldo Lake?

This forest paradise is only an hour away

Published: October 02, 2008

An ambitious outdoor enthusiast (or writer) could probably make a career out of Waldo Lake.

The second-largest natural lake in Oregon, Waldo is a Windex clear, forest-rimmed jewel in the Cascades, west of Willamette Pass. The 21-mile Shoreline Trail loops the lake and delivers mountain bikers and hikers to the most beautiful white-sand-pocket beaches I've seen this side of Kona.

It's somewhat jarring to emerge from a forest primeval and come upon these little slivers of shoreline paradise — at 5,414 feet above sea level.

According to the Forest Service, there are more than 150 miles of hiking trails in the immediate vicinity, leading to small wilderness trout lakes, streams, peaks and stands of big trees. In the winter, snowshoers, snowmobilers and nordic skiers hold sway.

It's fall — Indian summer — and the place was pretty much deserted Monday.

I felt as if I'd made this groundbreaking discovery, even though, I'm told, Waldo Lake isn't a secret. And how could it be? It's sprawling and scenic and not far off state Highway 58.

A visitor could choose to bike the loop and get a fast-paced glimpse of the entire lake, or bite off a chunk of the Shoreline Trail and take time to poke around the coves and mosey to the soothing beat of the lapping wavelets.

I began hiking at Shadow Bay, on the south end of the lake, heading counterclockwise. The first thing that struck me was the clarity of the water. Waldo's water is gin clear (pardon the cliche, but it's an apt description) because the lake has no permanent inlet to deliver nutrients into the lake to foster plant growth. The lake is recharged by underwater springs and snowmelt.

"The lack of plant life contributes to its purity," according to the Willamette National Forest Web site.

All I know for sure is that you can see a long way into the water. Boaters are said to be able to see 120 feet down on a windless day.

The lake, formed by scouring glaciers, is 427 feet at its deepest point.

The only limiting factor I can see for hikers, bikers and canoeists is that motorized boats are allowed in Waldo Lake, with a 10 mile per hour limit. It was a moot point Monday, but summertime can bring noise pollution to the lake.

From Shadow Bay, it's a little more than a mile and a half to the South Waldo Lake Shelter, located in a meadow, back from the lake. On the way back and forth, there are several small wooded islets creating sheltered coves that would be inviting swimming spots on a hot day. Keep in mind, the Shoreline Trail loops the lake and can be accessed from several points.

Old Waldo hands speak of the voracious mosquitoes in June and July. But late September is gloriously non-buggy in this neck of the woods.

The hiking is sublime. But Waldo is a good overnight destination as well. And there's still time before the snow starts flying. Shadow Bay Campground and Islet and North Waldo campgrounds to the north offer full services, including toilet facilities, drinking water, boat ramps, garbage service and recycle centers for a fee. For the more adventurous, there are unimproved campsites dispersed around the lake that can be accessed by boat or on foot. The Forest Service reminds campers to "leave no trace" when enjoying these remote spots.

Forest Road 5897 skirts above the east shore of Waldo Lake at about 6,000 feet. The north and east side of the lake has no roads and is bounded by the backcountry hiking trails of Waldo Lake Wilderness.

If You Go:

GETTING THERE: From Bend, drive south on U.S. Highway 97 and turn right (west) on state Highway 58. Turn right at the sign for Waldo Lake, three miles past Willamette Pass. It's eight miles to the Shadow Bay turnoff and another two miles to the lake. To reach the north part of the lake, continue another seven miles on the upper road. It's about an hour-and-15-minute drive from Bend.

CONTACT: 541-225-6300.

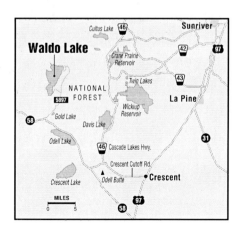

Dead trees add to the ecological diversity of the lake, promoting insect proliferation and fish growth as well as providing habitat for birds.

photo by Jim Witty

An Uncluttered View

A short, isolated hike at the Crane Prairie Reservoir

Published: August 03, 2005

Crane Prairie Reservoir has long been synonymous with outsized trout.

But this sprawling (more than 5 square miles) impoundment in the Central Oregon Cascades has a lot to offer nature lovers, even if they're not carrying their long rods.

A camera, however, is essential.

Poke around the edges of Crane Prairie and you can see swooping osprey, bald eagle, great blue heron, azure skies, cerulean waters and, if you're lucky and time it right, nary a soul.

We had the trail to Osprey Point all to ourselves, which is always a pleasant surprise on a summer day in Central Oregon. It's a short trail - about a half-mile each way - and well worth the effort. The path takes you through a lodgepole pine forest, complete with scampering chipmunks and kamikaze mosquitoes (don't forget the repellent anywhere you go in the high country this time of year).

The trail ends in a loop fronting an open marsh and the western shore of the reservoir. Interpretive signs point out what's going on out there beyond trail's end: the fish-eating osprey use the high platforms to nest. If you're patient, you'll see one of these large, white-chested raptors dive bomb into the water and come out with a fish grasped head-forward in its talons. According to naturalist Stan Tekiela, the birds might mate for life but take a sabbatical each October, migrating to separate wintering grounds in Mexico, Central and South America.

There's a thin user trail out past the loop, but the ground gets muckier the closer you get to the reservoir. So take a long lens if you want to photograph the avian goings on at the water's edge. Binoculars are recommended as well.

A word about the fishing. It's good. According to the fifth edition of Sun Publishing's *Fishing Central Oregon and Beyond*, during the last 50 years, Crane Prairie has yielded more big trout than any other body of water in the region. Rainbow and brook trout grow to lunker status in the big lake and so do the largemouth bass (a species introduced illegally about 25 years ago).

"In 1928 the Upper Deschutes River was dammed below a meadow named Crane Prairie, forming a reservoir which currently covers over 5 square miles," according to *Fishing Central Oregon and Beyond*. "Trees, previously bordering the channels of the Deschutes, Cultus and Quinn rivers, were left standing as the reservoir filled and now occupy about 10 percent of the water's surface as silvered snags."

Those dead trees add to the ecological diversity of the lake, promoting insect proliferation and fish growth as well as providing habitat for birds.

Back at the trailhead, it's just a few hundred yards' walk to the Quinn gravesite. Again, well worth the limited effort. Billy Quinn was a 25-year-old sheepman who was accidentally shot during a hunting trip north of Waldo Lake in 1894. The family packed him out of the backcountry toward the Deschutes River as another family member sped to Prineville for a doctor. Billy Quinn died on the banks of the river that bears the family name before help arrived.

His headstone is surrounded by a rough-hewn fence and a stand of lodgepole pine. On this day in this splendid place, it's not difficult to imagine the sorrow and drama that unfolded here 111 years ago.

There's a resort with a marina, store and campground around the other side of Crane Prairie Reservoir, which is a great place to stock up for a fishing trip. But, if it's quiet and wildlife you're seeking, poke around the edges. You won't be disappointed.

If You Go:

GETTING THERE: It's about 45 miles SW of Bend on Century Dr. Look for the sign for Osprey Point on the left past Cultus Lake.

ROUND-TRIP DISTANCE: About one mile to and from Osprey Point.

ACCESS: Hikers.

PERMITS: Northwest Forest Pass required to park at the trailhead.

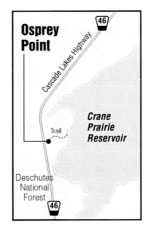

Tumalo Mountain is a popular winter outing for snowshoers, telemark skiers and snowboarders.
photo by Jim Witty

Tumalo Mountain

Snowshoe adventure with Mr. and Mrs. Map Guy

Published: February 18, 2004

Tumalo Mountain looks way different in the winter.

When Map Guy and I hiked to the top of the 7,775-foot mountain last July, birds chattered and flitted through the pine forest, wild flowers poked up through the duff and sunlight dappled the trail.

This weekend, the sun dappled, but the trail was an indentation carved by snowshoers and skiers heading straight up the hill.

And everywhere, white.

This time, Map Guy, his wife and I made the trek. True to form, Map Guy grumbled about the pitch, Mrs. MG commented a lot on the wonder of it all, and I didn't say much because I was breathing too hard.

It's a mile-and-a-half to the top, which feels twice that on snowshoes (they don't give you credit for vertical, just distance).

The trail begins at the Dutchman Flat parking area and climbs through a thick canopy of mixed conifers. Our snowshoes, big, fat oversized affairs that we rented at Pine Mountain Sports, afforded us surprisingly good traction, even up (and down) the steepest sections.

After a good climb, about midway up the mountain, you break out into the full sun and get the first of many views of Mount Bachelor towering behind you.

Look hard enough and you can see the skiers, tiny moving dots carving turns down the opposite hillside.

The upper portion of the climb takes you across an open snow field and on to the summit, where, on a clear day, you can see South Sister, Broken Top and the High Desert as well as Mount Bachelor.

Chances are, if it's the weekend, you won't be alone. We encountered a fairly steady procession of other snowshoers, telemark skiers and snowboarders. There was even one guy with a device that looked like a modified body board.

We encountered a fairly steady procession of other snowshoers, telemark skiers and snowboarders.

photo by Jim Witty

And one thing's for sure, getting down is way faster than going up.

The skiers and the boarders flew down the mountain through the trees; we rambled back the way we'd come.

I'd come to the conclusion that snowshoes are great tools for getting from Point A to Point B but are lacking a bit in the thrills department. But watching Mrs. Map Guy take off through the fluffy new snow headed down with a big grin on her face, spoke otherwise.

The one piece of equipment I wished I'd brought was a set of trekking poles. I was envious of those who had them because they give you added locomotion and stability.

It took us just under three hours round-trip; you may be faster or slower. But give your party plenty of time; you definitely don't want to be racing darkness on the return trip.

If You Go:

GETTING THERE: From Bend, drive about 20 miles SW on Century Dr. toward Mount Bachelor. The Dutchman Flat parking area is on the right side of Century Dr. just before the main Mount Bachelor parking lot.

ROUND-TRIP DISTANCE: About three miles.

DIFFICULTY: Moderate.

PERMITS: A sno-park pass is required to park.

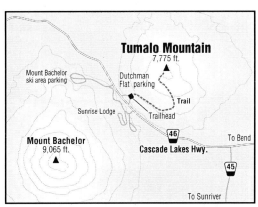

Lucky Lake is a 30-acre body of water just inside the Three Sisters Wilderness boundary.
photo by Mark Quon

Lucky Lake

A full-fledged wilderness lake in an Alpine setting

Published: June 29, 2007

    The key to a happy hike with Map Guy is to make sure the payoff is bigger than the expenditure of blood, sweat and boot leather. I suspect there's a little of that in most of us.
    In this regard, we got Lucky.
    Lucky Lake is a full-fledged wilderness lake in an Alpine setting. It has everything the day hiker wants and needs: big green trees, blooming wildflowers and enough mosquitoes to keep you goal-oriented.
    At the end of the rainbow, there's a picture-perfect little lake you come upon after about one and a half miles. The trail goes about halfway around Lucky Lake (30 acres and about 52 feet deep in the middle, according to Mr. Three Sisters Wilderness, Les Joslin) before breaking away and continuing on to Senoj Lake. Map Guy didn't have the time for an additional eight-mile round trip (he had to go to work), so we lingered at Lucky Lake, snapping photographs, eating juicy, roadside-stand peaches and swatting mosquitoes.
    This is a hike that's tailor-made for those who have only a half day to spare or who feel comfortable keeping their walk at about four miles, including side excursions. For

those who want more, Senoj Lake is up the trail and so are Doris and Blow lakes.

In fact, the map shows a plethora of little blue dots, small lakes within striking distance of the southwest of Lucky Lake and northeast of the Winopee Lake Trail. In fact, there are so many high mountain lakes within the Three Sisters Wilderness, it would take an ambitious hiker a long lifetime to get to them all (make sure you check on snow conditions before heading out).

That Lucky Lake is on the inside edge of the wilderness boundary doesn't diminish its wilderness qualities. You won't see mountain bikes here or four-wheelers or people with chainsaws.

According to Joslin, a Bend-based wilderness educator who wrote *The Wilderness Concept and the Three Sisters Wilderness,* the term wilderness means different things to different people.

"At one extreme, it is a damnable idea that 'locks up' otherwise valuable resources," Joslin writes in "Three Sisters." "At the other, it is the romanticizing and perpetuation of pristine nature. Somewhere in the middle, where most people stand, it has long been and generally remains the proposition that preserves wild places for a variety of outdoor recreational and spiritual experiences. And, as (Wallace) Stegner observed, the wilderness is 'important to us when we are old simply because it is there, important, that is, simply as an idea.'"

Jim Witty on a half day hike to Lucky Lake.
photo by Map Guy

One of the beautiful things about Lucky Lake is that it is the idea incarnate of an easily accessible slice of genuine wilderness. One you can see, smell and dip your feet into.

And that's a happy thought, especially if you have to be back in town by early afternoon.

If You Go:

GETTING THERE: From Bend, drive SW on Century Dr. toward Mount Bachelor. Lucky Lake is just past Lava Lake. The trailhead will be on your right.

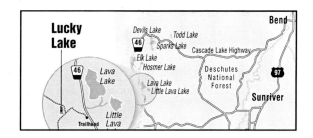

Todd Lake, with Broken Top in the near distance, is an ideal fall day-hike destination. It's easily accessible and a great place to hike, picnic and fish.

photo by Jim Witty

Todd Lake Welcomes Fall

Get out and enjoy the changing colors before winter arrives

Published: September 27, 2006

Ever notice how you appreciate things more when you realize they're not going to be there forever?

While the mountains and the valleys around us are about as permanent as it gets for us humans, the fall season is not. Part of the aching beauty of autumn is impending winter.

The other parts are good trails, pleasant weather, fewer hikers, active wildlife and an absence of mosquitoes. Are there more? I'm sure of it. Fall offers outdoor enthusiasts a cornucopia of reasons to head out for the day.

While the eastern desert can be nice this time of year, the mountains beckon.

An old Southern California high school friend of mine stopped by unexpectedly last week, just in time, as luck would have it, to accompany me into the Central Oregon Cascades for the day. With cameras in hand, we hit the high points, ending up at the Todd Lake trailhead around lunchtime.

Stuart Brenner and I used to walk the desert trails around Hemet, Calif., back in the old days, but a home in Orange County and a demanding sales job had pretty much kept him away from the rivers and trees through the years. He couldn't recall the last time he'd seen anything quite like this (it's nice to have an appreciative audience).

Our timing was impeccable.

Late September on the trail that circles Todd Lake offers all of the above and a nebulous inkling that you're here in this place because you should be and that if you could stand time on end, you would. But you can't. There's an end-of-the-summer, boarded-up-beach-house feel that hangs over the lake, even though the place is pristine and undeveloped.

At 6,150 feet, Todd Lake is a 45-acre gem nestled between Mount Bachelor and Broken Top. Lodgepole pine and fir crowd the shore around most of the lake, but the trail opens up to an expansive meadow at the north end.

Here, several streams seep off the hillside above, making for some marshy moments. A series of squat wooden bridges keeps hikers out of the soggiest spots and relatively dry.

Earlier in the season, this meadow was ablaze with wildflowers. But it's late in the year - especially at this elevation - and the blooms are mostly gone. Mount Bachelor looms back over your shoulder, and the jagged summits of Broken Top are just over the next rise out ahead.

There are picnic tables near the south end of the lake, a good spot to rest and relish the alpine splendor. Todd Lake is stocked with trout from time to time; fly anglers fish it from float tubes or pontoon boats. Motors are not allowed on the lake.

"I like fall hiking because the crowds are less, and it's a comfortable time to hike," said Larry Berrin, a naturalist with the High Desert Museum. "The birds are active; it's my favorite time."

Berrin noted that wherever you go in Central Oregon, you can witness the changes. The deciduous trees are turning color, the rabbitbrush is blooming and the red-winged blackbirds are forming large groups and getting ready to fly south. In addition, mayflies (genus Ephemerella because they're here today, gone tomorrow) are reappearing along rivers and creeks.

At Todd Lake, small toads are taking advantage of the wet and the lingering warmth, hopping underfoot. These days, when a cloud glides between you and the sun, you might shiver, but it passes. As a reminder.

Like high school escapades and summer vacations gone by, hiking up here in the fall is laden with finite possibilities. You'll appreciate them today, next week and long after the snow starts flying.

If You Go:

GETTING THERE: From Bend, drive about 27 miles SW on Cascade Lakes Highway, past Mount Bachelor. Turn right at the turnoff to Todd Lake. The trailhead is on the left, about a half-mile from the highway.

DISTANCE: It's a little more than a mile around Todd Lake.

PERMITS: A Northwest Forest Pass is required to park at the trailhead.

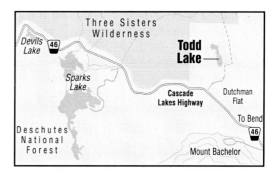

Sparks Lake was formed 10,000 years ago when lava flows clogged the Deschutes River.
photo courtesy of Tim Gallivan

Calm, Cool and Collected

Take time to unwind at this Central Oregon gem: Sparks Lake

Published: July 11, 2007

A friend of mine was sitting in a kayak toward the middle of Sparks Lake on Sunday, admiring the panorama, going with the lazy flow.

I was in another craft, close by, doing much the same.

"I'm glad you invited us to your wedding," she said, and I knew exactly what she meant.

If we hadn't done that three summers ago, it might have taken them years longer to discover Central Oregon and find themselves considering South Sister, Broken Top and Mount Bachelor from the enveloping cool of this alpine lake in mid-July. It's the kind of realization that gives you a psychic pinch, lest you ever begin taking this stunning country for granted (no, I'm not dreaming).

This is what it's all about.

A shallow 779-acre lake, Sparks can be explored by land or water. The Ray Atkeson Memorial Trail is a 2.5-mile loop on the east side of the lake where lava meets lodgepole pine, and there's a postcard view of the lake at almost every turn. It's a must-see, must-do in Central Oregon, and the first 1/4-mile or so is paved and wheelchair accessible.

Summer is cool at Sparks Lake. Here, kids play in the shallows near the boat ramp as kayaks cruise.
photo by Jim Witty

During the heart of the summer season, though, paddling Sparks Lake is the preferred method of transit. And there's no need to be proud (but do be safe). Rubber Sevylor rafts, kayaks, canoes and prams are all good, as long as you carry a couple of paddles or oars in good working order. And always wear a properly fitted personal flotation device when on the water; Sparks Lake is relatively shallow, but 8-feet is still over most people's heads. It's just sound boating practice.

We set up our day camp along a sandy little inlet at the end of the road just past the boat ramp. Beach chairs, coolers, a blanket or two strewn with tubes of sunscreen, potato chip bags and bottled water. And the lake, seductive in its turquoise accessibility.

Ah summer.

The beach scene is nice. Being on the lake is better.

I'm no limnologist, but given that Sparks Lake is so shallow, is filling with sediment and meadowlike islands seem to be forming there, the lake might not be there in 100 or 1,000 or 10,000 years. We'd best enjoy it while we can.

According to the Forest Service, Sparks Lake, at 5,400 feet, was formed 10,000 years ago when lava flows clogged the Deschutes River. Those 10,000-year-old flows are evident all around the lake, but especially on the east and south sides. There's a marvelous knife-back lava island not far from the boat ramp where the lava cooled into bizarre shapes, and hardy shrubs, wildflowers and even evergreen trees cling to the volcanic rock.

The spine-like island runs tight and parallel to the shore, making a cozy 1/4- to 1/2-

Calm, Cool and Collected *continued*

mile passage that was a highlight of our float. Paddlers can loop around the island and back to camp or push out on the open lake for more exploration.

Sparks Lake is no secret anymore, if it ever was. We were joined on Sunday — a warm summer's day — by an armada of like-minded boaters. There were lots of smiles and the good-natured small talk made it a social outdoor experience. Those seeking a little more solitude should schedule their Sparks Lake outing during the week or a shoulder season when the weather isn't quite as warm and the kids are back in school.

Sparks Lake was named after "Lige" Sparks, an early day stockman of the region, according to the Forest Service. While trappers and American Indians likely passed through the region early on, the first organized group of white Americans was a Pacific Railroad survey party that traveled the Green Lakes Trail in August 1855.

Sparks Lake was named after "Lige" Sparks, an early day stockman of the region.

photo by Mark Quon

Today, there are trout in Sparks Lake — both stocked cutthroat and holdover brookies — but there are better places to fish in the Central Oregon Cascades. The clear water makes for tough fly-fishing, the only type of angling allowed in the lake.

Better to relax, paddle, float and enjoy.

Summer's short. Winter's long. Get out while you can.

If You Go:

GETTING THERE: From Bend, drive 25 miles west on Century Dr. and turn left at the sign for Sparks Lake. Take the left fork on Forest Road 400 (the right fork takes you to the campground) and drive to the end of the road. There's a parking area and a boat launch.

ACTIVITIES: Hiking, mountain biking, fishing, photography, boating (engines are permitted with a 10-mph speed limit).

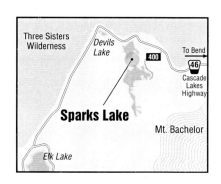

PERMITS: A Northwest Forest Pass is required to park here.

CONTACT: Bend-Fort Rock Ranger District of the Deschutes National Forest, 541-383-4000.

Donald M. Kerr, a native of Portland, Oregon, founded the High Desert Museum out of a passion for natural history.

photo courtesy of High Desert Museum

High Desert Museum

A world-class place of wonder for the kid in all of us

Published: December 07, 2007

Daniel liked the otters best.

No, on second thought, I believe the porcupines got the nod. Or maybe it was the longnose snake, all coiled up with no place to go. The Native American masks?

It's difficult for a 7-year-old to decide. For all its scholarly trappings and glossy veneer, the High Desert Museum is a world-class place of wonder for a kid.

Son Danny was hooked before we made it to the front door.

"What fish? I don't see them," he said, peering down into the little stream that fringes the patio outside the Schnitzer Entrance Hall. "Whoa. There they are, Dad."

The museum trout, inured to a steady procession of four-limbed gawkers, don't dart for a safe haven the way their wild desert brethren would. But with their mossy backs and subdued speckles, they're able to hide in plain sight.

According to its goals statement, "The High Desert Museum exists to broaden the knowledge and understanding of the natural and cultural history and resources of the High Desert for the purpose of promoting thoughtful decision-making that will sustain the region's natural and cultural heritage."

First grade is a good place to start.

High Desert Museum *continued*

"That trout is huge. He must be the dad of all those other guys."
"Look at the lizard. He's cute. He's so harmless. They like to hide, don't they?"
"This teepee is so middle ages. Back when they had lanterns for light."
"How do they get all the sound effects?"
"Dad, let's find out about the snake."
"I was thinking I'll share about this when I go back to school."
"In memory of Fre-der-ick W … I wonder who he was. It wasn't George Washington was it? Come on, camera breath."

And it was off to see the otters, Daniel leading the way.

If the youngsters in your household are getting antsy, take them down to see the otter (there were two at the time of this visit; currently there is one).

They're inherently cute, intelligent and playful to a fault.

They're really friendly. Danny said that.

"If an otter can't have fun doing something, it simply won't do it," is something otter expert and author Ed Park said that was so right on that the museum made it part of the exhibit.

The otter lives in an exhibit that can be viewed outside from above and inside from under the surface of the water. You can watch it gambol and cavort on your own or time your visit to coincide with one of the periodic lectures about their life history.

"Want to go look at the porcupines?"

I was following Danny this day. We were pretty much bypassing the history-heavy exhibits. It was the living, breathing, slithering creatures of the High Desert that held this kid's attention.

At the High Desert Museum in Bend, visitors can meet wild raptors, like this Harris hawk, in close-up wildlife encounters.

photo courtesy of High Desert Museum

The river otter is a popular attraction at the High Desert Museum.

photo courtesy of High Desert Museum

Two owlets born to America's only northern spotted owls to have bred in captivity.

photo courtesy of High Desert Museum

When the museum fires up the Lazinka Sawmill, with its engine powered 48 inch blade, the sawdust flies and the whistle sounds as the timbers are sliced into boards.

photo courtesy of Bob Speik

"I just love porcupines."

The porcupine is the anti-otter. You'd only cuddle one once. Porcupines are slow of gait, rolly-polly and exhibit a prickly appearance that only a mother could love.

"Aren't they cute?" said Dan.

He especially liked the baby porcupine that got way out on a limb only to have its mom help it gently back down to terra firma.

"Let's go find some more animals."

And we did, inside the museum's Donald M. Kerr Birds of Prey Center. The "Raptors of the Desert Sky" gave us a close-up view of a number of these fierce predators including a golden eagle, bald eagle and spotted owl.

There's much more to see at the High Desert Museum, and if your kids are a little older (i.e., longer attention span), you'll probably want to show them the Lazinka sawmill, the 1869 vintage Robbin's homestead cabin, the Changing Forest Exhibit that shows how fire is essential to the ecosystem, the Silver Sage Trading museum store and the various galleries and rotating exhibits.

All that walking and talking and thinking, however, left young Danny with a powerful hunger. So after a couple of hours at the museum, we were off in search of a burger and fries.

But we vowed to return again one day soon to see "the rest of the stuff."

And look in on the otters.

If You Go:

GETTING THERE: Drive three miles south of Bend on U.S. Highway 97. Museum entrance will be on the left. The museum is open 9 a.m. to 5 p.m. daily.

COST: Adults $15; seniors 65 and older $12, youth 5-12 $9, children 4 and younger free. Admission costs drop slightly during fall and winter months.

CONTACT: 541-382-4754 or www.highdesertmuseum.org.

Wizard Island is probably the most photographed landmark at Crater Lake National Park.
photo by Mark Quon

Big, Beautiful, Blue

Enjoy the wonders of Crater Lake from every angle along Rim Drive

Published: August 22, 2007

    The water is so blue.
    I take it on faith that it's actually water. From up top, it's an other-worldly azure, somehow better than blue, but I'd have a hard time pinpointing the precise quality that makes it so. It reminds me of the picture on an expensive, high definition television screen, but not quite. Or a scene through one of those 3-D stereoscopic viewers, but that's not it, either.
    People have been trying to describe Crater Lake for hundreds of years, and the best most can do is "wow" or "aah" (or the monosyllabic American Indian equivalent).
    At 1,943 feet, Crater Lake is the deepest in the United States. According to the National Park Service, "Light gets absorbed color by color as it passes through clear water. First the reds go, then orange, yellow, and green. Last to be absorbed are the blues. Only the deepest blue gets scattered back to the surface, where you see it as the color of the water. The water is, of course, no more blue than the sky is blue."
    Yeah, right.
    Crater Lake was formed a mere 7,700 years ago when Mount Mazama blew its top, scattering ash over eight states and three Canadian provinces. Ash lies 50 feet deep in

Phantom Ship is a smallish island in Crater Lake.
photo by Mark Quon

Crater Lake National Park's Pumice Desert, and there's a lot of it in the topsoil of Central Oregon.

When the eruptions wound down, there was nothing left for the volcano to do but collapse. About 5,000 years ago, springs, snow and rain began to fill the caldera. Today, evaporation and seepage balance the incoming flow of water. If it really is water.

The sheer magnitude of the Crater Lake experience can send the human mind on extended flights of fancy.

A colleague of mine suggested that if there's not a dragon or mythical monster lurking in the barely fathomable depths of Crater Lake, there ought to be. A grizzly bear that sprouted gills and preys on God knows what way down there.

Or a freshwater shark that grows to ghastly proportions and scares the bejabbers out of park visitors on its rare forays to the surface of the 5 trillion-gallon lake.

We weren't the first to think about this kind of thing.

The 1977 movie, "The Crater Lake Monster," had a meteor crashing into the lake, which incubated a prehistoric egg. The baby plesiosaur grew to ghastly proportions and terrorized the community.

But the reality is that Crater Lake National Park is an American treasure right here in Oregon. If you've never been, this month or next is the time to do it. If you want to spend a whole day, drive all the way around and take a few side trips on foot. The last time I was there, in June during a healthy snow year, the Rim Drive was still closed (the winter is a good time to ski there and experience that season's beauty at 6,450 feet).

This time around, the 33-mile Rim Drive was clear sailing, and we stopped at all

Big, Beautiful, Blue *continued*

30-plus pullouts for a slightly different perspective and a photograph. My mother-in-law, Helen Holder, who lives in Maryland, was enthralled with the lake and the Castle Crest loop trail that swings through a dark forest of fir and hemlock, then opens onto a sunny meadow on the back side. The meadow was full of wildflowers, freshened by myriad springs on the hillside, but the show peaked a couple of weeks ago. Allow as much as an hour so you can stop every so often and soak it all in.

On the Rim Drive, you can check out Wizard Island from just about any overlook you choose (Watchman on the west shore is closest), and Phantom Ship, the lake's "other" island, on the east side. The 400,000-year-old rock structure looks more like a castle than a ship, but it's captivating either way.

Volcanic Spires at Crater Lake National Park.
photo by Mark Quon

Vidae Falls is a cascading waterfall on the south end of the lake that, even in late August, is a good place to photograph Indian paintbrush and other wildflowers flourishing in the moist environment.

If you get to the park early enough (7:30 a.m. is a good bet on a summer weekend), you can buy a ticket for a boat tour of the lake ($25.50 for adults, $15 for a child 11 and younger). The tour involves a 1.1 mile hike down to (and back up from) the Cleetwood Cove boat dock; tours typically leave the dock at 10 a.m., 11 a.m., noon, 2 p.m. and 3 p.m. Contact: 541-594-3000.

We finished our day at the Crater Lake Lodge, an historic old building with a charming restaurant and renovated rooms. Not surprisingly, the view of the lake from the veranda was breathtaking, stunning, awe inspiring.

Three hundred feet below, the surface of Crater Lake seethed with the sepulchral depth of a billion opulently blue sapphires.

Almost. But no.

If You Go:

GETTING THERE: From Bend, drive south on U.S. Highway 97 to Route 138 west. This will take you to the park's north entrance. The park's north entrance is typically closed for the winter season from mid-October to mid-June.

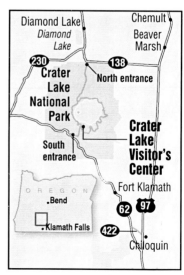

Northwest Region

Three Sisters and Broken Top / photo courtesy of Mike Putnam-Pacific Crest Stock

"Hmm. That road looks interesting. Since this is Central Oregon we're talking about, more times than not my suspicion is confirmed. Which is a batting average I can live with."

The Metolius River moves by fast on its way to Lake Billy Chinook.
photo by Mark Quon

Along the Metolius River
River begins calm, builds to chaotic whitewater, but remains beautiful

Published: May 10, 2006

The Metolius River burbles out of the ground on the back side of Black Butte, picks up steam where it converges with Lake and Jack creeks, and really starts ripping with the addition of Canyon Creek.

By the time it reaches Bridge 99 (or Lower Bridge), it's hard to believe this is the same river that slides along so peaceably back up around Camp Sherman.

While the Metolius upstream exudes a fairy tale-like sylvan charm with its friendly riffles, snug cabins and curling wood smoke, this downstream sector is brash, like an outspoken uncle who somewhere along the line decided diplomacy was for wimps.

Gone are the vacation homes, the cozy mill pond feel, the midstream hummocks thatched with grass. On this reach, there's water, lots of it, moving downhill fast. There are big trees, mostly ponderosa pines, lining both banks. And there's the emerald spine of Green Ridge looming over the treetops to the east.

It's the kind of place you want to be when you're looking for a little chaos to go along with your natural beauty.

From Bridge 99, there's a trail that follows the west bank of the river downstream to its confluence with Candle Creek. You can park in the lot just west of the bridge and

Along the Metolious River *continued*

walk up or down stream. You can't go wrong either way.

Despite the steep gradient and frequent patches of whitewater, the river is glass-clear. With polarized sunglasses, you can see the contour of the river bed and even an occasional rainbow trout, feeding on tumbling nymphs from the lee side of a subsurface boulder.

The bull trout are bigger. These "apex predators" - actually members of the char family - typically range from 5 to 15 pounds and look a lot like underwater logs, until they move. Their presence is indicative of a healthy, dynamic watershed.

Amid all this water thundering by on its way into Lake Billy Chinook, there are quieter pockets close to shore where the current eddies back on itself or is broken by a fallen log. Those downed trees also provide a respite for fish and a medium for streamside plants to take root. You expect to see a profusion of green in spring, but it's jarring in January to come upon green spraying from the middle of a snag when everything else is cloaked in white. Those who know the Metolius explain that since it's a spring creek, with little temperature fluctuation from season to season, the microclimate right next to the water promotes year-round growth.

Up on the bank, you might see a lizard, a snake, a chipmunk or a white-headed woodpecker. Osprey and bald eagles are common along this river corridor.

You might think about packing your fly rod for an out-and-back hike downriver from Bridge 99. The fast water is difficult to fish, but those quiet pockets hold fish. You can hike about a mile and a half down to the campground at Candle Creek, turn around and find your way back up.

The Metolius is a popular fly-fishing stream (and spin fishing is permissible downriver from Bridge 99), but the legions of long rodders have yet to descend on this challenging water this season. In a few weeks, the green drake hatch will be in full bloom, which means anglers will be casting their imitations to rising trout while the big, gangly mayflies helicopter by.

But for now, the trails are quiet, except for the sound of rushing water.

If You Go:

GETTING THERE: From Sisters, drive 10 miles northwest on U.S. Highway 20 toward the Santiam Pass. Just past Black Butte Ranch, turn right on Forest Road 14. The road joins Forest Road 1419; follow this to the left, ignoring a fork to the Head of the Metolius. Turn right at the stop sign; the Camp Sherman Store is just across the bridge. Follow the road to the left, then turn left on Forest Road 14 to follow the Metolius downstream. Bridge 99 is six miles from the Forest Road 11 turnoff.

CONTACT: Roger White and his employees at the Camp Sherman Store know what's going on in and around the Metolius River, 541-595-6711.

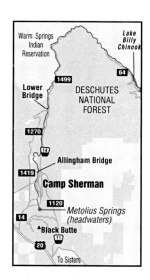

The Central Oregon Cascades provide a brisk backdrop on an unseasonably warm winter day.
photo by Jim Witty

Discovering Dry Canyon

Rock wall, rimrock and juniper

Published: February 20, 2008

      This year marks a chronologically significant milestone in my life.
      Since my pal Mark Quon is staring down the big Five-O right along with me, we're planning an early summer backpack trip into the bear-infested mountains of northwestern Montana. We have this (vague) idea that we'll cover 50 miles in the Northern Rockies, which will somehow prove to us that 50 is actually the modern equivalent of, say 48.
      What we're actually doing is getting all worked up over the prospect of spending several days in a wilderness known for its generous bounty of wildlife, including wolf, wolverine, mountain goat, black bear and a remnant population of Ursus arctos horribilis — the North American griz. There are many lakes, too, most teeming with large, voracious cutthroat and rainbow trout. Did I mention dumb? The trout up there are easily duped, or so I'm told.
      It's true. Half the fun is planning and anticipating and buying new backpacks and stuff. And, such a trip gives us a bona fide excuse to go hiking as often as possible. To get in shape, to prepare, to get outside on a regular basis and enjoy the best Central Oregon has to offer.

Discovering Dry Canyon *continued*

The top part of the trail into Dry Canyon is narrow. Parts of it stay in shadows most of the day.
photo by Jim Witty

So we were pleasantly surprised to discover an unobtrusive Bureau of Land Management trailhead off of Fryrear Road, just south of state Highway 126 between Redmond and Sisters. The trail leads to a series of doubletrack dirt trails, some of which have been churned up by motorcycles and ATVs. We also saw evidence that horses had passed this way.

We walked straight ahead from the parking lot and turned south to follow a fence line. At the end of the fence line, we headed left into a narrow canyon that still protected patches of icy snow. It was here that we stashed two bottles of Mirror Pond Pale Ale (buried neck deep in a bed of snow inside the crotch of a burned out stump). Planning ahead.

That's Dry Canyon, the upper end of the big gorge you see when driving by on the highway between Redmond and Sisters. We paused to take advantage of a break in the junipers and a photo-perfect glimpse of the snow-draped Cascades to the west. Soon, the country opened up a little and we were hiking gradually downhill with a rock wall and rimrock to our left.

This is juniper country, with a ponderosa pine thrown in here and there for variety.

Despite myriad tracks, we encountered just one off-road vehicle last Friday, a jeep at the bottom end of the hike, close to the highway. It was pretty muddy, so the driver opted to crawl back up and out.

On the way back up canyon, I heard (but didn't see) a canyon wren. I'm no expert, but I listened to the recorded call on the Internet and I'm pretty certain, even though it's a little early for them.

The Cornell Lab of Ornithology confirms that the canyon wren is aptly named.

"Found throughout the arid mountain country and canyonlands of western North America, the canyon wren nests and feeds in narrow rock crevices," according to the Cornell web site. "Often, it announces its presence by its beautiful and distinctive song, a loud cascade of musical whistles."

A couple more cool things I learned about the canyon wren from the Cornell Lab site: "The vertebral column is attached higher on the skull than it is on most birds," which allows a foraging canyon wren to thrust its bill forward into tight crevices without bumping its head. Also, researchers believe the canyon wren doesn't drink water. Rather, it gets the water it needs from its insect prey.

Good thing. This canyon is aptly named as well.

In all, we covered about five miles, out and back, trying to avoid the snowmelt mud when and where we could. This is a nice hike on a weekday and when so many spots to the west are snowbound.

There were no fish in this canyon and we didn't see any bear, but it was good to be out on a 60-degree winter's day.

We ferreted out the cold beer, sat on a couple of rocks and talked about Montana, the merits of pepper spray in warding off marauding brown bears, and big stupid trout. And I thought about the canyon wren.

That bird was exactly where it belonged. And so, for a few hours last week, were we.

If You Go:

GETTING THERE: From Redmond, head west toward Sisters on state Highway 126. Turn left on Fryrear Rd. (it's Holmes Rd. to the right) and drive about two miles to the trailhead parking area on the left.

DIFFICULTY: Moderate. It's about five miles to the old bridge supports next to the highway and back.

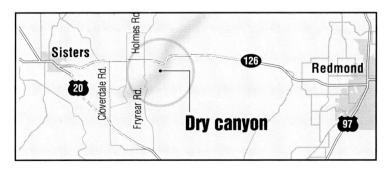

Grandview Cemetery is a rough-hewn old country graveyard west of Lake Billy Chinook.
photo by Mark Quon

Peaceful Resting Places

Old cemeteries offer glimpse into Central Oregon's pioneering past

Published: April 26, 2006

The best old cemeteries have a timeless feel.

There's one, for instance, near the now defunct town of Geneva on the back road between Lake Billy Chinook and Sisters. A post office was established there in 1914, where families worked the unforgiving grassland, living and dying in the rain shadow of the high Cascades.

If not for a chance discovery a few years back, I would never have known Grandview Cemetery was there.

You park in a dirt driveway that circles an old, gnarled juniper or two, and enter the graveyard through a rickety gate. The space, no larger than some backyards in Bend, is congested with headstones and flowers, artificial bouquets rising from store-bought vases and tiny, earthbound blooms having a go at spring.

It's a quiet spot and it is what it is. A place where people laid their loved ones to rest, where flesh and blood history awaits discovery.

There's a sobering aspect to be sure; death brings a jarring finality and it's difficult not to read the inscriptions and feel a little sad. Beloved wife. Loving husband. Rest in peace.

Camp Polk Cemetery is bordered by meadowlands. In the foreground is a typical 19th century headstone.

photo by Jim Witty

But there's a flip side. I think about the stories and the faces that must go with the headstones, the steadfast pioneers with the gumption to take on this amazing country of subtle beauty and brutal realities, and this unpretentious clearing in the wilderness comes to life.

Although it's an overcast day, an occasional sun ray slants in through the trees and illuminates a patch of newly minted grass. Little yellow wildflowers grow in scattered clumps all around.

This would be a good place for a picnic.

The same can be said for Camp Polk, perhaps my favorite pioneer cemetery. If the road's not muddy, you can reach Camp Polk from Grandview Cemetery by continuing west on Road 63, then turning left on Camp Polk Road after a spectacular tour through the Crooked River National Grasslands and privately owned rangeland (see directions from Bend in "If You Go").

Camp Polk dates back to the fall of 1865 when Capt. Charles Lafollett and a company of Oregon Infantry volunteers built eight cabins on a nearby hillside. According to an informational sign on the premises, the military abandoned the site in 1866 because it didn't deter hostile Indians. Samuel and Jane Hindman homesteaded the surrounding meadows in 1873. The frame of a barn there is the oldest one still standing in Deschutes County. The Hindmans also built a house, a rail-fenced enclosure and operated a small store and post office there. And they started a cemetery.

The oldest grave dates back to July 8, 1880. There are several headstones from the 19th century.

Peaceful Resting Places *continued*

It would be one thing to come across this kind of history in an urban setting, scrunched between sky scrapers. It's quite another to wander about out here, with the wind sighing through the big pines, rubbing elbows with the past among the bunchgrass and juniper.

The cemetery is adjacent to Whychus Creek and Camp Polk Meadow preserve, a 145-acre tract in the meadow where the Hindman place used to be. The Deschutes Basin Land Trust and Portland General Electric saved the land from development a few years ago, primarily to help restore the passage of steelhead through the Upper Deschutes Basin.

The unspoiled setting makes for a fine place to spend a contemplative afternoon.

There are other pioneer cemeteries scattered across the High Desert. According to Pat Kliewer, Deschutes County cultural and historic resources planner, two of the most interesting are Paulina Prairie Cemetery (formerly Reese) and Laidlaw Oddfellows Tumalo Cemetery.

Paulina Prairie Cemetery on the old Reese homestead contains many old graves. To get there, drive 22 miles south from Bend on U.S. Highway 97 and turn left on Paulina Lake Road. Two miles up the road, turn right at the power line right-of-way. Park at the bottom of the hill and walk west to the cemetery.

Laidlaw is 1.8 miles north of the town of Tumalo on Cline Falls Road.

"It has a real variety of tombstones, back to little metal and wooden crosses," Kliewer said. "People will recognize the names as families the streets are named after."

That cemetery was officially established in 1913, but burials took place there prior to that, Kliewer said.

If You Go:

GETTING THERE:

- To **Grandview Cemetery** from Bend, drive north on U.S. Highway 97. Before Madras, turn left towards Culver at a sign pointing to Cove Palisades State Park and Lake Billy Chinook. Follow the signs to the lake and cross the Crooked and Deschutes river arms, switchback up the western canyon past the Lake Chinook Village Store and straight on to Forest Road 63, which is gravel and can get muddy after a storm. The cemetery is a few miles up the road on the left.

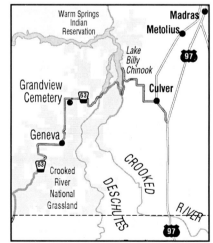

- To **Camp Polk Cemetery** from Bend, drive west on U.S. Highway 20 toward Sisters. Just before you reach the town of Sisters, turn right on State Route 126 toward Redmond. Turn left on Camp Polk Rd. The entrance to the preserve is a few miles up Camp Polk Rd. on the right. The cemetery is at the end of the gravel road.

Fish Lake is dry during the summer and fall months, but come winter, the lake bed fills up with life-giving water.

photo by Jim Witty

Fish Lake

Swimming in pioneer history

Published: October 23, 2008

Sometimes, readers' tips pan out quite nicely.

"Jim — I do not remember you ever writing about the Fish Lake Remount Station on the McKenzie River highway up near the beginning of the river. It is a fascinating reminder of the early days on the McKenzie. A beautiful spot. Some of the original cabins are still there. It is easy to picture the early pioneers living up there. It must have been very difficult. Down the road a ways is the Olallie campground. It is where the Olallie Creek joins the McKenzie. I think it is one of the prettiest camps in the Cascades. Yesterday the fall colors were at their peak along the McKenzie River. Beautiful."

Alex Morley's e-mail piqued my interest (and the destination seemed like a splendid place to spend a shoulder-season afternoon). So I called Map Guy and we headed up there.

This time of year, Fish Lake is no lake at all.

It's an expansive meadow, blanketed in late-season wildflowers and fringed by fir and deciduous vine maples blazing red and yellow.

Fish Lake *continued*

Not far from the headwaters of the McKenzie River, Fish Lake is a geologic anomaly with a fascinating human history.

First, the geology. The lake was formed 3,800 years ago when lava vents dammed Hackleman Creek. Given its porous lava underpinnings, the lake goes dry in the summer. Its trout have adapted to heading back up into Hackelman Creek in the dry months, spilling down into the lake come winter and spring.

Despite a steady rain Monday, the "lake" was in full meadow mode. Map Guy and I hiked along a trail that bisects the lake bottom, noting that what looked like prime elk habitat would actually be home to insect-gulping trout a few months on.

Fish Lake is rich in history of the human kind as well.

Located along the Old Santiam Wagon Road, Fish Lake was a stopover for pioneers traveling between the Willamette Valley and Central Oregon in the late 1860s. According to the McKenzie online visitor guide (http://mckenzie.orenews.com), there was a hotel and livery stable there until 1906.

About that time, the Forest Service built a log cabin ranger station on the lake's northeastern shore, according to Bend's Les Joslin, whose *Uncle Sam's Cabins* is the definitive guide to historic Forest Service ranger stations of the West. The original

Old Forest Service cabins speak of an earlier time at Fish Lake near the headwaters of the McKenzie River.

photo by Jim Witty

cabin, built in 1908, was crushed by snow during the winter of 1912-13. The cabin was replaced and other buildings were added. Still in use are the dispatcher's cabin (1921), the supervisor's cabin (1924) and the commissary cabin (1924).

"During the 1930s, Fish Lake became an important fire fighting remount station for crews and pack animals sent to forest fires throughout the Central Cascades, and served as a Civilian Conservation Corps work camp on the Willamette National Forest," Joslin writes. " … By 1940 the station comprised just over a dozen major structures."

These days, the dispatcher's cabin and the old commissary house the Fish Lake Guard Station. The outbuildings and rock walls, built in 1934 by the CCC, are now the Fish Lake Remount Depot, which provides pack animals for wilderness, trails and fire management missions, Joslin writes.

Wildflowers still bloom in October in the volcanic soil of Fish Lake.
photo by Jim Witty

The Forest Service has provided informational signs on the 20-acre site that relay some of the history that went down there. The place reeks of it.

From the main cluster of buildings, we walked up a dirt road framed by big firs, There's a grave there beneath the fallen leaves, the final resting place of Charity Ann Marks and her infant child. The pioneer woman died in childbirth in October 1875 after an early snowstorm barred the way through the Cascades.

Morley was right. "It is easy to picture the early pioneers living up there. It must have been very difficult."

This place is worth a visit.

If You Go:

GETTING THERE: From Sisters, drive west on U.S. Highway 20 and turn left on state Highway 126. Fish Lake Campground is about a mile south of U.S. Highway 20 on the right. Visitors can walk up the Old Santiam Wagon Rd. through two gates to the Fish Lake Remount Depot.

NOTE: Keep in mind, Forest Service personnel still use the depot. Be thoughtful and don't disturb any relics there.

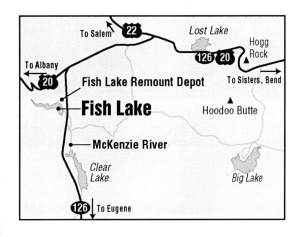

CONTACT: McKenzie Ranger Station, Willamette National Forest, 541-822-3381.

North and Middle Sister dominate the skyline along the McKenzie Pass. Several trail options, including the Pacific Crest Trail, branch off of this roadway.

photo by Jim Witty

Don't Pass This Up

Clock is ticking to tour the McKenzie Highway

Published: October 16, 2008

Last call.

Analogous to the watering hole that sets the clocks 15 minutes ahead to shoo out the early-morning die-hards, the summer hiking season is winding down. It may be seasonally mild this week, but the clock is ticking. It's 1:30, or is it 1:45? Either way, the party's almost over.

Last year, the snow gates on the McKenzie Highway clanked closed in early November. So, there's probably still time to trek in the high country. But don't dawdle.

The McKenzie Pass doesn't get much better than this. Unless, of course, you read this, drive up there and it's socked in and spitting snow. You never can tell this time of year.

On Monday, the pass was reach-out-and-touch-North-Sister brilliant. Patchy white from last week's early season snow persisted on the north-facing slopes along the Pacific Crest Trail, which was deliciously moist, not dusty. My fleece pullover went into the pack not far from the trailhead.

But it was far from hot. That's a beauteous thing about fall hiking. Especially on this stretch of the PCT, which skirts Belknap Crater through the lava flow, and can be one of the driest, most sweltering sections between Mexico and Canada during the summer.

From the PCT trailhead, the West Coast's most celebrated hiking path continues north through a mixed conifer forest and on through lava, which poured from Little Belknap and Belknap craters between 1,500 and 4,000 years ago. The relatively young flow spread 15 miles west into the McKenzie Valley and 10 miles to the east.

On the way, there are consistently awe-inspiring views of North and Middle Sister as well as funky lava forms that speak of geologic cataclysm. From the trailhead, Little Belknap is about five miles round trip; 6,872-foot Belknap is about eight miles (with some cross-country scrambling).

On Monday, there were no long-distance hikers on the trail, no vacationing tourists, no other people at all.

Designated a National Scenic Trail by an act of Congress in 1968, the PCT runs 2,500 miles through California, Oregon and Washington, from international border to international border. Each summer, hundreds of so-called through-hikers pass through Oregon, most northbound. Canada or bust.

Countless others enjoy it a little section at a time, via day hikes or backpacking jaunts to the myriad lakes athwart the trail.

Scott Lake, west of McKenzie Pass, is accessible by vehicle. It's near the trail that leads to Benson and Tenas lakes.

photo by Jim Witty

Don't Pass This Up *continued*

There are plenty of hiking options once you reach McKenzie Pass.

Another pass hike climbs 7,251-foot Black Crater from a trailhead off state Highway 242, just west of the pass. The walk up Black Crater is difficult, but rewards hikers with commanding views of Central Oregon and the Cascades.

About 4.5 miles west of McKenzie Pass is the Hand Lake Trailhead. The short trail to the lake starts out with the west side's drippy characteristics and ends up in an alpine meadow surrounding a mountain lake. Farther on, the trail hits the lava. A left turn takes hikers to Scott Lake, which can also be reached by gravel road off state Highway 242.

Hand Lake offers some of area's iconic vistas.

photo by Jim Witty

That road, about a mile to the west of the Hand Lake Trailhead, runs along the west shore of Scott Lake and ends up at the trailhead leading to Benson and Tenas lakes. It's only a mile and a half to Benson and another mile or so to Tenas.

Of course, a discussion of the McKenzie Pass country wouldn't be complete without mentioning the Dee Wright Observatory. It's a charmingly crude outpost complete with lava tube viewing portals that frame several Central Oregon Cascades' peaks.

Atop the structure is a rock and bronze peak finder that provides 360-degree identification of the mountains thereabouts. It's an easy walk-up in the strictest sense of the word, which means it's a wonderful place to take out-of-towners who don't feel too much like sweating.

Better get out now and drink it all in. It's just about closing time.

If You Go:

GETTING THERE: To reach the Pacific Crest Trail from Bend, take U.S. Highway 20 west through Sisters and turn left on to state Highway 242, the McKenzie Highway. The trailhead is on the right, a half-mile past McKenzie Pass. A rock slide that closed the highway several miles west of the pass has been cleared. A loop drive onto state Highway 126 along the McKenzie River is once again possible.

TAKE NOTE: High elevation fall weather can turn on a dime. Even on a day hike, go prepared to spend the night out. If the forecast looks nasty, better to read a book by the fire.

CONTACT: Sisters Ranger District, Deschutes National Forest, 541-549-7700.

This wooden bridge, along the South Pyramid Creek Trail, is a bit tweaked but still functional.
photo by Jim Witty

Hike West, Hike Green

Western Cascades trails offer pleasant change from brown High Desert treks

Published: August 07, 2008

Before our most recent hike, on Monday, Map Guy served fair warning.
"I don't do funny anymore."

I was thinking, "I never knew that you did," but at the time, I had a delicious Sno-Cap jalapeno pepper jack hamburger shoved most of the way into my mouth, and my reply was mostly unintelligible.

Besides, Map Guy was working on his own regrets: a large vanilla milkshake that was beginning to do a slow churn and was prompting him to complain a little about his current lot in life.

By the time we were on the trail, heading downhill toward a creek called South Pyramid on the west side of the Cascades crest, he was in full snarky stride.

I had to chuckle. A bit. Under my breath.

Then we were close to the bottom of the canyon, and my trusty companion said something that struck me as humorous.

"This is definitely the downside of hiking."

Hike West, Hike Green *continued*

He was glaring back up the way we'd come down and was voicing what I'd been toying with around the rough edges of my mind - what I usually toy with when contemplating an impending climb - but he was somehow making it an original and lugubrious thought. Cheerful pessimism is what Map Guy does best.

I just had to laugh, louder than the spotted owls would have liked.

I'm convinced, nothing makes Map Guy happier than hiking uphill. And complaining about it.

Hiking on the west side of the mountains always makes me feel as if I'm stepping into another world altogether. Everything's different. The fir, cedar and hemlock (massive, with branches that begin 10 or 12 stories up the trunk), the ferns and rhododendrons and vine maple, the banana slugs that stop you short on the trail.

My dog flushed a pair of grouse, one of which perched on a branch not far from where we were standing (the birds even look different in that drippy, primeval forest setting).

The South Pyramid Creek Trail is the candy store for two east side boys more accustomed to manzanita than trillium and bizarre shelves of fungus. (I use the term candy store in the figurative sense only; some plants are poisonous. Don't eat them. Duh.)

We actually began our journey by pulling into the Three Pyramids Trailhead parking lot, not far from South Pyramid Creek, but there was another party booting up there, preparing to hit the ground walking. Call me an aloof and antisocial ascetic or one of those other "a" words, but I can't see sharing a trail on a weekday if I don't have to.

The other party, a friendly guy with a Sierra Club daypack and his wife or girlfriend, got to hike two miles up to three volcanic plugs and the Old Cascade Crest Trail. And they were able to see most of the Central Oregon Cascades peaks from Mount Hood south. And they had the trail to themselves.

We opted for South Pyramid, which bore us through a second-growth and old growth forest, with occasional peek-a-boo views of clear cut scars across the valley. We covered about four miles, out-and-back or down-and-up, and got a real feel for this sun-dappled, west-side environment. We crossed several small streams and a misshapen bridge over a larger creek.

Take advantage of a hiking trip to the west side of the Cascades by taking a tree and plant identification guide along. Plants occupy just about every square inch of the ground there; the trees are big and beautiful and way different from their brethren to the east. *Northwest Trees* from The Mountaineers Press is a good place to start. Also, for sheer scientific wonder and gravity-defying adventure, tap into *The Wild Trees*, by Richard Preston (Random House) about redwoods and the people who study them. It's one of the best books I've read in the last couple of years.

Sometime during our ascent back to the trailhead, I noticed that Map Guy was wearing a "Life is Good" T-shirt with that optimistic little stick figure logo.

"Gravity sucks," he mumbled.

But he was grinning ear to ear.

Light (and dark) looks different in the forests west of the Cascades crest. Pictured are maple leaves in the early-afternoon light along the South Pyramid Creek Trail.

photo by Jim Witty

If You Go:

GETTING THERE: From Sisters, drive west on U.S. Highway 20 over Santiam Pass and veer right on state Highway 22 toward Salem. Drive just less than five miles northwest and turn left on Lava Lake Meadow Rd. at the sign to Old Cascades Crest trails. About two miles in, you'll cross a bridge (there's a great photo opportunity of the mountains from the middle of the bridge) and turn right on Forest Road 560. Follow the main road (avoiding several side roads) for about 3.5 miles to a signed junction. Turn left to the South Pyramid Creek Trailhead or continue straight to reach the Three Pyramids Trailhead.

CONTACT: Willamette National Forest, 541-225-6300.

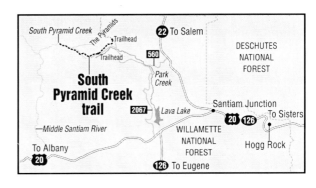

Water-skiing is big at Big Lake, near Hoodoo ski area. The Patjens Lakes Trailhead is nearby.
photo by Jim Witty

There and Back Again
Loop trail offers different views of Patjens Lakes

Published: July 31, 2008

After a half summer's worth of out-and-backs, it was nice to be in the loop.

The thing about hiking out a trail and retracing your steps is that the trip back out can be anticlimactic, a mindless race back to the trailhead and the car and the ice chest with the (cold) water in it. If you let it.

The trail to Patjens Lakes is a pretty six-mile loop that winds by three lakes and a couple of smaller ponds before circling back to the trailhead.

The thing about a loop is that you have to put your faith in those who have gone before. When you're hemmed in on all sides by lodgepole pine and fir, it's not hard to think you're heading in a direction that you're not. Without consulting my GPS or the Forest Service map in my pack, I had to fight the feeling that I was headed deeper into the Mount Washington Wilderness. You've got to keep the faith.

The Patjens Lake Trail begins at Big Lake, just south of the Hoodoo ski area. It's a raucous start to what turned out to be a soothing half-day walk in the Willamette National Forest. Big Lake is popular among water skiers with their souped-up boats as well as motorcyclists and ATVers. The trailhead is across the road from a lakeshore campground with a decidedly un-wilderness feel.

But once you're a half-mile down the trail, you'll leave all that behind.

Less than 200 yards into the trail, it forks. I stayed right and headed counterclockwise around the big lazy loop. The forest is alive here, with flowering lupine and blooming bear grass, its conical white heads brightening the path.

The trail takes you up and down and up again, but with only about 400 feet of elevation gain, there's nothing outrageously steep.

The most significant climb offers sidehill views of Sand Mountain Lookout. Along the way you'll also see Mount Washington, the Three Sisters and Hayrick Butte.

The combination of meadows, wildflowers, mountain views and the lakes make this outing a highly scenic alternative to others in the area that regularly attract hordes of hikers (I didn't see another soul on the trail Monday).

There's still patchy snow in protected areas along the trail, which my dog found highly refreshing on a hot summer's day.

It's always nice to see a lake shimmering beyond the trees. And sometimes you can sense one coming. In this instance, the mosquitoes were a dead giveaway (be sure to pack plenty of repellent).

The first of the Patjens chain is on the right, the second about a half-mile farther, on the left. The third, and final Patjens Lake is also to the left of the trail, surrounded by meadows. There are short side trails to all the lakes.

Rumor has it that there are small brook trout in the big lake, rainbows in the middle lake. There was no surface activity when I passed by, but the only way to tell would be to cast a line.

Wildlife sightings included an osprey, unidentifiable waterfowl way out on one of the Patjens Lakes, and several woodpeckers. An early-morning walk here would probably be more fruitful.

On the return, you'll come to Big Lake again, but this time you'll be on the undeveloped southern shore that offers a full-on view of flat-topped Hayrick Butte across the lake.

The trail leads back along the shore for about a half-mile, then climbs away from the lake and toward the trailhead to an unsigned junction. Left will get you back to the trailhead. We went right to the campground and walked several hundred yards along the road back to our vehicle.

It was nice to walk six miles and, save for the parking lot, never see the same country twice.

If You Go:

GETTING THERE: From Sisters, take U.S. Highway 20 west. Just past Santiam Pass, turn left at the sign for Hoodoo ski area. Follow Big Lake Rd. about four miles to the trailhead on the right.

PERMITS: Fill out a wilderness-use permit at the trailhead. It's free and gives the Forest Service valuable information.

CONTACT: Willamette National Forest, 541-225-6300.

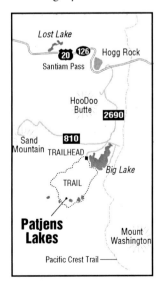

The Trout Creek wetland is a special 28-acre tract that's home to several rare plant species.
photo by Jim Witty

Taking the Path Less Traveled
Side road leads to adventure in Trout Creek Swamp area
Published: July 24, 2008

    Hmm. That road looks interesting.
    Since this is Central Oregon we're talking about, more times than not my suspicion is confirmed. Which is a batting average I can live with.
    Sometimes, I have a specific destination in mind, such as, "I'm going to Irish and Taylor lakes today." But sometimes it's just a general area on the map, as in, "That country west of Sisters looks promising." That way, I leave things open for fantastic "eureka!" moments, or rarely, the polar opposite — the completely lost, irretrievably wasted opportunity.
    The turnoff that caught my fancy this time around was Forest Road 1018, a gravel way off state Highway 242 (Old McKenzie Pass Highway), a little way west of Cold Spring Campground.
    Had I not acted on my impulse, I never would have discovered Trout Creek Swamp, where the Upper Deschutes Watershed Council and the U.S. Forest Service are in the midst of an ambitious effort to bring the compromised wetland back into shape.
    I saw a little sign to my left, braked to a stop and backed up through a cloud of dust to investigate.
    According to the Upper Deschutes Watershed Council, the 28-acre brown moss fen

There are a couple of creek crossings on the Scott Pass Trail.
photo by Jim Witty

beyond the sign historically supported a gee-whiz cast of plants such as the insectivorous sundew, bladderworts and a brown moss that's "extremely rare" outside of Canada. Some of those plants are still there, but the construction of ditches in the 1930s significantly lowered the water level and altered the habitat. Since then, lodgepole pine and the exotic reed canary grass have encroached on the swamp.

The two-year Trout Creek Wetland Restoration Project, recently completed, aimed to eliminate the man-made ditches that drained the wetland, retain more water there and increase late summer flows in Trout Creek.

"So far we're pretty happy with it," said council Executive Director Ryan Houston, who credits the Forest Service with the heavy lifting. "One of the primary objectives was to hold water in the wetland longer into the season." And, he said, that is happening. "There are some cool plants out there," he added.

The sundew, for instance, produces a sticky, gelatinous liquid that looks like morning dew. But if a fly or other insect lands on the sundew, it's likely there for the long haul, to be digested slowly by the rare carnivorous plant.

I continued up the road, hoping never to be reincarnated as a fly. I turned left at another sign a couple of miles farther on and came to the Scott Pass Trailhead after about a mile.

Time for a hike into Three Sisters Wilderness.

The trail, which eventually leads hikers to Scott Pass on the crest of the Cascades, begins as a path through a mixed forest of lodgepole pine and fir. Look for a couple of stream crossings and wildflowers on the bloom.

Taking the Path Less Traveled *continued*

After a little more than a mile, there's a junction. To the left is the way up to Scott Pass via alpine meadows and Cascade views.

I went right - the path less traveled - and quickly discovered why. There are multiple downed logs across the trail and the hike became an exercise in trailblazing, which can be satisfying if you maintain the proper mindset. That side trail intersects with the Millican Trail that leads to Lava Camp Lake Trailhead, gateway to the Pacific Crest Trail.

Although part of this forest has been compromised by a beetle infestation, it's still pretty, with plenty of stream crossings, blooming flowers and little pastel-blue butterflies. Lower down, you'll also get peek-a-boo glimpses of North Sister through the trees. Pack your mosquito repellent; they're out by the droves.

A mysterious wetland and a wilderness hike.

Eureka!

A view of North Sister from a forest road west of Sisters.

photo by Jim Witty

If You Go:

GETTING THERE: From Sisters, take Highway 242 west to Forest Road 1018. Turn left and drive four miles; Trout Creek Wetland Restoration Project is on the left. To reach the Scott Pass Trailhead, continue on Forest Road 1018 and turn right at the sign for Scott Pass Trailhead. Trailhead is about one mile up the road.

DIFFICULTY: For hikers, it's easy to difficult, depending on distance and which fork you choose.

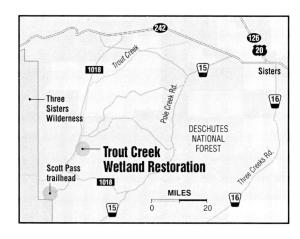

The North Santiam is a multiple-use river. Its waters are used for recreation as well as power generation, irrigation and flood control.

photo by Jim Witty

Where the River Flows

North Santiam offers old-growth beauty, challenging steelhead

Published: April 19, 2006

For those of us accustomed to our rivers banked by sagebrush or ponderosa pines, the North Santiam is a different animal.

At less than two hours west of Bend, North Santiam State Park is an ideal day-tripping destination for oldgrowth, west-side trees in a verdant, mossy setting and flowing water in a soul-stirring turquoise. This is a steelhead river, big and characterized by high flows at times and rainfall levels that leach nutrients from the soil and send them packing downstream. To the Willamette, into the Columbia and out to sea.

Which is the route the anadromous steelhead travel, out and back.

Fishermen haunt this section of the river near Mill City, casting and hoping and casting again. And again. Patience is the most important virtue of all where steelhead are involved. Once hooked, the hefty, sea-run trout turn into rockets, after-burners honed in the waters off the Pacific coast.

Although there are resident fish, the North Santiam River is not known as a classic trout stream; you can tell by the look of it that it's not your typical east-side-of-the-Cascades redsides factory. The huge evergreens lock up much of the important stuff

Where the River Flows *continued*

essential for vigorous growth. Despite habitat challenges downstream, the pure water is the perfect vehicle for steelhead to fulfill their biological imperative, then get back down to the ocean, more than 85 miles distant, where their appetite returns.

"The North Santiam River is the best example of a multiple-use river we've got," said veteran fishing guide Bill Sanderson, 66. "We have 60 percent of all the salmon and steelhead above Willamette Falls."

The river and dam upstream, according to Sanderson, are also used for flood control, power generation, irrigation and, of course, recreation.

"It's magnificent," said Sanderson, who's been guiding the river for nearly 40 years.

Finicky steelhead notwithstanding, North Santiam State Park is a good spot for a picnic. Located along one of the more picturesque reaches of the river, the day-use park offers picnic tables, running water and restroom facilities.

You can lunch at the tables in the grass or stroll down by the river and pick a rock. A good trail runs east along the north bank of the river.

You might even be better off if you neglected to pack a lunch. Giovanni's Mountain Pizza along Highway 22 in nearby Mill City is a magnificent reason to "forget" the tuna sandwiches (and fall off the heart-healthy bandwagon for one hedonistic afternoon in April). It's unpretentious (you can watch a guy behind the counter hand-tossing the crust) and reminds me of a little mom and pop place we used to frequent when I was a kid. Then you get your pepperoni and onion pizza slathered with cheese and savory tomato sauce and you vow never to buy a corporate pie again (at least for the next week or two).

A few miles east of Mill City is the dam that spells an end to the steelhead's epic journey. Behind the dam is Detroit Lake, a 400-foot-deep impoundment with 32 miles of shoreline. The lake is ripe for fishing, boating and all the warm weather recreational activities that sound like fun in a hypothetical sort of way right now. I remember driving through the area during a drought a few years ago and seeing docks and beaches left high and dry by the low water. The people of Detroit want you to know, the lake is back and they're anticipating a busy summer.

From Detroit Lake, it's a hop, skip and jump back to more familiar territory: Hoodoo, Suttle Lake, Black Butte Ranch, Sisters. But it's nice sometimes to sneak over the mountain and into a different world.

If You Go:

GETTING THERE: From Bend, drive east on U.S. Highway 20 and continue straight on to State Route 22 past Santiam Pass. West of Detroit Lake, turn left at the sign to North Santiam State Park. It's about 100 miles from Bend.

Bikers come from all over the world to ride the McKenzie River Trail. Here, Willie McClure from Calabasas, Calif. negotiates one of the many bridges that cross the river.

photo courtesy of Michael McClure

McKenzie River Trail: A Fat Tire Favorite

McKenzie River trail has it all - speed, fear, fatigue and pure bliss

Published: September 04, 2002

The McKenzie River Trail lives up to all the fat tire hype.

Variously described as "one of the best mountain bike trails in the U.S." (Adventurerivercenter.com), "one of the best rides anywhere, and that's not limited to Oregon" (John Zilly in *Kissing the Trail*) and "a sweet trail" (a guy we met near the Blue Pool at Tamolitch Falls), the McKenzie River Trail is outright gorgeous. And the biking offers some of just about everything: speed, fear, fatigue, bliss and technical back-of-your seat plunges on snaky rock and root festooned single-track.

And just when the careful maneuvering gets a bit tedious, the trail opens up and you're zipping between massive old-growth cedar and fir with the wind in your face and the river burbling alongside.

Then you're crossing the McKenzie on a narrow log plank bridge, then concentrating on keeping to the trail with a mountain side on the right and a sheer cliff on the left, then blasting down hill amongst the ferns and moss and big old Doug firs.

Last week, Mike Prescott, his wife Carolee, his brother Monte and I rode the McKenzie River Trail from Clear Lake downstream to the lower trailhead below

McKenzie River Trail: A Fat Tire Favorite *continued*

Paradise Campground. It didn't take long to see what all the fuss was about.

Sahalie and Koosah Falls present themselves during the first part of the ride as does the Blue Pool. We ate lunch above the limpid turquoise waters of the Blue Pool, where the McKenzie reappears after running underground for a few miles.

Not far below the Blue Pool, the trail gets maddeningly technical again; there's one spot where you could launch off into space if you don't have your wits about you. This is one trail that you'll want to ride completely in control.

And it's a trail you wouldn't want to ride without packing some food, water, clothing and extra tubes. The lava is sharp and, although no one in our party had a flat, it was reassuring to know those tubes were there if we needed them.

The 25-mile ride (we started a mile-and-a-half downstream from the upper trailhead at the Clear Lake Campground) took us 6+ hours, which included a leisurely lunch break and several shorter pauses to drink in the west-side-of-the-Cascades beauty.

Allow five to nine hours depending on your skill and fitness level. I wouldn't try riding this trail with little kids. There are some scary sections and it's a long haul.

But there are many alternatives to riding the entire thing, top to bottom. Several good mountain biking books cover the McKenzie River Trail, including Zilly's *Kissing the Trail Northwest and Central Oregon,* which provides a mile-by-mile description of the ride. Another good resource is www.adventurerivercenter.com/biking.html, which features a bunch of rider trail reviews.

As for the Prescotts and me, we agree with the eloquent rider we met at Tamolitch Falls.

Very sweet.

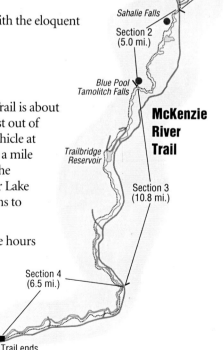

If You Go:

GETTING THERE: The McKenzie River Trail is about 75 miles from Bend. Take Highway 126 west out of Sisters. This involves a shuttle. Leave one vehicle at the Lower McKenzie River Trailhead about a mile north of McKenzie Bridge and another at the starting point 26 miles upstream near Clear Lake at the Santiam Wagon Rd. (look for the signs to the McKenzie River Trailhead).

DIFFICULTY: Advanced. Allow five to nine hours for this ride. There are several sections of technical riding, which may, depending on your skill level, involve some walking. Some sections of narrow trail have a sheer drop on one side.

DISTANCE: 26.5 miles one way.

Dee Wright Observatory was completed in 1935. It's built of lava rocks.
photo by Jim Witty

A Good Outlook

Showing off the McKenkie Pass and Dee Wright Observatory

Published: August 15, 2007

The Old McKenzie Pass Highway, officially known as state Highway 242, is the one place I'd take out-of-town guests if I only had one place to take them.

There's nothing like that surge of pride that comes with showing off the good old backyard, especially when the reaction includes ooh, aah and wow. Trust me: McKenzie Pass will elicit the desired response.

West of Sisters, the road climbs through a dense fir forest, a feel-good cocoon of green on a sunny August day. Then, before you reach the pass, you pop out into the open. There's a viewpoint on the right side of the road that's worth a look. It offers primo views of Black Crater, Mount Washington and Mount Jefferson. And the golden-mantled ground squirrels that hang out in the rocks up there are sociable with a capital S.

Stand still for a few moments admiring the view, and several of the jaunty little chipmunk look-alikes will sally forth in hopes of a handout. When they get lucky, the ingratiating critters store the morsels du jour in their cheek pouches, and, when they have accumulated a full load, pack it back to their burrows among the boulders. That way, they'll have a little something to chow on after they wake up in the spring.

A Good Outlook *continued*

At about 5,000 feet, the sun was beating down, but the breeze carried a faint feel of fall. We left the squirrels to their relentless gathering and headed for McKenzie Pass and Dee Wright Observatory.

Located amid a sea of long-cooled lava at 5,187 feet, the observatory is not what you'd expect. Unless you figured all along that it would be a stone memorial that looks more like a bunker than an observatory.

According to the Willamette National Forest, it was built in the 1930s by the Civilian Conservation Corps Camp F-23 of Company 927, and foreman Dee Wright made ingenious use of the materials at hand. He was charged with building a structure that enhanced the tourist potential of McKenzie Pass. The result is a charmingly crude outpost complete with "lava tube" viewing portals that frame several Central Oregon Cascades peaks. Atop the structure is a rock and bronze "peak finder" that provides 360-degree identification of the mountains thereabouts.

And there are many. Mount Jefferson, Cache Mountain, Bald Peter, Dugout Butte, Green Ridge, Black Butte, Bluegrass Butte, Black Crater, North Sister, Middle Sister, Little Brother, Four-in-One Cinder Cone, The Husband, Condon Butte, Horsepasture Mountain, Scott Mountain, South Belknap Cone, Belknap Crater, Little Belknap and Mount Washington are the volcanic peaks you can study from the top.

Along the paved trail up to the observatory, there are interpretive panels that tell the story of the observatory construction and the geologic and human history of the area. The observatory is accessible via wheelchair.

If you're looking for further background and more compelling photo ops, the nearby Lava River Interpretive Trail is a short (½-mile) complement to the observatory jaunt.

Taken as a whole, it would be difficult not to be enchanted by the fiery origins of the place and the irrefutable evidence all around you.

Most years, you can follow the narrow road west until it meets back up with state Highway 126. But this season, the Oregon Department of Transportation is repairing the highway to the west of Dee Wright, between Scott Lake and Alder Springs. As it stands now, it won't re-open until just before Labor Day, according to Deschutes National Forest spokesman Chris Sabo.

But rest easy.

"They aren't making it a freeway by any means," Sabo said.

He pointed out that the old highway does become a freeway of sorts for bikers during a brief window in spring after most of the snow has been plowed or melted off and before ODOT opens the gates to cars. During that period, cyclists cruise the scenic highway without the threat of motorized traffic looming around every bend.

But summer's the time to load up the out-of-towners and head for McKenzie Pass. Even though there are plenty of worthy day-trip destinations (after all, this is Central Oregon), Dee Wright is the hot ticket for mid-August.

They will be impressed.

This rock and bronze "peak finder" provides a 360-degree identification of the nearby mountains.
photo by Jim Witty

If You Go:

GETTING THERE: From Sisters, drive west on U.S. Highway 20 and turn left at the junction with state Highway 242. Follow the highway about 15 miles to the observatory. It's a winding, narrow road, so proceed with caution.

PERMITS: None required.

CONTACT: Sisters Ranger District of the Deschutes National Forest, 541-549-7275.

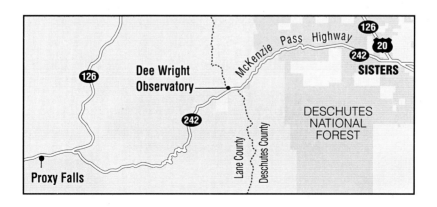

Shevlin Park is an ideal place to view fall colors. Here, aspen and pine trees grow side by side.
photo by Mark Quon

Shevlin Park

An urban escape that's conveniently close to town

Published: September 16, 2004

There's a lot to be said for convenient. And when we're talking Bend, Ore., convenient could easily find you miles away from everything just five minutes out of town.

Shevlin Park is like that, a Cascades east sanctuary abutting the boundary of creeping urbanization. We love Shevlin Park for lots of reasons, not the least of which being that a townie can get out there for a run, ride or hike at lunchtime and get back before the boss calls out the militia.

I go there whenever I can and, so far, I've flown under the middle-management radar.

But I'd never explored the extension of the park across the street. Operated by Bend Metro Park and Recreation District, the tract is home to Aspen Hall, Shevlin Pond and Tumalo Creek.

Aspen Hall is a top-tier meeting facility in a sylvan setting. It rents for $625 a day and gets lots of use.

Right outside is a picnic area and Shevlin Pond, a still-water component of Tumalo Creek where youth 17 and under can (and do) catch stocked rainbow trout from April through October.

Over the weekend, Bruce Ottenfeld of Bend brought his children and grandchildren to the banks of Shevlin Pond for some fishing, some picnicking and some exploring. "It's a good place to bring the little kids," he said.

And sure enough, Ottenfeld found time to relax with the other adults while a couple of the children cast small jigs to the trout and a couple chased lizards among a garden of sun-warmed basalt boulders.

According to caretaker Lori Maxwell, who lives on premises, the lake is stocked with catchable trout every couple of weeks during the summer months.

Lori and Jim Witty pose inside the covered bridge at Shevlin Park.

photo by Mark Quon

If you go, be sure to check out the trail that meanders downstream from the park area. You'll quickly leave the happy shouts of children at play behind and enter a typically Central Oregon realm of seriously large ponderosa pines, clear running water and volcanic geology.

It's such an amiable place, you might catch yourself dawdling along the tall grass of the creek bank, contemplating the assonant rhythm of rapid and rock. Or cocking your neck at an improbable angle to watch a soaring raptor. Hawk? Eagle? Buzzard? Too high up to tell.

There's even a swimming hole not too far downstream; a good place to cool off in midsummer. Barely 60 degrees and a little breezy this day, though. I passed on the opportunity.

There are so many sublime places in Central Oregon, it's easy to overlook the ones right under our noses. Don't. It's good to have a close-in destination like Shevlin Park/Aspen Hall in your outdoor repertoire.

But be wary. I think I saw your boss out there.

If You Go:

GETTING THERE: From downtown Bend, drive west on Greenwood Ave. which will turn into Newport Ave. Continue straight through the roundabout at Mount Washington Dr. to Shevlin Park Rd. Shevlin Park entrance is about 2 miles on your left. Aspen Hall is on your right.

ACTIVITIES: Hiking, jogging, fishing, cross country skiing and picnicking.

CONTACT: 541-389-7275.

This horse sculpture greets you on the east side of town.
photo by Mark Quon

Shop Sisters the "Witty" Way

One writer's itinerary in and around the quaint town of Sisters

Published: May 23, 2001

How to describe Sisters to an out-of-town visitor?
Charming? Rustic?
Cozy? Quaint?
Fine adjectives all, but they don't adequately convey the feeling you get when you're looking west on Cascade Avenue, a light breeze mussing your hair - a morning of browsing behind you, a possibility-filled afternoon ahead.
What to do when you're all shopped out, even as some in your party have yet to hit full stride?
Here's a possible day's itinerary:

10 a.m. - To Sisters Coffee Company for double shot Cafe Americano. Bid adieu to half your party.
10:25 a.m. - Finish coffee while walking to Fly Fisher's Place. Browse, drool and dream. Buy tippet spool, three flies, a single strike indicator. Talk fish with proprietor Jeff Perin until paying customers interrupt.
11 a.m. - Stop in at Mountain Man Trading Post for no particular reason other than it's a very cool place to be.

11:10 a.m. - Enter Paulina Springs Book Company. Pour a complimentary cup of java. Browse the titles. Buy a book on mountain biking and make a mental note to come back when you've got more money. (You know, however, you'll return well before that.)

11:40 a.m. - Pepsi and pit stop at Sno Cap. Caffeine is a mild diuretic.

11:45 a.m. - Stand on Cascade Avenue looking west, a slight breeze mussing your hair. All shopped out.

11:46 a.m. - Picnic at the Village Green, on Elm Street a couple of blocks west of U.S. Highway 20. Discuss options for the afternoon.

12:45 p.m. - Drive west on Elm about four miles. Turn right on to a Forest Service Road and park. Walk a few hundred yards down to Squaw Creek, in full spring runoff. Sit on a rock, watch the stream cluck amiably by and experience a profound sense of well-being.

1:45 p.m. - Hike back to the car and drive back into town but not before admiring the Three Sisters from a different perspective.

2 p.m. - Hop on the cell phone and confirm the other half of the party is still fully engaged in its thorough exploration of the cozy-yet-deceivingly-expansive business district.

2:05 p.m. - Turn left on U.S. Highway 20 and roll west. Suttle Lake or the Metolius River. Either way, you can't go wrong. Why not do both?

2:25 p.m. - About 13 miles west of Sisters, turn right on Forest Road 14 at a sign for Camp Sherman.

2:40 p.m. - Park at the Camp Sherman General Store and Deli and engage proprietor Roger White in conversation while sipping a latte. Drool some more as White shows off 1,100 bins of dry flies, streamers and nymphs as well as the world's largest selection of Metolius River and Camp Sherman T-shirts in the known world.

3:15 p.m. - Walk across the road and watch the Metolius for a while. Cuss at yourself because you forgot to pack the fly rod.

3:20 p.m. - Pit stop at public bathroom near the store. Flowing water and caffeine ... well, you know.

3:40 p.m. - Back out at the highway, turn right and drive about three miles to the Suttle Lake turnoff on the left. Circumnavigate the mountain lake on a four-mile loop trail, then return to Sisters.

5:30 p.m. - Pull up in front of The Gallimaufry. Load bags in trunk, people in back seat.

5:31 p.m. - Bask in the sweet afterglow of a perfect day of shopping.

Editor's Note: Shops mentioned in article may no longer be in business.

If You Go:

GETTING THERE: From Bend, take U.S. Highway 97 north to U.S. Highway 20 NW and continue for about 18 miles to Sisters.

Camp Sherman and the Metolius River just west of Sisters could be the prettiest place on this planet.

photo by Jim Witty

Scenes from Autumn

As fall descends, driving through the Oregon wilderness grows more beautiful every day

Published: October 19, 2005

It's Sunday (or Wednesday or Friday), it's autumn - the best season of the year in Central Oregon - and gas is a few ticks below $3.

Time to go for a drive.

Last weekend, we explored one of the countless variations on an ageless seasonal theme: fall colors.

While this is an ideal time to catch those eye-squinting yellows and blazing reds nearby at such places as Drake Park in Bend, the Deschutes River Trail west of town and on the road to Tumalo Falls, the colorful display is even better to the west, along the McKenzie Highway on the other, wetter, side of the Cascades.

Of course, it's alright if you get sidetracked on the way. We did.

Just west of Sisters on Highway 126, the turnoff to Camp Sherman and the Metolius River always seems to beckon, never more than in the fall.

This could be the prettiest place on this planet.

There's the head of the Metolius, a short walk from the parking lot to the place where it all begins, where the water wells up from underground and begins its journey

The viewing platform in Camp Sherman has educational information about the fish that inhabit the Metolious River.

photo by Mark Quon

to Lake Billy Chinook. Now's the time to look for kokanee salmon on their annual spawning migration from the lake up the Metolius. And there's the town of Camp Sherman, a rustic little burg hard by the banks of the river where you can pick up an espresso, rent a fly rod or just stand on the viewing platform and marvel at all the sylvan serenity.

Middle Earth with vine maples.

The contrast between the deciduous and coniferous here is stunning.

According to the Metolius Recreation Association, the Camp Sherman store was actually a tent prior to 1917 when a more permanent structure was built. The post office moved out of the store and to a permanent home next door in 1976. These days, besides providing sustenance for the road, the Camp Sherman Store is the spot for information on just about any local subject. Proprietor Roger White will be glad to fill you in on the state of the kokanee run (light this year) the state of the fall show (some of the trees got "nuked" by an early frost) and the state of the fishing on the Metolius (pretty darn good some days).

After taking some photos and scouting the river bottom for bull trout, we drove back to the highway and forged ahead to the Santiam Pass and the headwaters of the McKenzie River.

Scenes from Autumn *continued*

Clear Lake, off Highway 126, is a cold, clear lake that sits behind a dam formed by a 3,000-year-old lava flow. Ghostly, petrified, 2,900-year-old submerged trees are visible below the surface of Clear Lake. And the deciduous trees here - mostly maples - are putting on a spectacular show all around. It's pretty much that way between there and Eugene.

After exploring Clear Lake and environs, we wended our way back the way we'd come. There still may be time before the snow flies, however, to drive the Old McKenzie Highway (242) back over the McKenzie Pass and in to Sisters. Motorists can catch the turnoff just downstream from McKenzie Bridge.

That whole country is full of lava fields and evergreens and the dramatic colors of autumn.

Leaf pigments, the duration of night and the weather all affect when leaves change color. According to the U.S. Department of Agriculture, as nights get longer, the trees

A row boat sits calmly on Clear Lake.

photo courtesy of Gary Calicott

produce less chlorophyll and eventually stop making it all together. Brown, yellow, orange and even purple pigments move in to replace the green. Sunny and cool is the best weather combination for vivid fall colors.

If You Go:

GETTING THERE:

• **Camp Sherman:** From Sisters, drive 10 miles northwest on U.S. Highway 20 toward the Santiam Pass. Just past Black Butte Ranch, turn right on Forest Road 14. The road joins Forest Road 1419; follow this to the left, ignoring a fork to the Head of the Metolius. Turn right at the stop sign; the Camp Sherman Store is just across the bridge. Follow the road to the left, then turn left on Forest Road 14 to follow the Metolius downstream. Bridge 99 is six miles from the Forest Road 11 turnoff.

• **Clear Lake:** From Sisters, take Santiam Pass U.S. Hwy. 20/OR-126 for about 29 miles. Turn left onto OR-126 Clear Lake/Belknap Springs Hwy. Continue about four miles. Clear Lake Resort will be on your left.

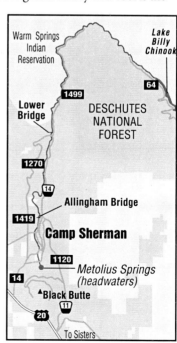

Three Creek Lake is 6,500 feet above sea level.
photo by Jim Witty

Three Creek Lake
It's popular, but still peaceful
Published: June 15, 2005

It's early in the season at Three Creek Lake.

The snow has retreated up Tam McArthur Rim, but a chilly wind still blows most mornings up here at 6,500 feet above sea level.

Hiking weather. And not so bad for fishing, either.

My dog Zeke and I poked around the lake and its environs one recent afternoon, walking the trails, watching the trout rise and observing the fly fishers in their float tubes and pontoon craft trying to get them to take.

Around the far side of the lake, a bald eagle exploded from near the top of a tree, soared for an instant, then dipped down and snatched a fish from the lake. A while later, we spied an osprey flying high over the water, hunting.

Which bodes well for anglers as long as the birds leave some fish for us.

Donna Sandver, who runs the tiny store on the lake, reports that fishing has been lively. There are brook trout in Three Creek Lake and the Oregon Department of Fish and Wildlife stocks rainbows during the summer.

The state isn't scheduled to dump more fish in there until the end of the month, so the rainbow trout that have been pulled out thus far this season are last year's class.

Three Creek Lake *continued*

They're bigger and hungrier than they were last fall. Donna and Jerry Sandver stock basic fishing supplies such as hooks, sinkers, worms, salmon eggs and Power Bait along with soda, beer and snack foods. They also rent row boats and paddle boats. Motors aren't allowed on Three Creek Lake and the result is serene audio to go with all that picture-perfect video.

A row boat can be rented at Three Creek Lake.
photo by Jim Witty

"It's very quiet," said Donna Sandver. "It's right outside the wilderness area. It's getting more popular all the time. People come up for the day and picnic on the beach and swim."

And they hike.

Tam McArthur Rim, named for the author of *Oregon Geographic Names*, looms above the south end of the lake. A trail that begins on the east side leads hikers and horseback riders on a lung-expanding climb to the rim and a spectacular view of Three Creek Lake, Little Three Creek Lake, the High Desert to the east and the Cascades peaks.

Another trail, this one around the north side of the lake and west about a mile to Little Three Creek Lake, offers hikers extreme Alpine vistas with less huffing and puffing. Or you can just mosey around Three Creek Lake, observing the people and the fish and the predators that swoop from above. There are two Deschutes National Forest campgrounds on Three Creek Lake and a horse camp down the road.

If You Go:

GETTING THERE: From Sisters, turn south on Elm St. (which turns into Road 16) and follow it to Upper Three Creek Sno-park and an open gate. Drive on through the gate. The pavement ends before you get to the lake, but a two-wheel-drive rig, driven slowly, should be able to make it in. Three Creek Lake is about 17 miles from Sisters.

ACCESS: Hikers, picnickers, horseback riders, anglers, swimmers.

PERMITS: None required along the lake; Northwest Forest Pass required to park at the trailheads.

CONTACT: Sisters Ranger District, 541-549-7700.

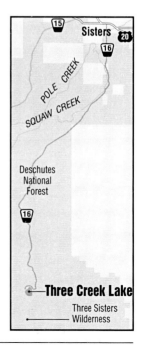

Mark Quon (left) and Jim Witty study rock formations along the Tumalo Creek Trail.
photo courtesy of Bob Speik

The Tumalo Creek Trail
Intrigue your mind and your feet

Published: May 18, 2005

A good day hiking is a day well-spent.

And a good hike is more than a vigorous walk through the woods. There's a social side; good company helps make the memory. Observing wild places and wild things always enhances the experience. And, a well-executed trail that rolls with the geological punches is a definite plus.

We had all that going for us last week on one of Central Oregon's most interesting hiking paths.

The Tumalo Creek Trail between Shevlin Park and the Columbia Southern Canal is challenging. It follows the blustery creek upstream for 4 miles of rock scrambling, eagle watching, photo snapping bliss. The wildflowers are just starting to pop and Tumalo Creek is in top turbulent form.

It's an 8-mile out-and-back (if you go all the way to the old canal) that takes hikers just below the rim of the basalt canyon, then closer to Tumalo Creek. The trail is off-limits to mountain bikers and equestrian traffic.

This section of trail was engineered and built a few years back but was upgraded recently by a Forest Service trail crew led by John Schubert. Their handiwork - freshly

The Tumalo Creek Trail *continued*

Bob Speik and Jim Witty on the Tumalo Creek Trail.
photo by Mark Quon

cleared areas, natural water bars and slash, steering hikers away from hazard and harm - was evident all along the way.

"Springtime along this trail, tucked at the base of south-facing Tumalo Creek canyon, brings warm temperatures, lots of wildflowers and exquisite views of multicolored cliffs and the rushing creek," said Schubert in an e-mail. "The trail can be reached from the back of Shevlin Park beyond Fremont Meadow, thus linking the city of Bend by trail all the way to the Pacific Crest Trail, and onward to Canada or Mexico."

Schubert also warned hikers of the ravenous ticks in this part of the Deschutes National Forest.

We opted to take it slow, stop for a creekside lunch and get back to Bend before a drizzle turned into a deluge.

But before all that, we watched a couple of golden eagles soaring right above the rimrock and noted some over-sized tracks in the damp soil, heading straight downhill toward the creek. It's the kind of place a big cat can go about its business without any major press coverage.

Those hiking this reach of the Tumalo Creek Trail can return the way they came, hook into the Mrazek Trail (an 8-mile loop) or hotfoot it back along the Forest Service Road on the northern rim. While there are straightforward sections, much of this trail is up, over and around rocks, which makes it both fun and a little hazardous. Take it easy to avoid turning an ankle. And allow plenty of time; the going can be slow.

And then there was the social side. After the hike we watched the rain bang down

Jim Witty and Mark Quon scramble on the Tumalo Creek Trail.
photo courtesy of Bob Speik

from the cozy confines of Parrilla Grill. That's where a friend noticed a speck of dirt on my neck that started moving and turned into a tick right before her eyes.

Always trust the guy who built the trail.

If You Go:

GETTING THERE: Drive west on Skyliners Rd. 2.4 miles past the Mount Washington Dr. roundabout. Turn right onto a dirt road and left after one-tenth of a mile onto Road 4606. Drive 1.5 miles to the bridge across Tumalo Creek. Park just beyond the bridge and hike up the spur trail to just below the ridge, or drive another half-mile to the top of the grade and park across from the trailhead on the right.

ROUND-TRIP DISTANCE: Eight miles out and back.

DIFFICULTY: Difficult; involves some scrambling.

The scars of the Booth and Bear Butte fires in 2003 can still be seen at Round Lake.
photo by Mark Quon

Devastation and Renewal

Forest near Round and Square lakes continues recovery from 2003 fire

Published: July 12, 2006

I was fearing the worst.

The last time I'd hiked from Round Lake to Square Lake in the Mount Jefferson Wilderness had been four Julys ago, before the Booth and Bear Butte (B&B) Complex Fire in August 2003 charred 92,000 acres of lush forestland. According to published reports, lightning caused two small fires that smoldered for nearly two weeks before erupting into the B&B fires. The two blazes merged and consumed a whole lot of beautiful timberland.

I recall a couple of pretty lakes, a moderate hike, intermittent mountain views and green as far as the eye could see.

In 2003, I wrote: "The sylvan path around the north side of (Round) Lake takes hikers through pines and firs and blooming wildflowers. The dominant hue is green; Round Lake is close enough to the Pacific Crest to take advantage of ample precipitation."

I noted that the Round Lake Christian Camp, about halfway around the lake and near the trailhead to Square Lake, was a good place to turn around if you merely wanted to scout Round Lake.

The Christian Camp burned up in the fire too. It's since been rebuilt.

As for the forest, it's in the process.

Everywhere there are the overt signs of rebirth. Trout dimple the surface of Round Lake. Ferns carpet just about every square inch of mountainside along the trail to Square Lake that isn't taken up by beargrass and lupine, blooming blue in the midsummer day sun. Yes, save for an intermittent green survivor, the firs and pines stand ghostly against the blue above and the emerald below. But the dominant theme along this roughly 2 1/2-mile route is new life - in profusion.

The trail to Square Lake winds through a carpet of ferns, lupine and beargrass.

photo by Jim Witty

One kind of life you can expect, but probably don't want to see, is the buzzy, obnoxious and invariably annoying snowmelt mosquito. Depending on the time of day, mosquitoes will likely find you quite tasty, especially along the banks of Square Lake. Pack the repellent and keep moving; that's all I can offer as far as advice.

The trail has been rerouted since the fire and the views of Three-Finger Jack are inspiring. Obviously, the character of the trail has changed, but open isn't all bad. And there's still that welcome lake at the end of the hike. A couple of parties had beat me to the lake, but there's plenty of room to picnic, swim or fish.

An equestrian family I met along the trail was headed farther into the Mount Jefferson Wilderness, possibly to Booth Lake. There's a junction on the far side of Square Lake where hikers can decide on Booth Lake or the Pacific Crest Trail, a little more than two miles southwest.

"In the time it takes to play 18 holes or sneak off to the Deschutes for a few casts, you can venture into untrammeled wilderness, crunch pine needles beneath your boots and get back before the boss calls out the dogs," I wrote the first time around, four years ago.

It's still a great place to escape to for a half day of rejuvenation. And while the pine needles are few and far between, this wilderness destination is on its way back.

If You Go:

GETTING THERE: From Sisters, drive west on U.S. Highway 20 toward the Santiam Pass for about 15 miles. Turn right on Forest Road 12, then veer left on Road 1210 and follow it about four miles to Round Lake. Park at the campground to explore Round Lake or turn right just past the campground and continue on to the Square Lake trailhead.

DIFFICULTY: Moderate.

ACCESS: Hikers, horses.

PERMITS: A Northwest Forest Pass is required to park at the trailhead.

South Matthieu Lake is a worthy topper to a most pleasant day hike. Relax and have a picnic before you return to the trailhead.

photo by Jim Witty

High Trailing It

Hiking a section of the Pacific Crest Trail to Matthieu Lake

Published: September 05, 2007

"I don't remember all this uphill on the way in. It seems like it's twice as far on the way back."

It was good to be hiking with Map Guy again. Frankly, I missed the running commentary, the tongue-in-cheek whining that bears enough resemblance to his true feelings to make the miles fly by in a cloud of cheerful pessimism.

Since Map Guy's work hours changed a year or so ago, we'd been like ships passing in the night. I'd offer an occasional "ahoy there" in the parking lot and he'd come back with something so deliciously snide that I decided, come hell or high water, we had to plot a return to the trail.

So it was that I found myself high tailing it back to the Lava Camp Lake Trailhead listening to Map Guy's comforting complaints and trying to figure out how a self-proclaimed introvert could be so damned extroverted.

We'd set out in the morning for Matthieu Lakes - Mark Quon, Map Guy and I - on a section of the Pacific Crest Trail through a deep forest on the cusp of a wide open lava flow that emanated once upon a time from the peaks and buttes hereabouts.

It's a six-mile out-and-back hike with a "nice little reward" in between. You get to North Matthieu Lake first. It's a typical mountain lake, shallow and inviting. We encountered a few mosquitoes, but recent cold evenings may be keeping the populations down. There are several unimproved campsites in the vicinity.

Up the hill and a half-mile or so farther along the trail, we came to South Matthieu Lake, a popular destination at the junction of a couple of trails. South Matthieu is the more dramatic of the two, with its tree-lined shore, mirrorlike surface and clear view of North Sister up ahead.

We met several day hikers there, soaking up the warmth of the sun and all that Three Sisters Wilderness beauty. Hikers from Eugene, Portland and Bend can get up there for the day and recharge their batteries in the high Cascades before descending back down to their day-to-day realities.

Simply by walking this trail, they're rubbing shoulders with an elite group of hikers who are tackling an extended section or the lofty, awe-inducing entirety of the Pacific Crest Trail. The PCT extends 2,650 miles between the Canadian and Mexican borders; it's a marvel of splendid geographic diversity and inter-agency cooperation. The nonprofit Pacific Crest Trail Association brings the U.S. Forest Service, Bureau of Land Management, California State Parks and the National Park Service together with dedicated volunteers in three states (California, Oregon and Washington) to keep the lengthy trail open and in good shape.

According to the Pacific Crest Trail Association, about 350 through-hikers try to walk the entire trail each year. Thousands bite off a shorter segment and are treated to some of the most spectacular wild country in the world.

It's enough to make a guy dream of an extended backpacking trip, say next summer, from one high point on the map to …

I was jostled from my pleasant reverie by a familiar, albeit persistent voice.

"I said, do you want an energy bar? Here, take it and eat it later. I'm trying to lighten my load."

Yep, it was good to have him back.

If You Go:

GETTING THERE: Drive west from Sisters on state Highway 242. About 1/2-mile before McKenzie Pass, turn left at the cinder road to Lava Camp Lake and the trailhead.

TRAIL DISTANCE: About six miles out and back.

TRAIL DIFFICULTY: Moderate.

CONTACT: Sisters Ranger District of the Deschutes National Forest, 541-549-7700.

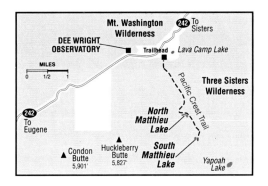

Northeast Region

Smith Rock State Park / photo courtesy of Alan D. St. John

"You ever have one of those pinch-yourself moments when you mutter under your breath, 'I actually do live in Central Oregon, don't I?'"

The call of Crooked River Canyon.
photo by Jim Witty

A Sunday Drive through Crooked River Canyon Country

Published: March 18,. 2004

I took a drive with Ed Abbey this weekend.
So naturally, we pointed east, choosing hard pan over snow - washed out, earth-tone, mono-chromatic rimrock over the hospitable greens and whites and blues of the Cascades.
Abbey died 15 years ago last Sunday.
I wasn't a friend of Cactus Ed's, never knew him when he was alive. But like so many others who cherish the West, I feel a certain kinship to this iconoclast, author and lover of wild places.
"The sun goes down," he wrote in *The Journey Home*. "A few stray clouds catch fire, burn gold, vermillion, and driftwood blue in the unfathomed sea of space. These surrounding mountains that look during the day like iron - like burnt, mangled, rusted iron - now turn radiant as a dream. Where is their truth? A hard clean edge divides the crescent dunes into black shadow on one side, a phosphorescent light on the other. And above the rim of the darkening west floats the evening star."
Abbey loved the desert, especially the canyon lands of the American Southwest.
I've a hunch he would have felt at home in Central Oregon.

A Sunday Drive through Crooked River Canyon Country *continued*

So we rolled by Alfalfa (out Powell Butte Highway off U.S. Highway 20, right on Alfalfa Market Road and on up Reservoir Road) - past pasture and barn and off-highway vehicle playground - and into the rolling juniper hills. Singing the praises of the Sunday drive (bring back the Sunday drive).

At the fork where Reservoir Road meets State Route 27, we've a decision to make. Right toward the Bear Creek Buttes and U.S. Highway 20 along the last unpaved section of state highway in Oregon or left toward Prineville Reservoir, Bowman Dam (easy Ed, this dam has made the farmers happy and the trout fishing sublime) and the Crooked River Canyon?

Abbey's choice. The canyon calls.

While it's not as grand as the Grand or Glenn or The Canyonlands where Abbey spent much of his time, the Crooked River Canyon country has many

The Crooked River meanders through the canyon.
photo by Mark Quon

of the bona fides. Slot canyons with sketchy tributaries and little hidden grottoes. Crenulated rimrock and bizarre hoodoos. Lonesome, wind-scoured mesas and a river running through the heart of it all.

"At evening, near sundown, the vultures would return. Friendly, tolerant, gregarious birds, they liked to roost each night on the same dead pine below," Abbey wrote. "One by one they spiraled downward, weaving transparent figures in the air while others maintained a holding pattern, sinking slowly, gradually - as if reluctant to leave the heights - toward the lime-spattered branches of the snag. They might even have had nests down in there somewhere, although I could never see one, with little buzzard chicks waiting for supper. Try to imagine a baby vulture."

Early spring, before the sun withers the grasses and beats down hard on a hiker's head, is a good time to go exploring here. Away from the refuge of flowing water.

I chose the trail to Chimney Rock, a few miles downstream from the dam on the right side of the road. It's about four miles round trip. The trail takes hikers over a sidehill, up a little canyon and over to a big boulder that resembles a chimney. From there you can see the Crooked River slithering at full Army Corps of Engineers throttle far below. And beyond that the opposite canyon wall. And beyond that the white-capped Cascades.

Between Chimney Rock and the western canyon wall, there was a big bird soaring. I couldn't see it clearly, but I'm thinking it was a Cathartes aura, turkey vulture, although it may be a little early yet.

They migrate south in winter, then head back up north when the weather turns.

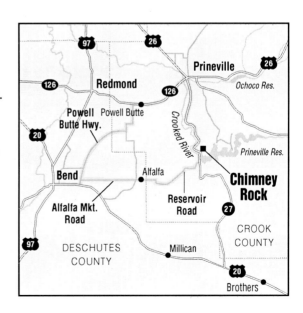

"I respect vultures myself, even like them, I guess, in a way, and fully expect some day to join them, internally at least," he wrote. "One should plan one's reincarnation with care. I like especially the idea of floating among the clouds all day, seldom stirring a feather, meditating on whatever it is that vultures meditate about. It looks like a good life, from down here."

Ed Abbey wanted to come back as a turkey vulture.

And who knows, maybe he did. I don't know much about those things.

I am relatively certain that Abbey was clandestinely buried, as per his request, in a shallow grave somewhere out in his old Arizona stomping grounds. And who knows, maybe one of those migrating buzzards found some carrion. Which means I could have been looking at Edward Abbey reincarnate or at least one of his metaphysical progeny.

Or perhaps not.

All I know is there was a big bird soaring above the river and the canyons and the rocks and it was a good day to be alive.

And to take a Sunday drive.

If You Go:

GETTING THERE: Take U.S. Highway 20 east and turn left on Powell Butte Highway. Take a right on Alfalfa Market Rd. to Reservoir Rd. At the fork where Reservoir Rd. meets State Route 27, turn left toward Prineville Reservoir, Bowman Dam into the Crooked River Canyon.

This rock formation along the trail to Steelhead Falls resembles a sand castle.
photo by Jim Witty

Finding Yourself in Sundown
Visit the Deschutes from Crooked River Ranch
Published: March 05, 2008

If you've never been lost in Crooked River Ranch, you've probably never been there.

Of course, if you carried a map from the get-go, you probably figured things out in a hurry. If you were winging it, the way I usually do, navigating "the ranch" can be a great adventure. I even get lost trying to find places I've been before. More than once.

On the plus side, it's a pretty place to lose your bearings, in a dusty, saddle-up-your-horse kind of way.

I found Sundown Canyon for the third or fourth time last weekend, after blundering my way up and down dirt drives with names like Shad, Chipmunk, Golden Mantle and Horny Hollow. (I didn't actually lose my way on Horny Hollow, but that's one of the better street names I've ever come across.)

There are several ways to get to the Deschutes River from Crooked River Ranch, each offering access to the dramatic rimrock canyon country of the middle reach of the stream.

There's a dirt parking area above Sundown Canyon and a narrow trail that snakes down to the river below. The trail continues upriver for a short distance but soon peters out into a jumble of river rocks that should be negotiated with care. We got to know them well. My son dropped his water bottle there, then unknowingly lost the walkie-talkie he was carrying when he bent down to pick up the bottle. When he realized my walkie-talkie was missing, we retraced his steps, paged it and heard it squawking down there in the shadows below the boulders.

He spent a good half hour trying to reach the radio - just beyond arm's length - in a dark crevasse beneath those immovable rocks. Maddening, but one of those things that can happen when you venture outside the boundaries of the amusement park. Best to rationalize and move on. It could have been my fly box. In which case, we'd probably still be there trying to fish it from the rocky recesses.

This time of year, the Middle Deschutes is as robust as it gets; unfettered by irrigation withdrawals upstream, there's plenty of water chugging through the canyon, depositing foam along the edges. Come spring, however, the irrigators open the gates near Bend and the flow goes from vigorous to anemic in the blink of an eye.

By midsummer, flows drop to about 7 percent of the natural, historic level, the water temperature spikes, and the rainbow and brown trout between Bend and Lake Billy Chinook must contend with one more challenge compromising their survival.

The encouraging news is that the Deschutes River Conservancy has brought farmers, irrigation districts, anglers, power producers, developers and the Confederated Tribes of Warm Springs together to restore some of the historic stream flow. There is hope for the river while balancing the needs of myriad users.

A fly fisherman plies the Deschutes River near the Folley Waters close to Crooked River Ranch.
photo by Jim Witty

Next stop was the Folley Waters upriver. A popular early season fly-fishing spot, it's a section of the river accessible by a mile-long trail down to the water. There's a big tree-studded meadow there on the river's east bank, a pleasant place for a picnic. There's a sketchy fishermen's trail that leads up-canyon.

Downriver from the Folley Waters is the Steelhead Falls trailhead and, a half-mile beyond that on a well worn path, the falls itself.

There's a fish ladder there, built in 1922, which once offered steelhead and salmon a boost over the natural falls. That was before the Pelton-Round Butte Dam complex

Finding Yourself in Sundown *continued*

downriver slammed the door shut on anadromous fish in 1959 (they're being introduced into the system again as you read this).

Navigating our way back out of Crooked River Ranch, I began wondering how this sprawling rural subdivision came to be. Back home, www.crookedriverranch.com answered my questions to a tee.

In 1910, when nearby Redmond boasted a population of 210, a Texas oil man named Gates bought the 12,000-acre ranch from homesteaders. According to the Web site, the main ranch house, built in 1916, is now home of the Crooked River Ranch Senior Center. The Thomas Bell family bought the ranch in 1961 and operated it as Z-Z Cattle Co. for the next decade. Bill MacPherson developed Crooked River Ranch as a recreational site in 1972. It's now home to more than 4,000 people.

And a rugged reach of the Deschutes River that will make you forget about all those houses the moment you drop below the canyon rim.

Steelhead Falls is about a half mile down the trail.
photo by Jim Witty

If You Go:

GETTING THERE: To reach Crooked River Ranch from Redmond, drive north on U.S. Highway 97 to Terrebonne. Turn left on to Lower Bridge Rd., then right onto 43rd St. and left onto Northwest Chinook Dr. into the Crooked River Ranch subdivision. From that point:

- To reach **Steelhead Falls,** turn left on Badger Rd., then right on Quail Rd. After about a mile, turn left on River Rd. and left on Folley Waters to reach that trailhead, or continue on River Rd. to the Steelhead Falls parking area and trailhead.

- To reach **Sundown Canyon,** take Mustang Rd., turn right on Southwest Shad Rd. and left on Southwest Sundown Canyon Rd.

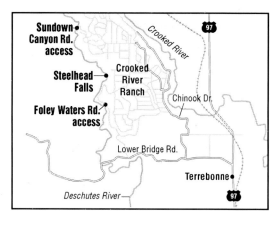

Looking upstream from above the Deschutes River canyon. Spring is a good time to hike the Tam-a-lau Trail.

photo by Jim Witty

A Scenic Edge

Tam-a-lau Trail offers preview of spring, views of Deschutes and Crooked rivers

Published: March 26, 2008

'This isn't going to work.'

Hiking pal Peter Howse chuckled as we both stopped in our tracks. Two more steps and we'd have been several hundred feet above Lake Billy Chinook, and falling fast.

What happens when you pay more attention to Howse's story about getting scammed in Buenos Aires than where you're going? You blow right past the trail junction and end up at the edge of the rimrock with a half-mile uphill climb back to where you went wrong.

But you really can't screw things up too badly on the Tam-a-lau Trail at Cove Palisades State Park (just don't step off the edge). It's a memorable day hike. There are vertiginous vistas, yellow bells underfoot and golden eagles overhead. I even spotted my first butterfly of the year.

Spring is the season to do this one. There are already scads of little blue, yellow and white wildflowers along the trail. You'll be thankful for the cool breeze, especially over the first mile of the trail, which climbs about 600 feet in that short distance.

The trail begins near the northeast corner of the Upper Deschutes day-use area

A Scenic Edge *continued*

parking lot on the Deschutes River arm of the lake, wends through a juniper forest back to the road and continues with a series of switchbacks on the other side. Carry your camera and you'll have an excuse to rest periodically on the way up. Views of the Deschutes, the Island between the Deschutes and Crooked rivers, and bizarre rock formations will have you zooming and snapping, and breathing a little easier.

The climb gets you to the top of the Peninsula, a plateau that separates the Crooked from the Deschutes before the two rivers come together in the reservoir. Up there, the trail is a relatively flat 5-mile lollipop loop that skirts the north end of the Peninsula.

You'll see the Crooked River from the east rim, and both rivers from the northern point. On a clear day, you'll also see the high Cascades, from Mount Hood to the Three Sisters.

The steep cliffs and deep canyons hereabout are the result of alternating layers of stream sediments, volcanic debris and basalt lava that flowed from the Cascades into a huge basin, according to an Oregon State Parks brochure. The Deschutes Formation was capped by lava 3 million years ago, forming the rimrock at the top of the cliffs. The canyons have been sculpted by eons of erosion.

If you hike on a Saturday or Sunday, you probably won't be alone. But this rugged country gives the illusion that you're walking in a remote corner of the West (even though the lake below attracts thousands of buzzing boats and sun-seeking visitors during summer).

State park crews built the Tam-a-lau Trail during the late 1990s when trails on the Island were closed to the public. According to Oregon State Parks, the Island contains "one of the last remaining ungrazed and unaltered ecosystems of its type in the United States."

Negotiate the loop and you'll be back where you started, atop the plateau. Get caught up in Howse's storytelling and you'll likely end up where the land ends and a great yawning chasm begins. But at least you'll know not to fall for the old fake bird poop pickpocket flimflam when rousting about South America.

If You Go:

GETTING THERE: From Bend, drive north on U.S. Highway 97. Before reaching Madras, turn left and head to Culver at a sign pointing the way to Cove Palisades State Park and Lake Billy Chinook. Follow the signs to the lake. The Tam-a-lau Trailhead is across the first bridge (over the Crooked River arm) and up the hill on the right near the Upper Deschutes day-use area parking lot.

CONTACT: Cove Palisades State Park, 541-546-3412.

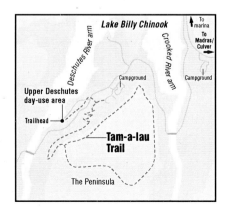

A semi-frozen Haystack Reservoir looking like lost continents or cumulonimbus.
photo by Mark Quon

Haystack's Snow White Look
Winter storm creates a surreal view

Published: January 30, 2008

    Due to factors beyond my control, I ended up doing this Outing on Sunday. Due to factors beyond my control, Sunday turned out to be an interesting day to be outside.
    While most sensible people were inside looking out, watching the snow pile up and the juniper boughs sag under the strain, my friend Mark Quon and I were watching the snow pile up all around us as we explored the winter white countryside around Haystack Reservoir.
    What we saw was quite remarkable. And we never would have been there had we followed our quite reasonable inclination to hole up and watch the storm unfold out the living room window or from the cloistered confines of the Deschutes Brewery & Public House. And, in truth, we never would have been there had we ventured down the steep hill to Lake Billy Chinook in Mark's pickup to go hiking at Cove Palisades Park. No, we never would have been there because we'd still probably be at the bottom of the grade trying to figure out how to get back up out of that hole.
    So we opted for our second choice, fighting the strong urge to retreat to the brewery for a shot of warmth and a pint of IPA.
    I wrote about Haystack Reservoir in 2003, so I had a mental image of the place.

Haystack's Snow White Look *continued*

Forget about it. It looks way different when it's laden in a muffling blanket of white, when fat chicken feathers are flying in your face and all that swirling snow has cast a gray pall over the road, the trail and the lake. What lake? From our perspective at the wooden fishing pier, then atop the dam and then again from way up the hillside to the east, the reservoir looked more like a vaguely familiar planet as seen from space, or the tops of clouds from a Boeing 737.

What it was, was a mostly frozen reservoir with big blotches of snow on the surface that looked more like lost continents or cumulonimbus than 62,000 acre feet of impounded irrigation water in a semi-frozen state.

It was difficult to fathom that six or seven months from now, speed boats will be buzzing around down there and anglers in shirtsleeves and shorts will be casting for crappie, bass and catfish. It was hard enough to remember that this was a reservoir north of Terrebonne smack dab in Central Oregon's banana belt.

But it is. Built in 1956 by the Bureau of Reclamation, Haystack stores irrigation water for the prime agricultural land in the surrounding Culver and Madras areas. The reservoir and immediate environs cover 271 acres, with five miles of shoreline.

Jim uses his GPS device to lock in his vehicle location before hiking to Haystack Reservoir.
photo by Mark Quon

In the warmer months (and during most of the winter, actually) Haystack gives off a pleasant, High Desert, family recreational vibe. Sunday, we could have been up near Circle, Alaska, or in Siberia somewhere battling the elements as we tramped out across the trackless tundra. That fantasy was bordering on the believable except for those darned juniper trees (with the snow-clotted branches) that were always popping up on the periphery, a Central Oregon reality check.

Mark and I tramped around the reservoir and the adjacent Crooked River National Grassland on Sunday, reveling in all that weather. We saw raptors and songbirds and the tracks of a deer that must have just passed by. All that new snow, and more falling all the time, made it an adventure.

Mark Quon walks towards Haystack Reservoir.
photo by Jim Witty

While writing this, I was reminded by a colleague that there are two kinds of people: Those who get a charge from the promise of a strong, low-pressure system, rapidly dropping temperatures and the distinct possibility of some full-tilt, batten down the hatches, crappy weather and those who don't (also a completely reasonable position).

No doubt where I fall on that question, though. Mark too.

And I've a strong hunch there are many more out there who get a little rush of adrenaline at the tantalizing prospect of a rapid drop in barometric pressure.

Later, over that beer at the pub, Mark and I noted that had we opted out of going out, we would have missed a great time and the surreal view of the reservoir, which was really quite memorable.

You can't catch a fish if your line's not in the water. And we'd never have seen Haystack Reservoir the way we did Sunday if we'd stayed home.

Then again, don't do it if it's not safe.

The view out the window is quite nice.

If You Go:

GETTING THERE: From Redmond, drive about 15 miles north on U.S. Highway 97 and turn right at the sign to Haystack Reservoir. Another right turn takes you to the west shore. Since conditions were snowy, we parked at the sign for the fishing pier and walked the half-mile to the reservoir, then skirted the shore to the dam. We crossed the dam and followed a doubletrack trail up the hill. Caution: The lake may look frozen solid, but it won't support your weight. Stepping out on the ice could prove fatal.

PERMITS: None required. Campsite fees.

CONTACT: Crooked River National Grassland, 541-475-9272.

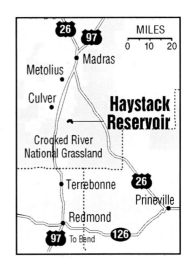

Haystack Butte, which rises up to 4,015 feet, is south of Haystack Reservoir in the Crooked River National Grassland. Inset: An old skull has been bleached by the sun and softened by time.

photo by Jim Witty

Central Oregon 'Butte-ies'
Haystack and Juniper buttes furnish the Crooked River National Grassland

Published: March 19, 2008

Central Oregonians are used to buttes.

There are black ones and gray ones, round ones, square ones and many that are named after prominent pioneers.

These "steep hills standing alone in a plain" - as *Webster's New World Dictionary* describes them - are as much a part of this High Desert landscape as juniper, sagebrush and ponderosa pine.

We might have a tendency to take them for granted, to pass them off for the lofty peaks to the west. That would be a mistake (Mount Bachelor, I'm reminded, is a lofty butte).

According to www.geology.com, a butte is "a conspicuous hill with steep sides and a flat top. The top is usually a cap rock of resistant material. This structure is frequently an erosional remnant in an area of flat-lying sedimentary rocks."

In Central Oregon, buttes are reminders of our volcanic underpinnings.

At 3,925 feet, Juniper Butte is accessible to explorers. It's part of the Crooked River National Grassland, located north of Terrebonne.

photo by Jim Witty

There are two imposing buttes north of Terrebonne that we all pass by while driving on U.S. Highway 97. Heading north, Juniper Butte is on the left and Haystack Butte is to the right. If you see the ODOT weigh stations, you can probably see both buttes.

Both have recreational significance.

Juniper Butte, every 3,925-feet elevation and sprawling, rocky top, juniper flanked bit of it, is part of the 155,000-acre Crooked River National Grassland. The run-up to Haystack Butte from the west is inside the federally administered grassland; part of the butte itself is privately held.

You can drive close to the base of Juniper Butte and explore the folds and creases of the butte. The higher you go, the better the view of the snow-mantled Cascades to the west.

Last week, my dog Hoss and I opted to poke around the plains and hills on the other side of the highway. A couple of miles past the Juniper Butte turnoff, we swung right on the road that cuts back south, parallel to the highway, then left (east) on a gravel road marked by a large pile of cinder. Be sure to admire the red-rock formations to the left where the road jogs to the northeast. That's Haystack Butte on the right. I pulled off the road so Hoss could scare up a jackrabbit or two and I could stretch my legs. We hiked about three-quarters of a mile up a gradual incline of sagebrush and an occasional juniper tree before coming to a barbed-wire fence. I could hear, but couldn't

Central Oregon 'Butte-ies' *continued*

see, cows bawling on the other side. Although Hoss made a couple of darting forays onto the private property, I didn't. The inholdings here (and everywhere) are to be respected. Maps are available through the Crooked River National Grassland office in Madras. Contact them at 541-475-9272.

While we couldn't access the butte from this side, we had a close-up view of the base of the butte, the forested hillside and the top (I wonder what it looks like up there). I spent a while imagining the country unseen, then looked back over the grassland toward the car and slipped into another reverie.

Back in the 1920s and '30s, farmers who had homesteaded this marginal ground and found it a tough row to hoe, began packing up and heading out. Farm prices had plunged and drought followed floods. For many, it was a struggle to pay taxes and mortgages. In the 1930s, the federal government bought back homesteads that had fallen on bad times, according to former Grassland District Ranger Kristin Bail. Some of those lands became the Crooked River National Grassland.

This wide open country hasn't changed much, if at all, since those difficult days.

As we walked back toward the road, the wind kicked up and a hard snow began peppering everything in its path, including my exposed face and sunglasses. In reality, it wasn't snow, exactly, and it wasn't hail. It was those little, solid white pellets that defy definition, except probably among Eskimos. Anyway, it was hard to see for a spell there, and I thought of great clouds of locusts and how much pluck it must have taken to try and wring a living from this land.

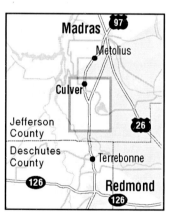

The snow and the gray pall moved on to the east and the sun shone bright. Hoss surprised a rabbit and bounded off in pursuit. An old pickup bounced by on the road. Back up on the butte, at 4,015 feet, the storm was picking up steam.

If You Go:

GETTING THERE:

- To reach **Juniper Butte** from the northern city limits of Terrebonne, drive seven miles north on U.S. Highway 97 and turn left onto the gravel road. Watch for a pullout and gate on the right. The butte is also on the right.

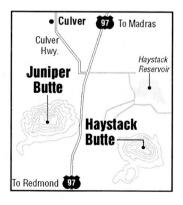

- The turnoff to the **Haystack Butte** area is nine miles north of Terrebonne, on the right. Look for the cinder pile one-half mile up the road on the left. Turn left. The road leads to Haystack Reservoir, with the butte to the east.

CONTACT: For maps or information, Crooked River National Grassland, 541-475-9272.

The Peter Skene Ogden State Wayside offers a breathtaking view of the Crooked River Gorge.
photo by Jim Witty

Peter Skene Ogden State Wayside Rich in Vistas

Published: January 21, 2004

You ever have one of those pinch-yourself moments when you mutter under your breath, "I actually do live in Central Oregon, don't I?"

When you can't quite believe the spectacular rimrock valley or the picture-perfect mountain lake you've stumbled across is real? When you gaze out over miles of empty and feel rich?

You don't always have to march for miles or ski your fanny pack off to put yourself in position either.

Stop off at the Peter Skene Ogden State Wayside, walk out to the edge of the Crooked River Gorge, and tell me you don't feel a little different about things.

It's about 300 feet straight down to the bottom of the canyon from where you're standing. The river sluices through a garden of boulders down there, and this time of year, the snow, the ocher walls, the juniper and the vertigo make for a heady brew.

And there are the bridges.

Three of them, each speaking of an era, each a vintage benchmark of engineering artistry.

On the upstream side is the new span, the Rex T. Barber Veterans Memorial Bridge, sleek, simple and businesslike. Many of us monitored the three-year construction process while we whizzed by at 60 mph.

Peter Skene Ogden State Wayside Rich in Vistas *continued*

The bridge, subsequently named after war hero Rex Barber, opened on Sept. 16, 2000, and was the first major cast-in-place segmental concrete arch bridge in the United States.

The concrete arch was installed in segments supported by two temporary towers and cabled until both ends met in the middle. Each segment was cantilevered like a bouncy diving board before workers attached the stay cables.

Standing at the overlook, you might wonder how they got the bridge to mesh perfectly in the middle. Or just how much chutzpah it would take to crawl out over 300 feet of nothingness tethered only to a skinny cable. There were no major injuries during construction.

But, Oregon Department of Transportation inspector Brady Pauls said, the gorge claimed a pile of equipment.

"There's quite a collection of hard hats and tools at the bottom of the gorge," he said. "One carpenter lost six hammers."

Just downstream is the old bridge (called the Crooked River High Bridge), built in 1926. According to ODOT, it's still structurally sound. It just couldn't accommodate all the north-south traffic in the booming region. Visitors can walk out on the High Bridge and contemplate the new span upstream, the old railroad bridge downstream and the river below.

The Oregon Trunk Railroad Bridge, built in 1911, was the first major structure to span the Crooked River Gorge, according to an informational sign at the site. In the early 1900s, the Spokane, Portland & Seattle Railway battled with Union Pacific to open up Central Oregon to rail traffic. SP&S won the fight in court, but night raids, dynamite and gunfire were the rule as the competing companies raced to be first from the Columbia River to Bend.

The roomy, greenbelt park is named after Hudson's Bay Company trapper Peter Skene Ogden.

He made the first recorded journey into Central Oregon in 1825 on behalf of the famed fur trading firm, and crossed the Crooked River Country just to the northeast. Ogden, Utah, was also named after him.

The park has an ample parking lot and restroom facilities.

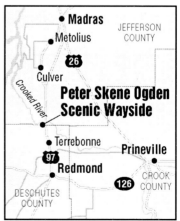

If You Go:

GETTING THERE: The Peter Skene Ogden State Wayside is on U.S. Highway 97 about 10 miles north of Redmond.

RESTRICTIONS: Leashed dogs are allowed in certain areas of the park. Keep your dog on a tight leash.

Young anglers fish from the dock at Walton Lake. Stocked rainbow trout kept them busy throughout the weekend.

photo by Jim Witty

Snug and Friendly

Ochoco's Walton Lake offers cozy warm-weather getaway

Published: July 05, 2006

Walton Lake in the summertime is intimate and inviting.

You know how big lakes impress with their depth, their breadth and their sheer magnitude? Often, those factors that make them awesome also make them chilly and a little impersonal. Think Crater Lake. You can't have it both ways.

Walton Lake is a popular warm-weather destination in the Ochoco National Forest because of its diminutive size and setting. At just 18 acres, it's surrounded by old-growth ponderosa pines and emerald meadows that beckon on a sunny day. It's snug and friendly, and so are the people.

While at 27 miles northeast of Prineville, it's not exactly on the beaten path, Walton Lake has definitely been discovered. Although the scenery is top-notch, it doesn't offer an untrammeled wilderness experience. But you know that going in.

Besides, there's something buoyant about young anglers' voices, their high hopes and audible excitement resonating from shore to shore.

"I got one." "What are you using?" "Powerbait." "Got another one."

The giddy sounds of summer.

Snug and Friendly *continued*

The Oregon Department of Fish and Wildlife stocks Walton Lake with pan-size rainbow trout on a regular basis, and the fishing can be productive.

Bait, spinners and flies all yield fish. The lake, at 5,156 feet above sea level, is no more than 20 feet at its deepest.

I got out in my pontoon boat, joining several other inflatables and even a drift boat on the water. Gas motors are not allowed on Walton Lake.

It's also a good spot to spy wildlife. Woodpeckers, belted kingfishers, osprey, Steller's jays, frogs and Belding's ground squirrels are among the cast of characters.

The lake is formed by a small dam near the head of Cady Creek. Spring water also seeps into the lake from surrounding meadows, according to the Forest Service.

A mile-long trail circles the lake and there's a 31-site campground that swings around three sides of the lake. The Round Mountain Trail, which begins on the southeastern side of the lake, is an option for those looking for a more strenuous jaunt. It's 16 miles up Round Mountain and back down again.

A boat ramp at the lake makes it easy to launch your canoe, raft or other craft.

The place was once a diversionary dam used to supply water to mines of Scissorsville downstream, writes noted local historian Steve Lent in his *Central Oregon Place Names: Crook County*. The lake was then known as King's Reservoir. But that changed in 1960 when the Izaak Walton League improved the facilities at the lake and filed water rights there. The lake was renamed after pioneer angler Izaak Walton.

We paddled around the lake, caught a few fish, and a couple of people in my party opted to swim (the water's colder closer to the bottom). I ate a sandwich on the beach and watched the swimmers and the anglers on the dock and some folks driving their radio-controlled boats from the shore nearby. The evocative scents of suntan lotion (SPF 30) and fresh-caught fish swirled, rounding out the day.

Inspiring. In a casual, Ochocos kind of way.

If You Go:

GETTING THERE: From Prineville, drive east on U.S. Highway 26 for 16 miles then jog right on to Forest Road 22. Keep left on Forest Road 22 near the ranger station and drive about six miles. Turn left on Forest Road 2220 to Walton Lake.

COST: Day-use fee is $5.

CONTACT: Ochoco National Forest, 541-416-6500.

Steins Pillar is a landmark in the Ochoco National Forest. It's composed of ancient volcanic debris flow deposits.

photo courtesy of Scott Johnson

Steins Pillar

Trek to view geology brings wildlife all the more in view

Published: September 06, 2006

I have the eerie feeling I'm being watched.

I'm hiking solo, pushing up the trail toward Steins Pillar, my senses heightened by the lack of human discourse and an underlying hunch that I am not alone out here in the Ochocos.

And, of course, I'm not.

There are dozens of species and hundreds of individual animals going about their diurnal routines here among the pines and firs and red-barked manzanita. I step over a furry, orange creature (caterpillar?) inching across my path with, what seems to this anthropomorphizing hiker, a single-minded intensity. Farther on, a small lizard darts across the trail and I wonder how it lost its tail. A little Buddha-like bird (mountain chickadee?) lights atop a boulder the size of a one-room cabin and surveys its prospects before I send it flapping.

At every twist, something new catches the eye. A chipmunk kicks up dust as it (literally) high-tails it up the trail in front of me. A red-tailed hawk soars. A fly buzzes in to invade my personal space, retreats and advances again.

Steins Pillar *continued*

I observe these things but can't shake the feeling that the watcher is being watched. It's a delicious prospect but discomfiting at the same time.

In all the hours I've spent tromping around in wild places, I have yet to see a mountain lion in the woods. But I saw one on the edge of the suburban sprawl in the chaparral country of Southern California many years ago and have been enthralled by these large, stealthy beasts ever since.

That chance encounter and the certain knowledge that just because I haven't seen them doesn't mean they haven't seen me, fuels the fascination.

And causes me to swallow hard when I pass beneath a rock, its topside obscured by tree branches and my line of sight.

It doesn't get much better than this. I'm traversing the side of a mountain on the cusp of the Mill Creek Wilderness, on my way to get an upclose look at one of Central Oregon's most unusual geologic anomalies. The hill is alive with the high-noon comings and goings of summer. This is cougar country, coyote country, elk country and quite possibly, bear country. I never see any of those animals, but maybe, just maybe, they see me.

It's about two miles from the trailhead to Steins Pillar, which, according to geologist Ellen Morris Bishop, is a volcanic remnant dating to the Oligocene Epoch, some 38 million years ago. The spire, which towers more than 300 feet from base to pinnacle, is composed of debris flow deposits, probably from the nearby Twin Peaks Vents, Bishop writes in her *Hiking Oregon's Geology*.

The pillar is impressive when viewed from a vantage on the valley floor; it's even more awesome from the trail looking over, not up.

Pack your camera.

At several points along the trail, the alfalfa fields in the valley below come into view, as do Powell Butte and the Cascades in the westerly distance. There are also a couple lesser spires - false pinnacles to borrow a mountaineering term - that come into view before you reach Steins Pillar.

It's an out-and-back hike, so I retrace my boot tracks to the trailhead.

That old feeling persists, but it's never confirmed.

Maybe, just maybe.

And that's enough.

If You Go:

GETTING THERE: From Prineville, drive eight miles east on U.S. Highway 26 to Mill Creek Rd. at the far end of Ochoco Reservoir. Turn left onto Mill Creek Rd. and follow seven miles to Forest Road 500. Turn right and follow the gravel road two miles to the trailhead on the left.

DIFFICULTY: Moderate. The hike is about four miles round trip.

CONTACT: Ochoco National Forest, 541-416-6500.

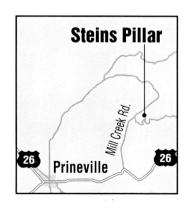

The Round Mountain Trail begins just west of the shelter at the sno-park.
photo by Jim Witty

On Walton Sno-park
Snowshoeing and nordic skiing in the Ochoco National Forest

Published: February 04, 2004

    The woman who cut my hair the other day was complaining that Bend is getting too crowded.
    Turns out, she grew up on a sprawling ranch east of Burns. She misses the unfettered fishing access, the wide open, unpeopled places.
    I have one word of advice for her.
    Ochocos.
    Those mountains to the east of Prineville never cease to enchant. And if it's solitude you seek, there's no better place in Central Oregon to seek it.
    The Ochoco National Forest is more than 850,000 acres of rolling ponderosa pine forest, open meadows and craggy outcrops. In my experience, your chances of seeing wildlife are far greater in the Ochocos than in the Central Oregon Cascades. Your chances of seeing other hikers, skiers or snowshoers are far less.
    I went cross-country skiing in the Walton Lake area last week. The snow was deep and pillowy, the trail beautiful. I saw nary a soul the entire afternoon.
    Walton Sno-park on the Big Summit District of the Ochoco National Forest has about 20 miles of ski trails that fan out from the parking area. Trails are marked and

On Walton Sno-park *continued*

there's information there on the length and elevation of the highest and lowest points, courtesy of the Ochoco Chapter of the Oregon Nordic Club.

There's an array of trails here, from short, relatively flat paths for beginners to longer, steeper runs for old hands.

The Corral Loop, for instance, is an easy five-mile path that's mostly flat but offers a few moderate slopes. Perfect for an easy ski through "park-like ponderosa pine and meadows," according to members of the Nordic Club.

The Round Mountain Trail, which begins just west of the shelter at the sno-park, joins the Walton Lake to Round Mountain hiking trail.

"The marked ski trail ends at a meadow near the base of the mountain," according to information supplied by the club. "The quickest way to the top, 6,753 feet elevation, is to go straight up if you have skins (for traction on the bottom sides of skis). Otherwise one can zigzag up the slope. In either case, the route is most difficult after it leaves the trail."

It's less than a mile to the top, but a 1,000-foot climb. Definitely for advanced skiers only.

I ended up at Walton Lake, which looks far different with its white winter frosting than it does during warmer months.

There are several other trails at Walton Sno-park as well as a spacious shelter near the parking lot. Inside the shelter is a stove and a big pile of wood, courtesy of the Nordic Club.

Speaking of which, membership to the Nordic Club is open to everyone interested in skiing the Ochocos. Annual dues are $9 for an individual and $14 for a family. The club schedules a variety of ski events throughout the winter months, including guided ski tours, ski lessons, a moonlight dinner and ski and a regular ski tour twice a month. Check out www.onc.org for more information.

And if it's a quiet skiing experience you're looking for (and what Nordic skier isn't), maybe it's time to check out the Ochocos.

During a good snow year like this, it's a great place to spend a day on skinny skis.

If You Go:

GETTING THERE: From Prineville, drive 16 miles east on Highway 26 to the junction of Forest Road 22. At the junction, keep right at a sign for Walton Lake. Travel on Forest Road 22 for nine miles to the Ochoco Ranger Station. Just past the station, look for an intersection and take a left. Walton Sno-park is about nine miles up the road. Traction tires or chains are recommended. The last few miles are steep, narrow and usually not sanded.

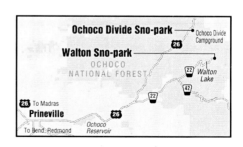

ACCESS: Skiers, snowshoers.

PERMITS: A sno-park permit is required.

Grizzly Mountain looms above the Crooked River National Grassland and Skull Hollow.
photo by Jim Witty

'Tis the Season to Ride Skull Hollow
Mountain biking in Gray Butte country
Published: April 09, 2008

April in Central Oregon is predictably unpredictable.

We took the mountain bikes out for a spin at Skull Hollow on Friday and ran smack dab into a typical spring slumgullion of rain, wind, peekaboo sun and those little Styrofoam-like pellets that are neither snow nor hail but a combination of both (snail?).

After a long winter of relative sloth, I felt a bit snail-like creeping up the Cole Loop Trail out of the Skull Hollow campground. It's a singletrack path that snakes out over the grassland and up-canyon into Gray Butte country. We saw plenty of signs that horses had passed this way; mountain bikers need to be vigilant for horseback riders on the trails in the Crooked River National Grassland.

We didn't see any horses, and the problematic Gray Butte gumbo wasn't an issue. But it can be, especially this time of year.

According to the Central Oregon Trail Alliance Web site, "The infamous Gray Butte gumbo is not to be messed with. At the first sign of gumbo, turn around and retreat. It will pack your tires to the point that they no longer roll through your frame and your bike is suddenly going to weigh 40 lbs as you carry it back to your car."

'Tis the Season to Ride Skull Hollow *continued*

Depending on the weather and conditions, it can get nasty. After a heavy rain, forget about it for a few days.

That said, this time of year and fall are the best times to explore the dirt roads and singletrack trails that ply the canyons and gullies on the back side of Smith Rock. I've ridden there in August. Trust me, if you're not partial to oppressive heat and dust, April is a better bet.

There are intersecting trails and gravel roads in the area that can make your loop long or short.

You can catch the Gray Butte trail or head toward the back side of Smith Rock State Park along a narrow, side-hill singletrack section known as "the traverse." Don't overthink it, but you wouldn't want to plunge over the downhill side.

Road 5710 from Skull Hollow takes riders (and vehicles) up and around to the west side of Gray Butte. You'll pass the historic McCoin apple orchard and a hiking trail to the top of the butte. The apple orchard was planted by homesteaders Julius and Sarah McCoin in 1886. Now owned by the federal government, the orchard still bears fruit.

Rocks are a major part of the landscape in the Skull Hollow area.

photo by Jim Witty

There are lots of options, one of which is to take a rest and consider the countryside. The canyons and arroyos with their scrubby juniper and rocky outcrops make the place look like a stage set for an old Western. "The Legend of Skull Hollow."

"It's a legendary thing," replied historian Steve Lent when asked how the place got its name.

According to Lent, who's assistant director of Prineville's Bowman Museum, a group of soldiers found a pile of skeletons and skulls up in the canyon sometime in the 1860s. They looked to be a couple of decades old at the time. Word was, the boneyard was what was left of the travelers in an ill-fated wagon train. The problem with that story, said Lent, is that there's nothing to back up that assertion and, given the lay of the land, it's unlikely wagons would have gone that way.

But Chief Paulina's raiders were active in the area during that time period (1840s) and the story persisted. More likely, the bones were the result of a skirmish between Indian bands.

Here's my advice. When riding out of Skull Hollow, pay the physical price and get yourself to a high place with a view. Reflect on the beauty below and the history all around.

Then hop on your bike, point it downhill and make your peace with Isaac Newton.

The clay hard pack of the Cole Loop trail usually makes for good riding.
photo by Jim Witty

If You Go:

GETTING THERE: From Redmond, drive north on U.S. Highway 97 and turn right on O'Neil Hwy. At the quarry, turn left on to Lone Pine Rd. Because the sign for Skull Hollow campground has toppled, look for the campground on the left (with Gray Butte looming to the west).

CAMPING: The campground is a wonderfully casual place used by climbers out of Smith Rock State Park, equestrians and mountain bikers. Camping is free in the 30 designated pull-in campsites, and fires in the grills are allowed. There are two pit toilets, but there is no water. Pack it in, pack it out.

CONTACT: Crooked River National Grassland, 541-475-9272.

The North Fork of the Crooked River flows near Big Summit Prairie.
photo by Jim Witty

Scenery Worth $4.31 a Gallon
A Sunday drive in the Ochoco National Forest
Published: June 19, 2008

The Sunday drive may be up against the ropes and reeling, but it's not dead yet.

With a gallon of regular going for $4.31 (and climbing) as of 10:45 a.m. Tuesday, no matter what day of the week you pick for your Sunday road trip, you better choose wisely. This is no time to bury your head in the sand, drop the ball, cloister yourself indoors.

It finally feels like summer out there, and it would be a shame to let the fleeting season sprint by under a scudding cloud of petrol panic. On the other hand, it's virtually impossible to ignore the gathering storm.

So I've been keeping my eye out for outings that offer maximum bang for the buck, mileage for the money, aesthetic delight per overpriced drop of fossil fuel.

From Bend, it's less than 100 miles to the far side of Big Summit Prairie in Ochoco National Forest, where the North Fork of the Crooked River flows clear and cool by Deep Creek Campground. To me, it was 200 miles (round trip) well spent.

For us, the trip essentially began in Prineville, where lunch can mean burritos at one of the authentic taquerias or a good old-fashioned drippy burger at Tastee Treet, a good old-fashioned burger joint.

A drive through Big Summit Prairie in Ochoco National Forest yields a plethora of Indian paintbrush within fields of wildflowers on display.

photo by Jim Witty

U.S. Highway 26 spools east out of Prineville, past Ochoco Reservoir and on into the Ochocos. Ochoco Creek Road (a right off the highway) delivered us to the ranger station where we opted to jog right for the drive up to the Independent Mine. The old cinnabar mine is now a couple of rustic wooden buildings in an emerald meadow of grass and false hellebore (a fine place for a picnic if you got past Prineville without stopping).

Back out on the pavement, we turned right on Canyon Creek Road (Forest Road 42), crested the pass and descended onto Big Summit Prairie.

Although wildflowers bloom there all summer long, the next week or two will be special up there. It's not just single blooms, but a riot of purple, white, yellow and orange. Indian paintbrush, yellow wyethia, arrowleaf balsamroot and many other species abound on the flat prairie. The interior of Big Summit Prairie is privately held and off limits to the general public. Most of the land along the roads that circle the prairie, however, is administered by the Ochoco National Forest and the Prineville District of the Bureau of Land Management.

Several gravel roads head south from the main road and offer more flower viewing and hiking opportunities.

Beyond the far eastern side of Big Summit Prairie, you'll meet up with the North Fork of the Crooked River, a wild and scenic waterway that looks more like a creek up there than a full-fledged river. The headwaters of the North Fork are within Big Summit Prairie.

Scenery Worth $4.31 a Gallon *continued*

East of Deep Creek Campground, which is temporarily closed because of a logging operation, we parked and explored a short reach of the North Fork. We found wildflowers, willows, alder and a profusion of butterflies along the banks. In river, rainbow trout seek refuge under log jams and beneath the protective blur of riffles.

Depending on your time and gas tank constraints, you can continue east, making a big loop to county roads 113 and 112 through the town of Paulina and on to Paulina Highway through Post and back through Prineville.

We headed back west through Big Summit Prairie, turned north and ended up at Walton Lake via Forest Road 2220. The 18-acre Ochoco oasis, formed by a small dam near the head of Cady Creek, was once a diversionary dam used to supply water to nearby downstream mines.

Now, there's a 31-site campground here, the Round Mountain Trailhead (16 miles round trip), a boat ramp and a fishing dock. The latter attraction was the reason my 11-year-old son, Daniel, endured 100 miles of starting and stopping and photographing and starting again.

One 14-inch rainbow trout and a small bullhead had that kid lobbying to start a new family tradition: the Sunday drive.

If You Go:

GETTING THERE: From Prineville, drive east on U.S. Highway 26 for 14 miles to the sign for Ochoco Ranger Station. Turn right and drive about eight miles and turn left on Forest Road 22 to reach Walton Lake or right onto Forest Road 42. The road to Independent Mine is on the right toward the top of the pass. Continue on Forest Road 42 into Big Summit Prairie.

CONTACT: Ochoco National Forest, 541-416-6500.

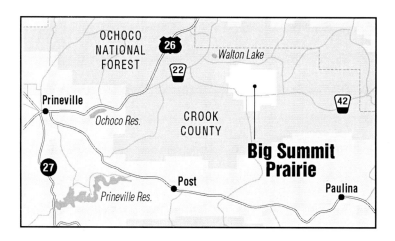

Mill Creek meanders through Mill Creek Wilderness in the Ochocos east of Prineville.
photo by Jim Witty

Leave It All Behind at the Mill Creek Wilderness
Rugged area in Ochocos an escape from civilization
Published: November 29, 2006

It's comforting to know that there are places close at hand where you can leave roads and cars and even mountain bikes behind along with the niggling stuff that follows you around from appointment to appointment.

When we crossed over the line into the Mill Creek Wilderness last week, it was time to trade the housebound baggage for something simpler, more elemental, if only for a few hours. Of course, wilderness boundaries don't poof to produce an instant trade of worries for wonder, but if you walk and sweat and open yourself to the possibilities of big trees, shadowed grottoes and the mystery of the next ridge over, your reality can't help but shift, even if only slightly (an aircraft carrier can't turn on a dime, a day hike can't blow out all the sludge). The heavy-handed artifice back there beyond the gates makes the wilderness seem random. Trees fall and rot into the soil where they lie. Small animals set up housekeeping inside - or not. Bigger animals, meat eaters - coyotes, bobcats, mountain lions and black bears - move stealthily through these forested hills just beyond perception, but sometimes, not often, cross your path. I listen and peer into the firs, try to will a bull elk into the daylight, a dusky bear onto the trail up ahead.

It doesn't happen. Nothing but the crunch of the trail and the whisper of the creek below.

Leave It All Behind at the Mill Creek Wilderness *continued*

And the kind of stillness that dates back further than any of us can remember.

Much of the 18,000-acre Mill Creek Wilderness burned in the lightning-caused Hash Rock Fire during the summer of 2000. From the Twin Pillars Trailhead at Wildcat Campground, the fire's impact appears minimal until you climb higher up the Mill Creek drainage. Here, the fire blazed in a mosaic pattern, leaving stands of ponderosa pine and Douglas fir untouched. There are also a few stands of old-growth ponderosa pines remaining in the wilderness.

With the fire and subsequent years of regeneration, the wildflower season in the wilderness this spring should be showy.

The Ochocos are often overlooked, especially at this time of year. We didn't see another soul on the trail.

The trail was snow-free late last week, but that's not always the case. Snowshoes would be a good bet as the season settles in.

The trail continues six miles (with several creek crossings) all the way up to Twin Pillars, a pair of 200-foot basalt spires that lord over the Ochocos. The upper section of the trail will soon be clotted with snow, off-limits to all but the most tenacious.

According to Wilderness.net, the southwest flowing Mill Creek drainage makes up 85 percent of the Mill Creek Wilderness, which Congress set aside for protection in 1984.

There are three other trailheads leading into the Mill Creek Wilderness, and about 18 miles of trails. Trails also lead from Bingham Prairie, White Rock Campground and Whistler Point. Wildcat is the most accessible this time of year.

My 10-year-old son Daniel and I ventured a couple miles up the trail, pausing often to look, listen and throw rocks. Along the trail, there are grassy meadows, deep forest and open, lightly timbered areas typical of this mountain range.

On the way back out to the trailhead, we were disturbed to find an empty beer can glinting from a mossy spot just off the trail. Coors Light. I cursed under my breath, stuffed it in my pack and bit the (silver) bullet. The anger passed.

But I could feel a subtle shifting as we crossed back over the line. I hope he had a nasty hangover.

If You Go:

GETTING THERE: From Prineville, drive nine miles east on U.S. Highway 26 to Mill Creek Rd. Turn left and drive 9.5 miles on paved road that turns into dirt/gravel to the Wildcat Campground. The trailhead is at a small parking area just before the campground. Walk over the bridge that spans Mill Creek and through the campground. The trail begins here.

DISTANCE: From three miles to 11 miles, depending on how ambitious you are and where the snow line begins.

Cedar Island can be seen here in a section of the Lower Deschutes.
photo courtesy of Greg Burke

Riding the River

It takes only about a day to ease into the rhythm of the Deschutes

Published: September 11, 2002

    It takes about a day to downshift into river gear.
    It goes like this. You're working then you're packing then you're attending to the last-minute stuff that life inevitably throws at you. Then all of a sudden you're afloat and the world is reduced to basalt canyon walls, sun, clouds, wind and water. Water that slides serenely along in places, seethes and boils in others. It's free and wild and indifferent to your daily struggle, to the baggage you've packed along with your duffel. Gradually, like the sun slipping up and out over the plateau to the east, you start shedding your city skin, tapering down, easing into the rhythm of the river. Then the Deschutes, submerged in morning shadow, explodes into sunlight, the riffles sparkling in the sudden luminescence. And you're more here than there, more what is than what if.
    It takes about a day.

Riding the River *continued*

The three-day float from Mack's Canyon to the mouth, where the Deschutes flows into the Columbia, slides and rumbles through some of the wildest, most elemental country in the state.

The hillsides are crackling dry, mostly treeless, stark. That's contrasted by the green ribbons along both banks and the water beneath your hull that dances from blue and cheery to inky and foreboding to coppery and dazzling depending on the changing light.

We're here - veteran river guide John Judy and I - in search of steelhead, magnificent silver bullets that pour up the Columbia each summer and fall, and shoot up the Deschutes to fulfill their biological imperative. They've done so for eons - salmonids that spend part of their lives in the salt, part in the cold, clear and fresh inland waters of the Northwest.

For Judy, who spends most days teaching and rowing and positioning clients for angling success, but not fishing much, this is a boatman's holiday, a chance to immerse himself in something he loves. For me, it's an opportunity to learn and observe and perhaps, to hook a steelhead or two on the fly.

The fishing is good. Days - from before sunrise to just about dark - are spent floating from run to run, wading the pushy current and probing for secure footholds amid basalt boulders and cobbled flats. The angling is methodical: cast, swing the fly, move a couple steps downstream and cast again.

Writing in his book, *Deschutes*, Dave Hughes describes the hooking of a steelhead as a "detonation." It is. But you detect more than you hook, hook more than you land.

Hooking and landing a steelhead on the fly is about as good as it gets.

But so is the dazzling night sky, the family of raccoons at the river's edge, the dizzying flash of enlightenment when you begin to grasp what the steelhead are up to beneath the cover of standing waves and shifting currents.

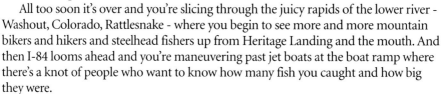

By day three, you forget the stops you made on day one, the specifics of the past blur into the general Now. River time, according to Judy, is a bit of a time warp.

All too soon it's over and you're slicing through the juicy rapids of the lower river - Washout, Colorado, Rattlesnake - where you begin to see more and more mountain bikers and hikers and steelhead fishers up from Heritage Landing and the mouth. And then I-84 looms ahead and you're maneuvering past jet boats at the boat ramp where there's a knot of people who want to know how many fish you caught and how big they were.

You give them the score as motorists sail by on the interstate. The boat engines rev, the moment slips past and soon you're sailing, too.

If You Go:

GETTING THERE: From Madras, take U.S. Highway 97 to the junction and 197 to Maupin. From the little fishing/rafting village, drive north along the east side of the river (downstream) about 25 miles to the end of the road at Mack's Canyon.

Old railroad ties can be seen above sections of the Lower Deschutes River.
photo courtesy of Greg Burke

DISTANCE: About a 25 mile float.

DIFFICULTY: This stretch of river contains some long placid stretches as well as a series of nasty class III and IV rapids. Experienced rafters and drift boaters only!

ACCESS: From Mack's Canyon it's a float. From the mouth, a dirt road (off-limits to motorized vehicles) allows hikers and mountain bikers to penetrate several miles upriver on the east side of the river.

PERMITS: To float the river, you'll need a Boater's Pass available at sporting goods stores around Central Oregon or online at www.boaterpass.com. Steelheaders must have a valid fishing license and steelhead/salmon tag.

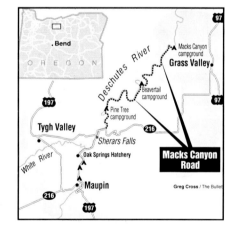

OPTIONS: Several Central Oregon fishing guides and raft companies ply the tricky waters of the lower river from Warm Springs clear to the mouth. Trips range from day-long excursions to multi-day adventures. Hiring a seasoned guide is often the best way to see the river, especially for those with limited experience with potentially treacherous class III and IV rapids.

Steelhead Falls is in the rugged middle section of the Deschutes River.
photo by Mark Quon

Steelhead Falls

Thoughts of insignificance, the power of nature... and fly-fishing

Published: December 01, 2006

Sometimes it's best not to fanatically cleave to your plans come hell or high water. Especially high water.

Turning back can be tricky, especially when you're psychically invested in a scheme that involves a hike along a big, boulder-strewn river, a deep High Desert canyon and enough wildlife to keep you craning this way and that for the duration of your particular adventure. Especially when you've been cooped up far too long.

But the weather was abominable. So, amid the driving rain, lashing sleet and road lakes that could swallow a Mini Cooper in a single gulp, I gave up on the Middle Deschutes and all that goes with it.

And I sulked. For a day.

But it turned out to be a good call because the following Sunday was beautiful out around Steelhead Falls. The rain had subsided, the temperature moderated and the sun even broke through a time or two. And the Deschutes River was a sight for housebound, cabin-sore eyes.

I wasn't the only one who felt the need to get outside and move, preferably to a place where the roads are rutted, the trails lonesome and achingly beautiful in a splendidly isolated, washboard sort of way. Mark Quon and Michael McClure were more than ready to bust loose after too many days on the inside looking out.

We parked at the little dirt parking area, about a half-mile upriver from the falls, next to a lone pickup, which, I deduced by the logoed cap on the front dashboard, belonged to a fly fisher from Eugene. I'll never know for sure, because he (she?) must have gone upstream; we never saw another soul.

We headed for Steelhead Falls, the trail damp, not soggy, perfect for surmising what had gone before us. Deer mainly, but the occasional small animal had passed this way as well. I couldn't tell exactly what left the little prints; need to brush up on my tracking skills.

Steelhead Falls, now in full winter flow, is the kind of place that conjures momentous thoughts of human insignificance, the awesome power of nature and the potential of some fair-to-middlin' fly-fishing come spring, before those notions go tumbling downriver and out of sight around the bend. At least, it's that way with me.

Before Portland General Electric built the Pelton-Round Butte Dam complex downriver in 1959, slamming the door shut on anadromous fish, steelhead, spring chinook and sockeye salmon battled their way up and over the imposing

A great blue heron blends into its surroundings along the river below Steelhead Falls.

photo by Mark Quon

falls each season. There's a crude and battered rock wall on the near side of Steelhead Falls that once served as a fish ladder to help the returning fish over the hump. Built in 1922, the ladder offered the steelhead and salmon a boost during low water months, particularly after irrigators began taking more water out of the Deschutes in the 1930s.

This time of year, if it could get past the dam downriver, a chrome bright, eight-pound steelhead could forgo the ladder and hurl itself up and over these falls. We saw none, of course, but there's a move afoot to reintroduce salmon and steelhead to the Upper Deschutes Basin. A tantalizing prospect.

After admiring the falls and thinking our thoughts, we forged on, downriver, to see what was around that next bend.

What's there is more rimrock, more river, more roadless country. It's that way from the falls down to Lake Billy Chinook. To the east is a chunk of land known as the peninsula because it's sandwiched between the Deschutes and the Crooked River, which also flows into Lake Billy Chinook (as does the Metolius River to the west).

Up top and back to the south is Crooked River Ranch country. The 12,000-acre rural subdivision was a working cattle ranch in the early 1900s. According to Crooked River Realty, the ranch went residential in 1971. Today, it's ranchettes, horse corrals and bands of wintering as well as resident mule deer.

On the return to the trailhead, we saw a golden eagle soaring, ducks, geese and a couple of great blue herons looking for trout.

Steelhead Falls *continued*

Back at the parking area, the white pickup was still there. I imagined its owner, somewhere upstream, happily fishing a pool lousy with big, hungry trout. Sometimes you don't realize how badly you need to get out until you do.

If You Go:

GETTING THERE: From Bend, drive north on U.S. Highway 97 to Terrebonne. Turn right onto Lower Bridge Rd., then right into the Crooked River Ranch subdivision. About 1 1/2 miles on, turn left on Badger Rd., then right on Quail Rd. After about a mile, turn left on River Rd. and follow it to the parking area and trailhead. It's about a mile roundtrip to Steelhead Falls, but the trail continues on, following the east bank of the river.

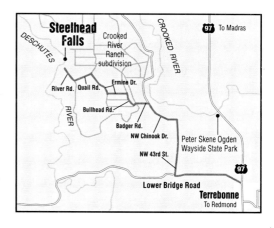

Jim Witty (left) shows visitor Michael McClure the way to Steelhead Falls.
photo by Mark Quon

The Lake Simtustus Marina and Store serves boaters, anglers and hungry travelers at the lake.
photo by Jim Witty

Sim ... What ... Stus?
However you decide to say it, Lake Simtustus is pretty as a picture
Published: May 17, 2006

Lake Simtustus is one of those wonder-what's-back-there places.

I can't count how many times I've driven by the turnoff to the lake, either coasting down that long grade into Warm Springs or pushing back up toward Madras, and wondered about the lake with the interesting name.

It turns out, the lake is on an access road about three miles from U.S. Highway 26. It also turns out that I'd been there before, but got there via a gravel back road from Culver. I didn't remember until it dawned on me that this strong feeling of déjà vu really wasn't.

Anyway, Pelton Dam is a delightful little impoundment brought to you by Portland General Electric and the Confederated Tribes of Warm Springs, the lowest major man-made obstruction on the lower Deschutes River before it empties into the Columbia some 100 miles downstream. That reach is a National Wild and Scenic River and known for its blue ribbon trout and steelhead fishing.

Bounded by the Warm Springs Indian Reservation to the west, Lake Simtustus is a different animal, but a pleasant place in its own right. The part of the lake not governed by a 10-mph speed limit is popular with water skiers, but most of it is a mecca for nonmotorized boaters, anglers and wildlife watchers. Those interested in

Sim...What...Stus? *continued*

geese, ducks, great blue herons and eagles like the Pelton Wildlife Overlook, just north of Pelton Park. At Pelton Park, operated by PGE, people can camp or picnic in a greenbelt overlooking the lake.

There are also viewing platforms from which you can admire the reservoir and the massive slab of concrete. No matter where you stand on dams, it's difficult not to come away impressed by human ingenuity and the big-picture engineering it takes to harness a river such as the Deschutes.

According to PGE, Pelton Dam allows the utility "to maintain a relatively constant flow on the Deschutes, mimicking that of a natural river."

Pelton has become a household word in Central Oregon because of a bold $62 million initiative to move juvenile steelhead and salmon downriver from Lake Billy Chinook. An underwater tower at Round Butte Dam will (hopefully) suck in migrating fish and spit them out on the other side. Trucks will then drive them around the series of dams and release them downstream of Pelton.

It seems the sea-run fish became confused on their downstream migration because of conflicting currents in Lake Billy Chinook.

Upriver passage had been less problematic, even after the dams went in. Adult fish moving upriver could hitch a ride on a set of pulleys and gondolas.

If the tower pans out, the Upper Deschutes, Crooked and Metolius rivers could host runs of anadromous fish for the first time in 50 years.

Meanwhile, the 7-mile reservoir behind Pelton Dam is home to kokanee, rainbow trout, brown trout and bull trout. According to PGE, rainbow and bull trout as large as 20 pounds are pulled from the lake each spring.

There are two other campgrounds on Lake Simtustus, Lake Simtustus Campground and Indian Park Campground on the far side of the lake.

As for the interesting name, Pipsher Simtustus was a member of the Warm Springs tribe and leader of the Indian Scout Platoon serving with the U.S. Cavalry in the 1867-68 campaign against the Paiutes. According to an informational sign at the lake, he was an "active force in bringing about a permanent peace for his fellow tribesmen."

He died in 1926.

Lake Pipsher just doesn't have the same ring to it.

If You Go:

GETTING THERE: From Madras, travel north on U.S. Highway 26, turn left at the sign two miles south of Warm Springs. The lake is about three miles up the road.

CONTACT: 541-475-0517.

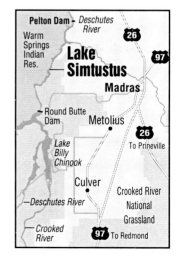

Skeleton Rock is a prominent landmark off North Shore Road. Legend has it that there's treasure buried there.

photo by Mark Quon

Skeleton Rock

Adventure, treasure and improvisation in Ochoco country

Published: March 10, 2004

The best adventures start with good friends and an element of spontaneity. And they end with the protagonists dog-tired and whipped.

When Map Guy, his wife and I set out for the Ochoco country Sunday with the canoe strapped overhead, we were mainly interested in enjoying a fabulously gorgeous day and possibly finding a geocache atop Skeleton Rock on the far side of Prineville Reservoir.

We were going to drive down the road along the north bank of the Crooked River and Prineville Reservoir, then paddle across the water to the rock. We'd find the cache, bask a little in the sun, wander around watching the wildlife and paddle back.

Bing, bang, boom.

Things didn't work out quite the way we'd planned.

The gate was locked. No motorized vehicles are allowed back there until April 15 because of the deer herds that winter around the reservoir.

So, as often happens when Mr. and Mrs. Map Guy and I go out day-tripping, our simple, hassle-free, straightforward outing got a little sketchy. And a lot more fun.

We improvised.

Skeleton Rock *continued*

The view from Skeleton Rock is worth the hike.
photo by Jim Witty

It turns out that what we did and what you should do if you try to replicate our journey are two different things.

We launched the canoe just upstream from where we had parked, and we paddled like crazy for the far bank. There, we stashed the canoe among some reeds and started marching for Skeleton Rock, some four miles distant.

When I consulted the map and talked to a helpful representative of the Bureau of Land Management the next day, I discovered that there's a small patch of private land not far downriver, and that we had probably crossed over it.

I can't lead readers across private land (I should have looked at the map beforehand, but with a guy named Map Guy along, you'd think ...).

So until the gate opens on Tax Day, you'll either have to float downstream a mile or so or carry your watercraft of choice the requisite distance before shoving off for the far shore (of course that means carrying it back, too, argggh).

But there is a payoff.

It always amazes me when we go someplace and get the whole area to ourselves.

In this case, an entire river valley without another soul in sight.

For five hours, just us and a gaggle of noisy Canada geese, a flock of snow geese, a curious river otter and myriad ducks, deer and a couple osprey riding the thermals.

And Map Guy grumbling about the inequity of vertical topography.

Skeleton Rock is a helter-skelter welter of basalt that juts from the south bank of Prineville Reservoir along what was once the Crooked River.

When we reached the rock, Map Guy pulled out his GPS unit and began homing in on the prize, in this case a weather-hardened box of trinkets placed here for the benefit of the growing legion of satellite-guided fun seekers who are after both wide-open places and the thrill of the hunt.

We found the cache, but the far more elusive treasure of Skeleton Rock remains unclaimed. That would be 50,000 pre-inflationary, 19th-century dollars' worth of gold.

In 1870, John Holt and a friend of his named Jack held up the mail stage carrying the Army payroll to forts in Southern Oregon and Northern California. Jack shot and killed the stagecoach guard and the pair made off with the mail sack and the strongbox, riding hard to the west toward the Crooked River Breaks.

Then they were ambushed by Indians, who chased them down Sanford Creek. The attackers shot Holt's horse out from under him and the robbers scrambled up onto the big jumble of basalt to make their stand. Both men took bullets; Jack died from his wound.

So the story goes, Holt buried his partner and the money up in the rocks, and, under the cover of darkness, made it to Prineville for medical treatment. But he was arrested by an Army patrol before he could return for the loot.

Since then, half of a skeleton turned up on what became known as Skeleton Rock. But no money.

You never know where spontaneity will lead. But it can be big fun finding out.

If You Go:

GETTING THERE: From Prineville, turn right on Combs Flat Rd., which turns into the Post-Paulina Hwy. (Highway 380). After about 16 miles, turn right onto the dirt road at the Crooked River. Drive a little over three miles in and park at the dirt parking lot on the left (just before the cattle guard). You'll see the Crooked River, Skeleton Rock and Sanford Creek out across the lake. From the parking lot, Skeleton Rock is about a half-mile across the lake bed. Access is by boat most years; by foot in a time of drought. No permits are required.

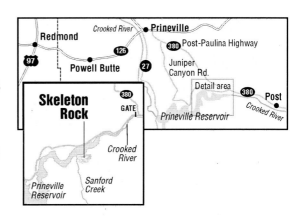

CAUTION: Always wear personal flotation devices when you're on the water. And never tackle any piece of water that could be beyond your abilities. Spring flows can rapidly change the dynamics of a stream or river.

Smith Rock State Park is a fine late-winter hiking destination.
photo by Mark Quon

Golden Opportunity

Thaw out, spy on eagles at Smith Rock State Park

Published: February 27, 2008

This is when Smith Rock State Park earns its keep.

It's that time of year when hikers have to work a little bit harder to find a place to go if they're hoping to wear boots, not snowshoes or skis. It's that time when the intellectual promise of spring clashes with the visceral reality of winter in Central Oregon.

There are dozens of places to go for winter fun. The snow is plentiful and the sno-parks are crowded.

But about this time every year, I long to take a bite out of the banana belt. Terrebonne can be comparatively balmy in late February. And there are eagles.

When it comes to the big birds, most people think of Lake Billy Chinook, site of last weekend's Eagle Watch event. But nearby Smith Rock State Park is also a fine place to view the wintering raptors.

While the bald eagle is the main attraction across the highway, the golden eagle merits most of the attention at Smith Rock.

And while the golden eagle doesn't sport the pure white pate and tail of America's symbol, it's arguably an even more impressive bird. What it lacks in wow it makes up for in pow.

Keep your eyes on the rimrock. It's where you'll see the eagles if they decide to fly.
photo by Dean Guernsey

A fierce predator, the golden eagle soars out over its hunting grounds watching for movement and swoops down on its unsuspecting prey. According to Stan Tekiela, author of *Birds of Oregon*, the golden eagle is capable of "taking large prey such as jack rabbits." I've heard accounts of golden eagle taking down fawns and baby sheep.

Smith Rock is home to numerous resident golden eagles.

According to Park Ranger Thad Fitzhenry, they use several well-established nests on the rimrock-cliff faces each year. Now is a good time to see them flying from their nests way up toward the top of the Crooked River canyon. The golden eagle is a uniform dark brown with a golden head. From below, it is sometimes confused with a vulture. The eagle can offer a formidable profile, with a wingspan of up to 7 feet across.

Tekiela notes that golden eagles are thought to mate for life, "renewing pair bond late in winter with spectacular high-flying courtship displays."

Fitzhenry said he also sees bald eagles, which focus more on fish, hunting near the river at Smith Rock occasionally.

During a late-winter day trip to Smith Rock State Park, you might also see mule deer, river otter or beaver (you probably won't see cougar, but they're known to be there). And you'll likely see rock climbers. There are more than 1,500 rock routes up and over the compressed volcanic ash (welded tuff) in the vicinity.

So, family-oriented day hikers and dog walkers often share the trails with extreme climbers.

Fitzhenry advised hikers to watch for ice in shaded areas. But he said that most park trails were snow-free at the beginning of the week. If you go, pick up a map when you pay your day-use fee at the parking lot and choose one of the trails. A stroll along the river at the bottom of the canyon is good for a two-hour outing, while a big loop around (and outside) the park can take up the better part of a day. Especially if you pack a lunch and take things slow.

Keep your eyes on the rimrock. It's where you'll see the eagles if they decide to fly.

Rangers ask that hikers stay on established trails to minimize the impact on sensitive vegetation and soil.

Barring extreme or unseasonable weather, this is the season I'm glad Smith Rock is a year-round park. There may not be any palm trees here (and you'll have to settle for Chiquita bananas), but the late February sun sure feels nice slanting off Monkey Face and on to yours.

If You Go:

GETTING THERE: See directions and map on page 228.

Massive formations caused by ancient volcanic activity come in many bizarre shapes and forms at Smith Rock State Park.

photo by Jim Witty

Smith Rock State Park a Mecca for Hard-core Climbers

A world-renowned playground among rock climbers

Published: March 31, 2004

The geologic drama always strikes me right between the eyes no matter how many times I go to Smith Rock State Park.

It's one thing driving up from Bend or over from Prineville and seeing those rocks in the distance. It's quite another when you're right there craning your neck up at them.

Spring and fall are the best seasons to pay a visit. It's not too hot, and if you're going to huff and puff up Misery Ridge, ride the Burma Road or just follow the Crooked River upstream or down, that's a good thing.

If you're a hard-core rock monkey, Smith Rock is a mecca. But if you're a mere mortal with a healthy respect for heights and a solid appreciation for natural beauty, the park still has plenty to offer.

The first things that impress a visitor are the massive tuff formations that come in many bizarre shapes and forms. They're the result of ancient volcanic activity and the erosive power of moving water. According to the official state park literature, lava flows entered the canyon millions of years ago and "crowded the ancestral river into the flanks of the main volcanic structure." The Crooked River responded by establishing a new channel and eroding the inside of the volcanic vent. The exotic rock formations are made of welded tuff — volcanic ash that spewed forth from an extremely hot and pressurized cauldron.

The rocks might be the main attraction, but there's much more to this place than climbing routes and vulcanism.

Like nesting eagles and skittering ducks and a river at full runoff.

After you cross over the bridge at the bottom of the canyon, you can go right upstream, left downstream, or straight up the switchbacks of Misery Ridge. This time around we opted for Misery Ridge, which got us up high in a hurry.

It's a steep slog to the top, but when you get there you'll get a commanding view of the surroundings.

Keep going down the back side of Misery Ridge and you can end up looping downstream and back up again to the footbridge. The trails of Smith Rock State Park are a good example of multiple use, with bikers sharing the space with hikers, runners and, in some places, horses.

Everyone, it seems, likes to stop and watch the climbers clinging spiderlike to the vertical faces.

Smith Rock is world-renowned among rock climbers.

Smith Rock was named after either early-day Linn County Sheriff John Smith, who discovered the place in 1867, or a soldier who fell to his death from the highest peak there in the 1860s.

Monkey Face is a popular vertical climb for experienced climbers.

photo courtesy of Ellen Jones

Even if you're not a rock climber, a hike up Misery Ridge can give you that rarefied feeling that comes from high places and vigorous exercise.

Plan on spending most of the day at Smith Rock, pack a picnic lunch and try several of the trails. And don't forget your camera.

Smith Rock State Park a Mecca for Hard-core Climbers *continued*

The Crooked River meanders through Smith Rock State Park.
photo by Jim Witty

If You Go:

GETTING THERE: From Redmond, drive six miles north on U.S. Highway 97 to Terrebonne. Turn right at the light where the road is marked with a sign for Smith Rock State Park. Follow the road down a hill and make a left at another sign for the park. Follow this twisting road for about two miles to another sign pointing to the park. Take a left and follow the road to the parking area.

DIFFICULTY: Easy to difficult, depending on your route. Misery Ridge is moderate to arduous.

ACCESS: Hiking, biking, rock climbing. Leashed dogs are allowed.

PERMITS: A $3 day pass is available from a vending machine at the parking area. Annual day-use permits are also available for $25.

Canyoneering into the depths of the Deschutes River Canyon is a steep, rugged challenge.
photo by Jim Witty

The Deschutes River Canyon is Ruggedly Lonely
Canyoneering in a landscape for the ages
Published: May 23, 2003

How low can you go?

In Central Oregon, you can creep pretty deep, hundreds of feet down into dizzying riverine chasms.

Canyoneering is a lot like climbing mountains except the descent comes first. Hiking partner Bob Speik, who never has tongue too far from cheek, often says the main drawback to mountaineering is the elevation gain. The same can be said for scrambling down ultra-steep, rock-strewn canyon walls, except in reverse.

I joined Speik, Paul Chance and Joy Newhart for an adventure in the Deschutes River Canyon between the mouth of Squaw Creek and Lake Billy Chinook. If you've not seen this country, adjectives are a poor substitute. But they're all I have.

Rugged. Craggy. Declivitous in spots. Downright precipitous in others. With its rimrock defiles and ochre walls scoured by ancient currents, the gorge is a landscape for the ages.

One moment you're walking along a flat desert of sage, bunchgrass and juniper, the next you're at a standstill, confronted with big air and a distant ribbon of blue at the bottom of the yawning hole.

The Deschutes River Canyon is Ruggedly Lonely *continued*

My companions were there to find a geocache, aptly known as The Hole of Inaccessibility, said to be stashed way down there along the river bank. The three of them are heavily into the adventure/navigation game and came equipped with the requisite GPS units, maps and computer printouts. I was there to relish the smell of juniper on the breeze, to taste the tang of sweat, to feel the burn of neglected muscles put to hard use, to listen to the river sounds. Come to think, my treasure hunting friends were there for the exact same reasons.

Paul Chance (left) and Jim Witty confer on the location of the elusive Hole Of Inaccessibility Cache.

photo courtesy of Bob Speik

The challenge begins at the beginning — finding a break in the rimrock cliff where you can make it down to the steep (but navigable) hillside below. We found our break - a place the geopundits have labeled Smokey's Gate because of a bear-shaped rock formation there - and got about the business at hand. Which was to scramble down the hill while making sure that we didn't go out of control, stumble and do a high-velocity face plant.

Our cross-country ramble took us into a dry stream bed, past a waterless waterfall and down a quarter mile or so to the mighty Deschutes, raging now with spring runoff.

According to those who have gone before, The Hole Of Inaccessibility Cache is along the trail in the roughly half-mile section between the mouth of that dry creek and Squaw Creek upstream. We had eight eyes, three GPS units, a constellation of satellites and a unified desire to succeed. But we never found the cache.

Not that we came up empty. We got to see a half-dozen golden eagles, hundreds of colorful caterpillars enjoying their spring incarnation, a coyote, delicate paintbrush spangling the slopes and a section of the Deschutes that few see up close.

Never one to admit defeat, Speik returned to the canyon Monday and found the cache not far from where we had been looking.

Our ascent back out of the canyon was more than just a long, steep haul. We succumbed to that siren song of day trippers, the seductive, all-tempting shortcut. Even though we knew they almost never work out, that we carried no ropes and had no way to scale an

With its rimrock defiles and ochre walls scoured by ancient currents, the gorge is a landscape for the ages.

photo courtesy of Bob Speik

intermediate barrier of rock, we bee-lined up the hill in search of a slot in the basalt that didn't materialize. So we angled back down and retraced our steps.

A great big word of caution: this trip (and others like it) is not for everyone. Only reasonably fit, well-prepared and experienced hikers should attempt it. Pack plenty of water and, as the weather warms, keep a sharp eye out for rattlers.

If You Go:

GETTING THERE: From Bend, drive North on U.S. Highway 97 to Lake Billy Chinook via Culver, cross the Deschutes and Crook river arms of the lake and top out on the other side. Drive straight on to the gravel roadway when the road makes a sharp right turn toward Perry South Campground. Follow Forest Road 63 to a Forest Service sign and gate on the left at Geneva. It's about three miles to the gorge from here.

The rainbow trout of the Lower Deschutes are vigorous and healthy. Spawning trout are usually darker than this one and can look beat up.

photo by Jim Witty

Floating and Fishing
Lower Deschutes is dramatic sampler of the rest of the river

Published: May 24, 2006

I'd floated the Lower Deschutes from the bridge at Warm Springs to Trout Creek before, but not like this.

I was with John Judy, an old-guard guide, author and fly-fishing journeyman who knows every bend, riffle, back channel and eddy in the river. He knows the ways of its fish as well as anyone, and better than all but a handful of his peers who have spent a lifetime lovingly learning the nuances of a delightfully complicated watershed.

The roughly 10-mile reach is best-known as the day-trip portion of the river where fly anglers put in of a morning, float downstream and make several fishing stops before taking out before sundown where Trout Creek enters the Deschutes River from the east. The balance of the river to its confluence with the Columbia River is best taken in multi-day doses.

Warm Springs to Trout Creek, with its swift, boulder-cobbled runs, sheer-side canyons and neck-craning, rimrock grandeur, is a dramatic sampler of the rest of the river.

And it's full of fish - crimson-slashed turbo-trout with an extra bottom gear borne of vigorous watershed-specific genetics and lives spent negotiating a consistent current that's somewhere on the far side of pushy.

At any given time, many of those rainbow trout are feeding, snatching bottom-tumbling insects in their nymphal stage from stations on the lee sides of rocks and other protective underwater structure.

But during spring and summer, some of those fish are spawning, perpetuating their kind with the single-minded determination of a perfectly adapted animal with more raw reproductive instinct than in-bred caution.

Trout on their spawning beds, or redds, are vulnerable.

As I said, I'd never floated the river like this before. Because I'd never seen the river like this before.

Besides being a fine fly-caster and angling mentor, Judy also has the eye of a naturalist. And it is possible, with the aid of such an eye, to see beyond the obvious, to glimpse (with the aid of polarized lenses) what's going on under the surface.

At stop after stop, Judy patiently pointed out the burnished gravel, the mounds and adjacent circular depressions in the sand - all telltale signs of a spawning ground. Through the refracting water skin, the fish appeared as dark cylinders moving to and fro at intervals, or torpedoes stacked like cordwood all along the gravel beds.

At one stop - a shallow gravel bar hugging the east bank with mounds and disturbed areas all along its length - we waded through, trying to avoid stepping on the humps where eggs could be deposited. Judy said he can tell when he's on a spawning bed by the nature of the terrain telegraphed through his wading boots. I began to see what he meant. Slogging back toward the drift boat, we stopped to examine a freshly excavated depression, just beneath the clear water. A 15-inch rainbow knifed from between my boots and stopped a couple of feet away, holding its ground. Far from a typical trout survival tactic.

"When I see fish spawning naturally in the wild it gives me great pleasure," Judy writes. "It indicates to me that the river I'm fishing is healthy, the habitat is good and the fish are strong and wild. What I am seeing, in most cases, is the payoff for the catch and release, the limiting of harvest that so many of us have practiced over the years."

What Judy also sees is people all season long fishing over the spawning beds - some wittingly, others not - to the detriment of the fishery.

It's tempting. The fish tend to be big and mature and they throw caution to the wind, hitting flies aggressively, more from territoriality than hunger.

"It's not easy to step away," said Judy. "You're giving up some of the best fishing you will ever experience."

But the spawners are usually several shades darker than a normal, healthy trout, much softer to the touch and are weakened from the nesting ordeal. Some have fungal infections. According to Judy, the last thing they need is the added stress of being caught and released.

Besides the somewhat subtle differentiation between prime fishable water and spawning sites, a good rule of thumb is if you catch two or three dark fish in a spot,

Floating and Fishing *continued*

you are likely over a spawning bed.

"Be aware even if you do know about spawning sites you will make some mistakes, that it's not a crime, it's really the effort that counts; it's your conscientiousness and concern that matter," according to Judy.

A few years ago Judy recognized the problem, printed up a bunch of bumper stickers and started talking up a solution. IPASS or I Pledge to Avoid Spawning Sites is one man's effort to give something more back to the river he loves.

Even if you don't fish but simply appreciate the Lower Deschutes and other waters, knowledge is power. It's satisfying to be able to recognize what's happening just below the surface as you float on by. We fished several nonspawning runs that day and did well.

A great day on the river. Mainly because I saw it in a whole new light.

A raft floats by downriver from Warm Springs.

photo by Jim Witty

If You Go:

GETTING THERE: From Madras, drive about 12 miles northwest on U.S. Highway 26 to Warm Springs. The put-in area is on the left across from the Rainbow Market. For maps to the take-out point, consult www.boaterpass.com.

PERMITS: To float the river, you must purchase a boater pass at $2 per person plus a service charge. See www.boaterpass.com. A tribal permit is necessary if you plan on fishing the Warm Springs side of the river. They run $8 per person for a daily pass.

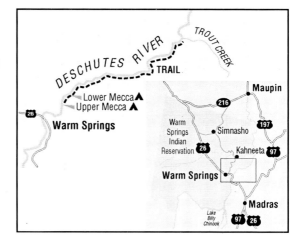

CAUTION: Extreme caution is advised when floating the river.

A section of the Middle Deschutes rambles below Steelhead Falls.
photo by Mark Quon

A Taste of 'The Middle D'

Borden Beck, Lower Bridge good places to check out the Deschutes

Published: April 30, 2008

Riverfest, that celebration of everything Deschutes, is coming around again, and it got me thinking about rivers. It doesn't take much.

Some of the troutiest and most scenic rivers in the country, including the Deschutes, are right here under our noses. The Deschutes has me spoiled. More on that later.

I was a product of a Southern California childhood. To me, rivers meant concrete flood control "washs" with nary a sliver of water in the summer, a mere trickle in the winter. I remember one stream, the San Gabriel, that actually resembled a river in that the reach closest to the headwaters spilled over rocks in the steep sections and formed pools where the gradient eased. Pine trees grew down to the high water mark and there was (and might still be) a beleaguered population of trout holding on there in the shady spots.

Before the hordes descended in waves on the pueblo of Los Angeles, the San Gabriel River ran unimpeded from high in the San Gabriel mountains west across the now urbanized plains and into the ocean between what are now Long Beach and Seal Beach. Today, there are five dams along its 75-mile course, and most of its urban reach

A Taste of 'The Middle D' *continued*

has been cemented and channelized. Graffiti despoils the boulders where the San Gabriel looks most like a river.

As a middle schooler, I would backpack with a group of friends in to one of the San Gabriel's tributaries, Bear Creek, catch pan-sized trout and enjoy a wilderness experience. I remember drinking the creek water from a Sierra cup (ignorance was bliss) and sleeping out under the stars (when we could see them through the haze). I really hope that place is still there, as I remember it, but who knows?

Anyway, picturing the San Gabriel River is all it takes for me to feel either smug about our relatively unsullied rivers in this part of the world or vigilant if I find myself getting complacent.

After all, grizzly bears once ruled the banks of the San Gabriel where street gangs now mark their turf with spray paint. There used to be grizzlies in Tumalo, too.

The Deschutes River runs through a deep canyon west of Redmond.
photo by Jim Witty

Riverfest, a 10-day celebration of the Deschutes River watershed, is all about what we Central Oregonians have and what we don't want to lose. See www.deschutesriverfest.org.

Besides participating in some of the activities set for Friday through May 11 (hike along Whychus Creek, help clean up the Deschutes and environs), perhaps the best way to mark Riverfest is to get out on a river or stream and appreciate what it is we have here.

This time of year — before it gets hot — is a good time to get to know the Middle Deschutes. That's the unique reach between Bend and Lake Billy Chinook. There are several places to access the river along this section, which is characterized by a rugged rimrock canyon and lower flows during irrigation season. One of the best places to get a taste of "the Middle D" is Borden Beck Wildlife Preserve near Lower Bridge.

Park at the Borden Beck lot and stroll upstream along the north bank of the river. Chances are you'll see geese winging overhead, ducks in the water. Rising trout often dimple the pools.

There's also a parking pull-out on the bank next to the bridge. From there, you can pick your way downstream.

Other access points along the middle river are Cline Falls, Tetherow Crossing and Tumalo State Park. There are also several "secret" spots with faint trails plunging into the canyon from the rimrock. Be careful: some are steep and can be dangerous.

According to Brett Golden, of the Deschutes River Conservancy, things are looking up for the Middle Deschutes. A major problem along this reach is compromised stream flow during the summer months, when irrigators take their portion out of the river upstream in Bend. In the last dozen years or so, flows have dropped as low as 30 cubic feet per second during the hot season. Low and warm conditions make life downright tough on trout, which thrive in cold, clear and abundant flows. Thanks to several broad-based efforts, including an innovative water-rights leasing program and increased canal piping (which conserves water otherwise lost to evaporation and seepage), flows in the Middle Deschutes should be 100 cfs or more during the critical months this summer, Golden said. Flows are running at about 70 cfs this week.

A good time to be a trout?

"It's better than it used to be," Golden said.

If You Go:

GETTING THERE: To reach Borden Beck Wildlife Preserve from Redmond, drive north about seven miles to Terrebonne. Turn left at the turnoff to Crooked River Ranch and follow the road about five miles west to Lower Bridge. The dirt lot is on the left, before the bridge.

PERMITS: None required.

CONTACTS: Deschutes River Conservancy, 541-382-4077; Upper Deschutes Watershed Council, 541-382-6103.

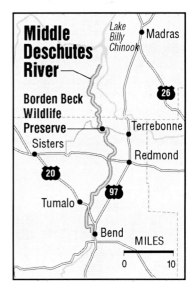

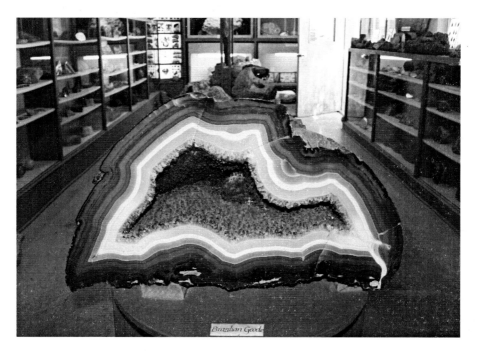

A huge Brazilian Geode is on display in the museum at Richardson's Recreational Ranch.
photo by Jim Witty

In Search of Thundereggs
Ranch is one of most plentiful sources of agate-filled nodules
Published: August 24, 2005

    Richardson's Recreational Ranch is 17,000 acres of juniper canyons, flat-top bluffs, bone-dry streambeds and hard-scrabble, cross-bred cows grazing out over the flats.
    It's also one of the most productive spots in the world to find thundereggs, those agate-filled nodules highly prized by rockhounds and collectors.
    Cut and buffed, the orbs with their dreamlike three-dimensional innards make exquisite paper weights (look, it's the Okefenokee Swamp; no, it's Aunt Harriet's Shih Tzu).
    But it's hunting them up and digging them out that gets in your blood. And it's visiting with Johnnie and Norma Richardson, browsing through their well-appointed rock shop and cruising around their ranch like Indiana Jones and family on a Sunday drive that makes for a full-fledged outing adventure.
    We walked into rockhound central and were greeted warmly by Johnnie and Norma, seated at far ends of the counter. A couple of baby chicks bobbed and weaved around Bonnie's feet ("they think I'm their mother") as she launched into the rules of the game. Grab a bucket and a couple of picks, she said, gruff but smiling. The picks are $30 apiece if you leave them out on the diggings. I don't care if you are writing a

story. Follow this road, then that. Got water? It's hot.

And then we were bouncing up a dirt road, bound for the interior of the ranch and the world-famous Priday thunderegg beds seven miles beyond.

Not far past the ranch headquarters, my wife volunteered to drive. The uncharacteristic offer had me scratching my head until we came to the first gate and I had to bail out and tend to the latches. Four gates in all for the round trip. That's cowgirl logic.

According to Johnnie Richardson, the Priday beds have been tapped since 1928 and show little sign of petering out. In 1976, he and his family bought 2,000 acres, which included the Priday thunderegg diggings, and added them to the Richardson holdings. It's a rich lode.

From the parking area just above the Blue Bed, we glimpsed snow-capped Mount Hood shimmering beyond the heat waves and a liberal sprinkling of intact thundereggs under a nearby juniper. So this is what we were after.

A short downhill walk and we were facing a rocky ledge, about four feet high and 50 or 60 yards long. Another party had arrived first; my initial pang of disappointment evaporated when I discovered we were literally rolling in discarded thundereggs (when we didn't watch our step).

We found an open section and started hacking at the rock. Soon, we had honed in on the prize, bulbous thundereggs raised in relief from the cross section of stone. Whack, chisel, chip.

According to Johnnie Richardson, the Priday beds have been tapped since 1928 and show little sign of petering out.
photo by Jim Witty

Whack, chisel, chip. Rats. An errant whack cracked my first egg before I could unearth it. But we got better at it and bucketed several nice specimens before the heat and the promise of an ice-cold drink drew us back over those rutted roads.

The Richardsons charge 75 cents a pound for the eggs you harvest. That includes cutting them in half, but the polishing part is up to you.

In Search of Thundereggs *continued*

Thundereggs generally run from golf-ball to soft-ball size, with about one in 20 becoming outstanding cut-and-polished specimens, according to the Richardsons.

Other than size, thundereggs look alike on the outside - nondescript and sandy brown. But each specimen is different on the inside, according to the company brochure. They were formed in layers of rhyolite lava flows, an estimated 60,000 years ago. Geologists postulate that thundereggs formed in gas pockets, which acted as molds. Over a long stretch, the gas cavities were filled with silica-rich water, leaving a dark matrix material and the crystalized inner core of agate or chalcedony.

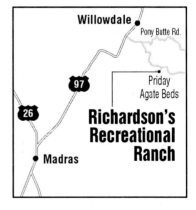

In addition to the generous supply of dig-your-own thundereggs, Richardson's Recreational Ranch offers a store full of finished (cut and polished) thundereggs and other rocks from all over the world.

Johnnie Richardson estimates that more than 65 percent of rock shops around the world carry thundereggs from the family ranch.

In addition to rockhounding, Richardson's Recreational Ranch offers stellar opportunities for photography and camping.

If You Go:

GETTING THERE: Take U.S. Highway 97 north from Madras - or south from Willowdale - until you see milepost 81 and the Richardson's sign. Follow the signs in for about three miles and you'll be at the shop! Located 11 miles north of Madras.

CONTACT: 541-475-2680 or 800-433-2680. Visit www.richardsonrockranch.com.

ADDRESS: Richardson's Rock Ranch, 6683 NE Haycreek Rd. Madras, Oregon 97741.

SHOP HOURS: 7 a.m. to 5 p.m., seven days a week. You must be there before 3 p.m. to go dig. Digging is "weather permitting." Roads may close due to rain. Be sure to call first to check on digging availability.

The author poses for a photo with Antelope Flat Reservoir in the background.
photo by Mark Quon

Antelope Flat Has It All

Who cares about fish?

Published: June 08, 2005

Sometimes a fishing trip isn't really about catching fish.

It's about solitude and killer sunsets, bald eagles and cowboy coffee - stout and chunky. It's about getting away from the everyday grind, spending time with people you like, singing old songs around the campfire, seeing so many stars you can't begin to count.

It's about ... OK. We got skunked.

But Antelope Flat Reservoir is a wonderful spot for an overnight camping trip or a day visit. And during the week, we had the place all to ourselves. That's a 170-acre irrigation reservoir nestled in the Maury Mountains with just the coyotes, the eagles and a swirling trout or maybe dozens for company. Nice.

Actually, the swirling trout thing was kind of frustrating. We'd heard good things about the fishing at Antelope Flat; we arrived with a half-empty ice chest and high hopes. Good thing we brought the chicken and the guacamole. Those hefty splashes about drove us nuts.

Despite all that, Antelope Flat Reservoir is an ideal place to get away to. It's remote, yet you can drive right to it and pitch your tent at the campground. There are 25

Antelope Flat Has It All *continued*

Jim Witty tries his luck in the early morning at Antelope Flat Reservoir.
photo by Mark Quon

campsites, tables, barbecue grills and standard-issue Forest Service bathrooms. And there's a little boat launch if you want to putt around a bit on the water.

Or you can take a walk as far around the irrigation impoundment as you desire. But there's no established trail all the way around. You'll have to make your own.

Springtime is busting out all over in the Maurys.

Thanks to recent rains, the hills are an emerald green and the wildflowers are beginning to pop. Indian paintbrush and columbine are everywhere.

The store in Post is always a point of interest and a good place to stock up on anything you might have forgotten back in civilization. We bought ice and mailed a letter at the post office.

On our return, we fished Prineville Reservoir near Bowman Dam. Which is where my little story had a happy ending. Prineville Reservoir is big, beautiful and full of trout, bass, crappie and bullhead.

Camping was fun. But it was nice to catch fish.

If You Go:

GETTING THERE: From Prineville, take Paulina Highway through Post then right on Forest Road 17 to Forest Road 16 and the reservoir. It's about 12 miles from Paulina Highway to the reservoir.

The Painted Hills Unit, just outside the small town of Mitchell, is known for its plant fossils and dazzling earth tones.

photo courtesy of Tim Gallivan

History Unfolds at John Day Fossil Beds
A lot can happen in 50 million years

Published: March 07, 2007

    Some things make an impression. And some linger long after the crucial moment has passed.

    Like 50 million years after.

    That's when tropical forests swaddled Eastern Oregon and Vulcan - incendiary and brash - was aglow over the land. Exotic mammals, ungainly and improbably large, browsed far and wide across the steamy woods. And the ocean lapped nearby.

    A lot can happen in 50 million years.

    Today, most of Eastern Oregon, more than 20,000 square miles from the Umatilla Plateau in the north to Hart Mountain in the south, Black Butte to the west and the Snake River to the east, contains a remarkably continuous fossil record of the last 40 million or 50 million years. Within that vast John Day Fossil Beds study area is the relatively compact 20-square-mile John Day Fossil Beds National Monument, cloistered into three units - Sheep Rock, Painted Hills and Clarno. The monument is where curious modern-day visitors go to wrap their brains around concepts more immense than this vast but infinitely less mind-boggling countryside. And do a little hiking.

History Unfolds at John Day Fossil Beds *continued*

The Painted Hills Unit, just outside the small town of Mitchell, is known for its plant fossils and dazzling earth tones. Sheep Rock, near Dayville, is the site of the national monument headquarters and is often canvassed by scientists seeking the fossils of mammals. And the Clarno Unit, 15 miles west of Fossil, is a hotbed of ancient flora etched into the volcanic rocks.

They're all worthy day-trip destinations; each offers a distinct flavor and some fabulously palatable education. The Clarno Unit teams bizarre rock formations, called lahars, with juniper canyons and rolling sagebrush swales and hummocks. The fossils discovered in the Clarno area are among the oldest in Oregon. They harken back to a time when this place looked more like a Hawaiian rainforest than an arid steppe. Fossil evidence of ancient palms, bananas, hackberries, yews, frankincenses and grapes have been found hereabouts, according to Park Ranger John Laing.

John Day Fossil Beds National Monument Park Ranger John Laing maintains an office across the road from the Palisades formation. He's there most days dispensing information to visitors.

photo by Jim Witty

"Generally, this is the oldest unit," he said from his tiny office across State Highway 218 from the Clarno Palisades. "This is known more for the paleobotany."

Which means scientists find lots of fossils imprinted with big leaves at Clarno and fewer bone fragments. Which, to me, is no less spectacular when you begin speculating about things like 18,250 million sunrises, the impermanence of cell and vessel and the unknowable history of the patch of soil upon which you now stand.

The journey to the Clarno Unit will take Central Oregonians through Madras (the low-key epicenter of Mexican cuisine in the region; try the adobada burrito at the new Mi Casa tacqueria on the north end of town), the tiny burg of Antelope, through Clarno and over the John Day River.

There's a parking area on the left side of the road in front of the Palisades, formed when a succession of ancient, ash-laden mud flows inundated the erstwhile forest. A trail winds around up to the base of the Palisades, with well-marked points of interest along the way. About half-mile farther east on the highway is the picnic area where a trail back to the Palisades begins.

Intrepid visitors can also access the monument backcountry from the picnic area, but, according to Laing, trails into Indian Canyon are neither signed nor developed. No bikes or dogs are allowed in the roughly 2,000-acre area and any fossils found must be left where they lie. Rattlesnakes will become a concern as the weather warms.

The road to the Clarno Unit is picturesque. Antelope can often be seen grazing on the hillsides. The bridge in this photo spans the John Day River.

photo by Jim Witty

"For those who want a backcountry experience, they can hike it," Laing said. "But if they hit a fence, don't cross it, it's private."

On the western side of the monument is Hancock Field Station, operated by the Oregon Museum of Science and Industry as an educational camp for kids. For more information, write Hancock Field Station, Fossil, OR 97830.

Spring (or when winter begins to feel like spring) is a good time to visit the Clarno Unit. The picnicking is sublime, the walking pleasant. And the history is nothing short of extreme.

If You Go:

GETTING THERE: From Bend, drive north on U.S. Highway 97 and continue on the highway northeast to state Highway 293. Turn right on Highway 293, then turn right again onto state Highway 218 at Antelope. The Clarno Unit is not far past Clarno, where the road crosses the John Day River. It's about a two-hour drive from Bend.

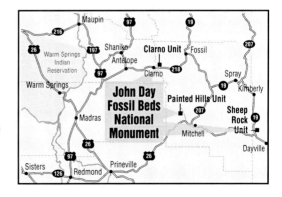

CONTACT: 541-987-2333.

Meet Me In The Badlands: Exploring Central Oregon with Jim Witty

The John Day Dam is just downstream from the mouth of the John Day River. It's part of the Columbia River Basin system of hydroelectric dams.
photo by Jim Witty

Past Meets Present
Oregon's mighty John Day River's power harnessed by hydroelectric dam
Published: November 13, 2008

Editor's Note: This was Jim Witty's last Outing written for The Bulletin before he passed away on November 17, 2008.

It's a little ironic that the first thing you see at the mouth of the John Day, the state's longest free-flowing river, is a dam.
A big one at that, making a lake of the mighty Columbia and the lower nine miles of the John Day.
These days, the mouth of the John Day River is Le Page Park, a U.S. Army Corps of Engineers facility that's become a center for drift boaters, campers, picnickers, hikers and anglers. There are trails along the river and above, but much of the uplands are privately held.
The park is neat and tidy and, with its RVs and vault toilets, friendly gatekeepers and uniformed rangers, it's the model of 21st-century industrialized recreation. It's a pretty place, and much changed.

But if you walk just upriver from the park, away from the manicured lawns and posted government regulations (camping units are restricted to one wheeled unit and one tent, or two tents per site), you can hear the echoes of the past. I swear it.

Geology is a powerful thing. If you listen, rimrock, basalt outcrops and eroded gorges speak louder than the traffic whizzing over the bridge on I-84.

Nowhere is that juxtaposition of modern development and primal forces more noticeable than on the Columbia River, whose waters meld with the John Day a few hundred yards from the park. The Columbia is wide there, and tamed, but the gorge speaks of its turbulent past.

Look over yonder
At the biggest river God put in the ground
Can you hear her roarin'
In the cold green water swirlin' 'round?
There's a lion in the water
And she makes an awful sound
She stands between the place I been
And the place where I am bound

The song, "Lion in the Water," written by a musician friend of mine, Mark Quon, is about the Oregon Trail family of Lindsay and Elizabeth Applegate, who opted to bypass the dense woods of Mount Hood and build flatboats to carry them downriver to the Willamette Valley.

The river took a son, a brother and a nephew.

Upriver from Le Page Park, the John Day remains wild and undammed, much of it designated as a national Wild and Scenic River and an Oregon Scenic Waterway. The main stem of the John Day begins at more than 9,000 feet in the Strawberry Mountains of Eastern Oregon and flows some 280 miles to its confluence with the Columbia at 265 feet above sea level. Forks include the North, Middle and South.

Named for expeditioneer John Day, who wandered lost through the region in the winter of 1811-12, the river was the longtime home of the Tenino Indians, who fished the abundant salmon runs and left pictographs on the rocks along the river's length. According to Judith Keyes Kenny, writing in the *Oregonian* in 1959, the river was originally named Le Page by Lewis and Clark.

The upper river was the site of a gold rush and still sustains a viable population of wild salmon and steelhead. Today, though, the river — roughly from Service Creek upstream to Kimberly, where the North Fork flows in — is chock full of smallmouth bass. Introduced to the river in 1971, the same year the John Day Dam (on the Columbia) was completed, the scrappy game fish have thrived and now attract thousands of anglers each year to the river.

State Highway 19 parallels the river between Service Creek and Kimberly; access is good. The flow along most of the John Day River is gentle. Nonmotorized rafts and drift boats are the most popular conveyances on the John Day.

After visiting Le Page Park on Monday, we drove a few miles west to the small town of Rufus and approached the dam from the downstream side to have a look. There's a nice park just downriver, used by Columbia River anglers and those wishing to get a

Past Meets Present *continued*

The John Day River, looking upstream from its confluence with the Columbia River at La Page Park, resembles a lake. Philippi Park is about three miles upriver, accessible by boat.

photo by Jim Witty

closer look at the big impoundment. Located 215 miles from the Columbia's mouth, the John Day Dam has a generating capacity of 2.2 million kilowatts, enough to power two cities the size of Seattle, according to the Army Corps of Engineers.

Sometimes I look at a dam and see a lot of electricity for a lot of people. Other times I see an imposing edifice, a remarkable testament to human ingenuity.

Last Monday, I saw right through it.

If You Go:

GETTING THERE: From Bend, drive north on U.S. Highway 97 to Biggs Junction. Turn north onto Interstate 84 and drive a few miles to Rufus. A road fronting the river leads toward the John Day Dam. To reach Le Page State Park, stay on eastbound 84 a couple more miles to Le Page Park on the right.

CONTACT: 541-506-7819.

Classic Central Oregon

The Deschutes River / photo courtesy of Scott Johnson

"Central Oregon isn't the only place you can have it all. But it just might be the best."

Jim Witty ties on a fly along a favorite stretch of the Crooked River.
photo by Mark Quon

Central Oregon Favorites

Crooked River, Prineville Reservoir, Lake Billy Chinook and The Badlands

Published: December 27, 2006

People often ask, "What's your favorite destination? What was your best outing? Where would you most like to go on your day off?"

I could, and often do, say something evasive like "My favorite outing is the one I did last." But that would be ... evasive.

Truth is, there are places I like better than others. It's just that there are so many of them.

The water gets muddied when you throw people in. Good company makes up for a multitude of flaws. The Mark and Linda Quons, Bob Speiks and Mr. and Ms. Map Guys of the world can skew the most earnest attempt at objectivity. So can the time of year. This week I'm in a looking east kind of mood.

It's not easy to rank fun. But, then again, it might be fun. So here goes. I hope it helps you figure out an accessible place or two to take your holiday visitors.

Crooked River

My all-time favorite spot (at least today) is the Crooked River, specifically the tailwater section below Bowman Dam downstream to Prineville. Mostly for personal

Central Oregon Favorites *continued*

reasons, but that's OK, because I have the soap box right now.

I began fishing the Crooked River in my early 20s, following in the boot steps of my brother, and my uncle before him. It's the place where my oldest son, now 20, learned to fly fish, and where I swelled with pride over the years as I watched his thrashing casts turn to easy loops and then to long, effortless arcs in dreamlike, seamless progression.

There's a lot to love about this rugged, rimrock river canyon. The water perks and tumbles downriver looking a lot like cowboy coffee and the whitefish outnumber the trout by a wide margin. But the juniper mingle with pine to the river's edge and the late afternoon sun bathes the eastern rim in a ruddy glow. It's not perfect but therein lies its perfection.

Visitors can fish, hike the trail to Chimney Rock or just wander the bank, taking photos.

The fish of winter may be a little sluggish, but they don't stop biting completely. Here, Keven Witty hooks a Crooked River rainbow trout.

photo by Jim Witty

GETTING THERE: From Prineville, head south on State Route 27 along the Lower Crooked River Byway. Bowman Dam is 20 miles up the road from Prineville.

Prineville Reservoir and Lake Billy Chinook

I like contrasts.

That's why Prineville Reservoir and Lake Billy Chinook are so appealing. In the summertime, these Central Oregon impoundments are bumper-to-bumper ski boats and big pickups with tow packages. But, come winter, they've got that cold, lonesome feel that makes these lakes a delicious off-season alternative.

The one million yearly visitors to Lake Billy Chinook are off snow skiing or tuning their outboards or hibernating. It's so quiet you can listen to what the place has to say.

Over at Prineville Reservoir, it's much the same. The fishing's not what it is during the warmer months and you'll definitely need a jacket. But if you enjoy resounding quiet, watching hawks and eagles and getting to know the reality of a place, why not take a drive?

GETTING THERE: Prineville Reservoir from Prineville, drive east on U.S. Highway 26, then right on Juniper Canyon Rd. The lake is about 15 miles out of town.

Lake Billy Chinook from Redmond, drive north on U.S. Highway 97. Before reaching Madras, turn left and head to Culver at a sign pointing the way to Cove Palisades State Park and Lake Billy Chinook. Follow the signs to the lake.

The Badlands is 30,000 acres of juniper, sagebrush, dry washes and a whole lot of empty.

photo by Joan Witty

The Badlands

The Badlands Wilderness Study Area is close to home, predominantly snow-free and brimming with subtle desert vitality. I go there often to hike with the dog and lose myself in the details. I went there earlier this year with High Desert Museum naturalist Larry Berrin, who's a stickler for those nuances that make this arid, volcanic steppe so fascinating. We noted the lichens on the rocks (algae and fungi coalescing), the microscopic cilia-like fibers that collect moisture for a sagebrush and the leavings of a mule deer.

The Badlands is 30,000 acres of juniper, sagebrush, dry washes and a whole lot of empty.

Editor's Note: On March 30th, 2009, President Obama signed the Omnibus Public Lands Management Act, designating the Oregon Badlands as wilderness.

GETTING THERE: From Bend, drive east on U.S. Highway 20. Turn left a few hundred yards past milepost 17. Drive about a half-mile to the Bureau of Land Management information board on the left. Grab a map and go explore.

Tumalo Falls may be Central Oregon's signature natural attraction.
photo courtesy of Kelly Haluska

"Wow"

Local sights pack a punch for those visiting from afar

Published: May 31, 2006

"Wow."

We had an out-of-town house guest last week and that was his oft-repeated exclamation of choice as he discovered Central Oregon for the first time.

The High Desert presents a series of high-relief contrasts if you're from the Atlantic seaboard.

This is the time of year when friends and family are passing through or destined to spend a few days camping in the extra bedroom. And it's fun and affirming to share the wonders of Central Oregon with them. Done right (and it's difficult to do it completely wrong), it can give visitors a new perspective and jumpstart your own. Every time I show someone Tumalo Falls, for instance, I get to see it through their eyes.

With snow still clogging the high country and touring time limited by work and commitments, I still wanted to give visitor Mike Haluska a tour that he'd remember long after he'd returned to the big city. There's so much to see and do here, my tendency is to overthink The Plan, to carom from one outing to another in my mind and end up with a hodgepodge of snippets and a budding headache.

The otter exhibit at The High desert Museum helps bring the region to life. River otters are precocious, fun-loving and, obviously, cute.

photo courtesy of Kelly Haluska

Better to keep it simple. Best to start with **The High Desert Museum.**

Visitors can soak up a basic understanding of the Great Basin country - its history and inhabitants - and are entertained in the process. Everyone gravitates to a different set of exhibits and comes away with a different set of memories. From river otters to wild horses, live birds of prey and a highly engaging stroll through the region's chapters of history, this is the High Desert.

With the museum under your belt, you and your guests should be primed and ready for some field exploration. And while there are countless variations on this theme, we opted for **Tumalo Falls.**

"Wow."

Twenty minutes west of town, the falls on Tumalo Creek gives us default tour guides plenty of bang for the buck. There's a reason the place is so popular. It's a slam-bang show of brute hydraulic force, especially during this time of high runoff, and it affords us the opportunity to showcase our firm grasp of the natural world.

"Lots of water."

And our local bona fides.

"Lots of snow along here in winter."

Hike less than a quarter-mile to the overlook at the top of the falls and your guests will have enough dramatic photos to wow the folks back home. If not, there are more falls up stream, and depending on the dwindling snowpack, they'll be accessible by trail later in the season.

"Wow" *continued*

From Tumalo Falls we headed for the southern section of the **Deschutes River Trail,** specifically the Benham East Picnic Area near Lava Butte. The ponderosa pine meadow has been used by indigenous people for 7,000 years, so it's a good place to throw in some history (there are signs). In 1910, the Shevlin-Hixon Lumber Co. began operations in Bend and saved the big trees there so the company could throw serious picnics for employees. As many as 2,000 were shuttled from Bend on railroad cars every year for the annual fandango.

There's a short, interpretive loop trail headed upstream that's worth the short hike. But downriver is where the action is. **Benham Falls,** in all its seething, boulder-gnashing glory, is a quick, half-mile jaunt. But first you'll cross a wooden footbridge to the west side of the Deschutes where a log jam constricts the flow. Logs were intentionally floated there more then 30 years ago to prevent debris from damaging the bridge pilings. Since then, silt has accumulated between the logs, and plants and trees have taken root. The log jam also prevents unwitting canoeists from sailing under the bridge and meeting their demise at Benham Falls downstream.

The Deschutes River is as scenic as they come.
photo by Mark Quon

Back up the road toward the highway is the **Lava Lands Visitor Center at Newberry Volcanic National Monument.** The visitor center goes heavy on the geology and archaeology of the region, thus rounding out your guest's informal education. Lava Butte, which spewed lava out over the area 7,000 years ago, looms over The Trail of Molten Land, a one-mile paved loop that offers unimpeded views of the Cascades peaks.

As I said, there are many permutations on The Plan, but this one worked for us.

I wish I could say one of Mike's parting words was "wow" as he boarded the plane for points east, but it wasn't.

It was "unbelievable."

Lava Butte looms in the distance at Newberry Volcanic National Monument.
photo by Jim Witty

If You Go:

GETTING THERE:
The High Desert Museum is three miles south of Bend on U.S. Highway 97. Turn left at the sign.

The Lava Lands Visitor Center is about 13 miles south of Bend on U.S. Highway 97. Turn right into the Visitor Center.

To reach the picnic area near **Benham Falls** on the Deschutes River, continue past Lava Lands out Forest Road 9702.

To reach **Tumalo Falls** from Bend, drive 10 miles west on Galveston Ave./Skyliners Rd. and veer right to cross the bridge over Tumalo Creek on to Forest Road 4603. It's less than three miles to the parking area.

PERMITS: A Northwest Forest Pass is required to park at Benham East and Tumalo Falls.

CONTACT: The High Desert Museum at 541-382-4754 and Lava Lands at 541-593-2421 for pricing and further information.

Benham Falls in all its seething, boulder-gnashing glory.
photo courtesy of Gary Calicott

Mare Schelz and son Hayden, both of Bend, enjoy a day on the water in The Old Mill District.
photo by Jim Witty

Going with the Flow

Paddling the river offers new perspective on life on the water

Published: *May 14, 2008*

If you really want to see a river, you've got to get on it.

Not in it, necessarily. But on it.

Paddling puts you right there, in intimate contact with the water and the denizens of the riparian zone.

Paddling is also a good way to get a whole new perspective on the country beyond the banks.

A walk along the Deschutes River through Farewell Bend Park and The Old Mill District to the Colorado Street Bridge and back again is a familiar diversion for many of us. But launch your boat and paddle that reach of river, and your point of view is altered. Considerably.

The same goes for any river, anywhere, but it's probably more dramatic on a local stretch, a piece of water that you know, at least think you do, from the outside looking in. I floated that "town" reach of the Deschutes the other day and discovered once again that there can be magic in the familiar. It just depends on your perspective.

Eye to eye with a great blue heron looks different from spying on one of the imposing birds downriver from the trail. The soggy timbers from the old wooden

The Deschutes River in Bend, as seen from on the water, is a different animal.
photo by Jim Witty

bridge from a boat passing below look quite different from the same span viewed from above. The bluffs up ahead. The bulrushes gliding by. The sparkling droplets flying from a paddle. The bugs — mayflies? — dipping and soaring and hatching. The swallows nabbing the bugs. All different and new from where I sat.

With summer giving Central Oregon a taste of things to come this week, many will be drawn to river and stream. A kayak, canoe or quality inflatable raft is a fine way to experience the river. Any river.

The best way to get started is to rent a boat (see Canoes and Kayaks listings in the Yellow Pages). Alder Creek Canoe & Kayak is right on the river adjacent to the Colorado Street Bridge. Renting kayaks there and making the run upriver to Healy Bridge and back makes for a fun family outing.

Sunriver Marina also rents kayaks and canoes and offers a serene stretch of river upstream and down.

There are also several companies offering guided whitewater rafting trips on the Upper and Lower Deschutes and other rivers in the region. Or you might consider toting your fishing gear along or hiring a guide to get you into the action.

However you choose to spend your time on the water, safety trumps all else.

Some of the rules to live by involve little but common sense: Don't mix drugs or alcohol with paddling, never venture out on the water without a personal flotation device (PFD or life jacket) no matter how calm the water, always be aware of hazards in the river and know exactly where you're headed and what you will encounter.

Going with the Flow *continued*

Other rules merit a closer look as warmer weather looms.

Pete Giordano, the author of *Soggy Sneakers: A Paddler's Guide to Oregon's Rivers*, offers numerous safety tips for whitewater kayakers, many of which apply to other paddlers as well. They include:

- "Be a competent swimmer."
- "Cold quickly drains strength and robs the ability to make sound decisions. Dress to protect yourself from cold water and weather extremes. When the water temperature is less than 50 degrees Fahrenheit, a wetsuit or drysuit is essential."
- "Boating alone is not recommended."
- "Test new and unfamiliar equipment before trusting it on a river."

Giordano also cautions paddlers to avoid dams, weirs, ledges, reversals and holes. "When water drops over an obstacle, it curls back on itself, forming a strong upstream current that can hold boats or swimmers," he writes. "… Hydraulics around human-made dams are especially dangerous. Despite a benign appearance, such water can trap a swimmer. Once trapped, a swimmer's only hope is to dive below the surface, where downstream current is flowing beneath the reversal."

One additional safety note: Even though it's warm outside, the water in the river this time of year is cold, fatally cold if you're not prepared. Go overboard and muscles will seize up quickly. Don't even think about paddling or floating without a life jacket.

The properly prepared paddler has a distinct advantage over those on the shore.

He or she can see the world from the inside looking out.

Owen Quon paddles down the Deschutes River and into Mirror Pond.

photo by Mark Quon

GO PADDLE:
- Alder Creek Canoe & Kayak, 541-317-9407.
- Sunriver Marina, 541-593-3492.

Micha Ollerton, left, and Joellen Colson, both of Wenatchee, Wash., skate ski at Virginia Meissner Sno-park.

photo by Jim Witty

In One Day, You Can ...

... carve through fresh powder ... wind through the desert ... enjoy it all

Published: April 02, 2008

Central Oregon isn't the only place you can have it all.
But it just might be the best.
A few days or weeks most years on the Big Island of Hawaii, you can actually ski atop 13,796-foot Mauna Kea in the morning and be surfing at Honolii or snorkeling at Richardson's on the windward side before lunch. But the snow, if it materializes, can be marginal, and a downhill run is closely followed by a lung-busting trudge back up the hill. There are no ski lifts in Hawaii.
Growing up in Southern California, we'd drive the Palms to Pines Highway from Palm Desert into the San Jacinto Mountains and back. It could be 80 degrees down below and hovering around freezing in the backcountry above the little mountain village of Idyllwild. But the snow in those southerly mountains is often latitudinally challenged (read: wet) and the desert is — well, the desert is real nice down that way in the winter (summer, not so much).
To borrow a phrase from the lexicon du jour: it's all good.
But perhaps it's even better where the High Desert meets the Cascades. Or maybe I'm just biased.

In One Day, You Can ... *continued*

The snow was as good as it gets at Virginia Meissner Sno-park over the weekend. The Tumalo Langlauf Club had recently groomed the trails for skate skiers, and slushy spring conditions were but a memory. The parking lot was full, the place was packed. But out on the trails, the crowds thin out and skiing is reduced to the individual sport that it is.

That was the morning.

It took me less than 40 minutes to drive out of the mountains, cross Bend and head east across the desert to Horse Ridge. Now is the time to ride the mountain biking system to the east, before the dog days of summer turn the trails to dust and the juniper hillsides into a sauna. It's a dry heat.

The singletrack there is not for the faint of heart or those used to riding flat, Forest Service roads. Expect healthy uphill sections and snaky, technical downhills with enough rocky impediments and vertical pitch to challenge the most advanced fat tire cyclists. Bundle up; it can get cold out there.

A lone Juniper tree stands on Horse Ridge.
photo by Mark Quon

But then, if you were skiing a mere hour before, you'd still have those layers of polypropylene and fleece handy.

Hiking conditions are ideal east of Bend this time of year as well.

Across U.S. Highway 20 from Horse Ridge, the Badlands Wilderness Study Area is inviting in early spring; there are tiny wildflowers popping up in the parts of the trail that get less traffic even though there are still patches of snow in the shady spots.

I bumped into my old friend Bob Speik out there, showing a couple of young wilderness activists the lay of the land. There's a concerted push to convince Congress to designate the Badlands an official, card-carrying wilderness and, not unexpectedly, Speik's right in the midst of it. I got caught up in their conversation and their enthusiasm at the Flatiron Trailhead, then broke away to take my dog, Hoss, for a walk.

I could see the soft, arching silhouette of Horse Ridge to the south and the snow-covered zigzag peaks of the Cascades to the west. A jackrabbit bolted from underfoot, pogoing out and away from immediate danger, and Hoss lit out in pursuit. But he slowed to watch a robin on the wing and veered off to re-excavate an old badger hole.

Linda and Jody O'Donell, of Bend, ride at Horse Ridge east of Bend.
photo by Jim Witty

Depending on where you are and who you're with, you really can have it all. Except, maybe, that tropical, black sand beach. Or sun-flecked swells, head high and feathering out over the reef. Or an In-N-Out Burger.

Guess we'll just have to make the best of it.

... wind through the desert ...

... carve through fresh powder ...

If You Go:

GETTING THERE:
To reach **Virginia Meissner Sno-park** from Bend: Drive 14 miles southwest on Century Dr. toward Mount Bachelor. The sno-park is on the right side of the road.

To reach **Horse Ridge** from Bend: Drive east on U.S. Highway 20. Turn right near milepost 17 onto old Highway 20 (across from the Badlands). The unsigned trailhead is on the left about one-tenth of a mile up the road.

The peaks of the Cascades are often in plain sight wherever you ramble in Central Oregon. This view is from near the Lava Lands Visitor Center.

photo by Jim Witty

You Are Here

No need to drive far to enjoy the many recreational adventures Central Oregon has to offer

Published: May 30, 2007

With gas prices running on the exorbitant side, a jaunt to Portland or the Columbia River Gorge these days costs about as much as a high-quality pair of hiking boots.

As much as I like to travel, I need the boots. And another fly reel. And a kayak; I think I want a kayak.

The point is, $3.50 a gallon petrol can eat into your recreation budget. If you let it.

I remember now that one of the several dozen reasons I moved to Central Oregon was proximity. It's a beautiful word and an even prettier concept. Unlike my friends clinging to existence in the suburbs of L.A., where a three-hour drive gets them to the outskirts of town, we've got worthy destinations every direction we turn, including up, many within 10 or 15 minutes of home.

I can't think of a better place to ride out the gas crisis, stick it to Big Oil or just have a whole lot of fun within pedaling distance of a half-caf skinny mocha, no whip.

Just 10 minutes south of Bend, **Lava Butte** looms into view to the right. Turn left on Crawford Road and check out **Lava Lands Visitor Center** for some education, the paved hiking trails there for some exercise (and more information). More often, I keep

The middle reach of the Deschutes River runs through Tumalo State Park.
photo by Mark Quon

driving west to the **Benham Falls East** trailhead and a sweet reach of the **Deschutes River** where I'm forced to choose among fishing, hiking, biking or simply lolling on the banks of the Big D.

The ponderosa pine meadow here has been used by indigenous people for 7,000 years, and a looping interpretive trail tells of them and those who came after. Shevlin-Hixon Lumber Co. began operations in the area in 1910 and saved some truly impressive old-growth monsters at Benham East for employees to picnic beneath.

Downriver, Benham Falls is an easy-but-dramatic 1/2-mile stroll.

Just to the north of Bend, it's the Deschutes River again that gets my attention. While there are several worthy spots along this, the middle reach of the Deschutes, **Tumalo State Park** has a lot going for it. It's close, it's High Desert beautiful, and it's an easy place to fish, hike and picnic. Water levels are up and down (mainly down) during the warmer months, but there's usually plenty of water there for swimming and angling. The state provides picnic tables, bathrooms and a campground with rentable yurts.

To get to Tumalo State Park from Bend, drive west on U.S. Highway 20 toward Sisters, then turn left onto the Old Bend-Redmond Highway. Turn right on O.B. Riley Road to the park.

I spend a lot of time east of Bend, walking the dog and wildlife and bird-watching and savoring the desert. **The Badlands Wilderness Study Area,** with its dusty arroyos and no-see-em slot canyons, is about 20 minutes east of Bend. If Congress ever deems

You Are Here *continued*

Kevin Fricke from Los Angeles, Calif. and Linda Quon view the Deschutes River from the bridge just upstream from Farewell Bend on the Deschutes River Trail.

photo by Mark Quon

it appropriate, it will be small for a wilderness area, at about 37,000 acres. But it's big country for you and the dog and all those old juniper trees.

To get there from Bend, drive east of U.S. Highway 20 to milepost 16 (there's a trailhead on the left) or just past milepost 17 and turn left. Drive about 1/2-mile in to the Bureau of Land Management information sign and trailhead. The interior of the Badlands is off-limits to motorized vehicles.

Now that the snow line has crept up the hill, there's lots to do to the west. A 10- or 15-minute drive will put you on the **Deschutes River Trail** or at **Tumalo Falls**. Hike upstream or down on the river trail and experience the heavy hydraulics of a series of serious waterfalls or check out the big one, Tumalo Falls, one of the area's most popular attractions.

Just drive about 10 miles west of town on Galveston Ave./Skyliners Rd. and veer right to cross the bridge over Tumalo Creek onto Forest Road 4603. It's less than three miles to the parking area. One way to access the Deschutes River Trail is via the **Meadow Picnic Area.** To get to the river trail from Bend, drive about six miles west on Cascade Lakes Hwy. A left turn on a gravel road just before Widgi Creek Golf Course takes you to the Meadow Picnic Area. From there, it's about 8 1/2 miles one way to Benham, from the downstream side. Or you can drive a few miles farther on the highway and turn left at the Deschutes River sign. From there you can drive to several recreational sites along the river, including **Dillon** and **Benham** falls.

Yep, I'm definitely in the market for a new kayak.

AFTERWORD

By Lori Witty

Completing Jim's book has been a journey - often therapeutic, often emotional, and often a sparking of happy memories, all at the same time. This effort has been a true labor of love not only for me, but Jim's family and friends as well. At times this adventure has been difficult, but for me the hardest part was figuring out what to say here.

As with every other aspect of the book, I wanted it perfect. I started numerous times, grappling with what I should write. I kept hearing the words of two people. The first, of course, was Jim. Whenever it came to writing, he would always say, "Less is more." He had a knack of conveying so much in so few words, always knowing the perfect thing to say. Unfortunately, that talent didn't rub off on me. The other came from Jim's longtime friend, Mark. After reading an initial draft, he responded, "This is from you Lor, it's your chance to say goodbye to Jim." That somehow hit me hard. How do you say goodbye to someone like Jim? It's impossible and something I don't feel I'll ever be ready to do. I've had to let Jim go in the physical sense, but his spirit and the essence of all he loved will forever remain with me. I carry his heart and soul, as do so many of us who were lucky enough to be part of Jim's life. Thus, our mission to complete Jim's vision of having this book published. It's a way for all of us to hold on to Jim for a while longer.

My hope is that you've thoroughly enjoyed reading Jim's articles and that you walk away with an urgent need to get outdoors. As you've discovered, my husband was an artist who painted pictures with words. He was also a loving, kind, gentle, funny, talented man who loved his family, friends, music, and the miracles found in nature. He had an innate ability of seeing the beauty in all things and people, no matter how large or small. Jim was loved by everyone who met him; that was part of his charm. He left our world much too soon, but his passion for life and for all the things he loved is his legacy. I miss Jim every moment of every day, but his memory will forever hold strong in our hearts and his writing will always be one mark he left on this world.

I know Jim would be proud of us all for our various contributions to the book, a memorial to him and a tribute to his passion for getting outdoors.

To my soul mate, my husband, my best friend, Jim: I know someday we'll be together again, wait for me, I'll meet you in the Badlands.

We did it babe, this one's for you – "IT IS!"

With Love and Blessings,
Mrs. Jim Witty (Lori)

ABOUT JIM

By John Witty

In the weeks after Jim's death in November of 2008, there was an outpouring of community reaction - support, sympathy and condolences, recounting of personal stories and memories and also wonderful expressions of respect and appreciation for Jim's work here in Central Oregon. All of us who cared for Jim were moved and supported by those efforts and sincere messages. Many of those reacting to his death reflected on his friendliness, his genuine interest in the people he met, how likely it was that you would share a laugh with him, and, of course, his ability to write so skillfully in a way that brought you along with him on his adventures. Many noted that they had never actually met Jim, but that they felt like they knew him.

One particularly moving note came from artist Ann Ingham, who lives in the beautiful little community of Camp Sherman, Oregon.

"Dear Jim,
I have been meaning to write to you for some time now, but I never seemed to get around to it. It is most unfortunately too late now for you to read this, but I am certain in my heart that you will somehow know that I am writing this letter."

Ann recounts a chance meeting with Jim and Map Guy on the trail to Doris Lake where the passing parties rested together for a few minutes, sharing a bit of humor about what Jim might be willing to pay for one of their mosquito netted hats.

"I often wondered after that if our paths would ever cross again. I don't think so, but I kept looking anyway.
What I enjoyed the most about your trips and resulting stories was your ability to take me with you, wherever you went. I was able to look at the photos, read the story, and be there with you drinking in the essence of the moment. You could take me with you to anywhere you went and I could feel what you were experiencing and enjoy the moment along with you. This is a great gift and one we will all miss very, very much."

Jim's "gift," his ability to offer up the "essence" of a place, to pick the right words, to take us along with him, and, as John Costa observed, perhaps even to give us "a glimpse of his soul" in the process, was indeed an expression of talent. But his work product was also more than that. It was the result of 30 plus years of perfecting his craft and of "paying his dues" as a journalist, and more importantly, as a writer. It is noteworthy that throughout all of his work life, Jim never strayed far from his desire to tell the story; he remained true to his aspirations as a writer.

Jim met his first wife, Donell, in a journalism class and they were married for 23 years. He graduated with a degree in Journalism from Cal Poly, San Luis Obispo, and worked for newspapers in Ferndale, Eureka, Corning, Redding and Vacaville, California. Jim's first son, Keven, was born during his stint in the central California town of Corning. During those early years, Jim covered city council meetings, sold advertising, wrote obituaries, and reported on the arrests over the weekend and the first birth of the new year. And whenever he could convince the editor it was a good idea, Jim wrote stories focusing on the outdoors.

In 1990, Jim and his young family moved to Hawaii, the place where our mother's family lived for many years, where our mother was born and grew up and where our father and mother first met. Jim worked for newspapers in Hilo and later in Honolulu. His youngest son, Danny, was born in Hawaii, and the family had terrific, happy times in their six years on the islands.

Hawaii was a time and place where Jim experienced a wholly different outdoor environment. There were picturesque spots everywhere, above and below the surface of the water. There were new birds, exotic plants, new insects, new fish to catch and always warm, easy weather. When we visited Jim in Hawaii he showed us "the sites," but his energy level increased and his enthusiasm peaked whenever he could take me to the wildest nooks and crannies he had been able to discover. I think he finally decided to leave Hawaii when the limited island geography began to impede his ability to find those places. Eventually, Jim wanted to get back to the wide open elbow room of the West, to cold water trout streams, to pine and fir forests and to the lonely desert canyons and sage flats.

His opportunity to return to the mainland West came with the newspaper in Longview, Washington. But it was when he arrived in Bend, a few years later, and about 10 years ago, that he found the place and the job that allowed him to do what he really loved and what he did best. All of us are grateful to *The Bulletin* for providing Jim with the opportunity and the freedom to create what this book now celebrates.

During his years in Bend, Jim enjoyed the best of times and the worst of times. His 23 year marriage ended and his family dealt with the collective personal trauma of a divorce. But life went on, as it has a habit of doing, and Jim remarried in 2004. We will never forget Jim with his guitar (with a little help from his friend Mark Quon) singing to his soon to be wife, Lori, in the old country church in the desert at Fort Rock. It was a day when Jim was surely in his element, and he was gloriously happy.

Jim's last years were spent enjoying his family in Bend, with Lori and her daughter Kelly, Kelly's fiancé Walt, with Keven and Danny, his two sons whom he loved and

ABOUT JIM

By John Witty • continued

cared about so very much, Keven's girlfriend Jen and Jim's new granddaughter Lexie, and with his dearest friends Mark and Linda Quon and their children Owen and Presley. Sister Deedee Sihvonen and husband Alan weren't too far away in Park City, Utah, and Joan and I and our mother Edna, were close by in Redmond. Jim was a truly devoted son to his mother and he loved her very, very much. He called Mom on the phone every single night, without fail, to share with her the news of each day. She was a constant, an absolutely unfaltering and unquestionable source of love and support throughout his life and he was a shining source of pride and delight in hers. In Central Oregon in his final years, Jim was in a place he wanted to be, doing what he wanted to do, surrounded by the people who meant so much to him.

At various stages in his career, Jim had opportunities to move away from writing, both inside and outside of the newspaper business. And even though his older brother sometimes urged him to look hard at something that might pay better, Jim stayed with what he loved to do. In retrospect, I believe he knew that he had the ability to write well and he knew that he was learning and getting better. He knew that he loved creating with the written word, and he hoped, probably dreamed, that he could make a significant contribution with his skills. He was right.

There was much Jim left unfinished and unaccomplished in his life when he died. He was working on this book. Jim was writing a western novel when he could get to it. We can only imagine what else he may have been able to give us had there been more time.

Ann Ingham met Jim very briefly on a trail, but she expressed a connection with him through his writing that was common to many of his readers. Many felt like they knew Jim, even though they had never actually met him, and many asked if he was really as nice a person as he seemed to be. All who are asked, his colleagues at *The Bulletin* and his friends and family, answer the question the same way – Jim was exactly what his writing suggests he was and he was exactly what you might imagine him to be. He was bright, affable, friendly and optimistic, interested in the people he met and a delight to talk to or spend time with. He was that same person as a child and for all of the 50 years I was lucky enough to live with Jim as a part of my life. My wife, Joan, first met Jim when he was nine years old and she was working in a summer recreation program in Monrovia, California. She remembers a bright, happy, friendly, skinny little blond boy who loved sports and could already beat her playing chess.

My older sister Deedee, Jim and I grew up in a middle-class Southern California family where we kids knew three important things. One, our parents loved us very much, and two, we were smart, fortunate, capable children who were expected to work hard, to go to college and to be successful. The third immutable truth in our family was that, at least in terms of our most recent lineage, we were solid cardinal and gold USC

Trojans! Our father graduated from the USC Dental School ("Fight on for old SC..."), our grandfather graduated from the USC Dental School ("... And then fight on..."), and our mother from the USC School of Music ("... To victory").

Deedee spoiled my parents terribly by playing the piano and singing beautifully, by being an outstanding student, and ultimately by earning an academic scholarship to USC. I often reminded Jim what a monumental favor I did for him by coming along just after Deedee and ten years before he belatedly arrived on the scene. I made it my personal mission (and I worked diligently at it for many years) to significantly lower my parent's inflated academic expectations in order to allow Jim to enjoy a much less stressful childhood. (Jim recognized and was very grateful for my efforts.) Although Jim did disappoint my parents a bit by tending to follow more in my academic footsteps than Deedee's, and although neither Jim nor I attended college at USC, Jim did demonstrate good breeding and good sense by developing into a dedicated, lifelong and very loyal Trojan fan.

Another joy in Jim's life was making music, sometimes with son Keven, but mostly with our immensely talented friends, Mark and Linda Quon. Mark and Jim grew up together as best friends in California and began singing and playing as teenagers. When Mark and Linda and their two children, Owen and Presley (also very talented), moved to Bend, Jim was able to again take full advantage of his nearly lifelong friendship with Mark and was also able to refresh his musical talents. Jim enthusiastically sang and played the guitar and the harmonica and, together with the Quons, Jim relished his occasional performances at local watering holes and events. Maybe most importantly, we had unforgettable times performing in our living room, complete with multiple microphones and amplifiers, serenading our mother and reveling in the approval of assembled friends and family.

Of course Jim was a frequent and exuberant participant in outdoor activities and his interests ran the gamut of Central Oregon recreation – hiking, biking, downhill skiing, cross country skiing, snowshoeing, geocaching, fishing, rafting, occasionally hunting with his brother, birding, or just taking pictures of all the fun. Fly fishing was a passion for Jim and he was good at it, but he was not a purist. There was no pretense in Jim and he always could be genuinely happy and engaged for hours trying to catch catfish or bluegill with a worm and a bobber with one or both of his sons.

Jim sometimes joked that his knowledge as a journalist was "an inch deep and a mile wide." He was partly right, he did know a little bit about a very wide range of diverse topics and it made him a remarkably good companion on a road trip or, if we were lucky, on an extended fishing expedition. But over the years he also learned a great deal about the geology, flora, fauna and human history of Central Oregon. And he became a competent woodsman, developing traditional skills and knowledge that are becoming increasingly rare today.

ABOUT JIM
By John Witty • continued

It was also evident that Jim cared very much about what was happening to the outdoor world he loved. He was deeply concerned that we were losing the amazing places and resources that were so important in his life. But in keeping with his personality and character, Jim was not dogmatic, even on something as dear to him as the environment. He listened carefully to the ideas and perspectives of those who held differing viewpoints and he tried hard to work his way thoughtfully through difficult environmental issues. His respect for the people he talked to and their opinions is consistently reflected in his writings.

Ann Ingham closed her poignant letter with the following passages:

"I will keep those stories that I have clipped and whenever I am anywhere outdoors exploring Central Oregon, I will think of you and hope that you are right beside me, enjoying the moment as I will be.

Over the years I have lost quite a number of relatives and friends and have developed a ritual of sorts. At this time of year I light a candle for those who have gone before me. This year as I light my candle, I will add your name, Jim, to my list of those whom I have loved, admired and respected during my lifetime. I wish it were not so."

Jim can rest assured that he has earned the love, admiration and respect of Ann, so many others he touched during his life and all of us who worked together to produce his book. There may be no higher tribute to a life well spent.

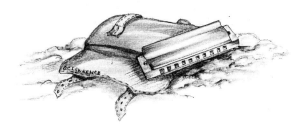

MESSAGE FROM MAP GUY

Dear Jim,

Wordsmiths. I have known few. "Mrs. Map Guy" would keep her eyes peeled for words that might stymie you. A couple of times she did — but you'd pull that word into your lexicon and craft it into your next story just to prove that you owned it. One thing confounded me, however, your penchant for "prolly." That simple three-syllable word - 'probably' - always came out "prolly" when you said it. And you said it a lot.

I'm prolly a little angry with you still. Less than I was, but a little. We were supposed to go for a hike the morning I got the call. I thought it was you telling me where to meet you for a breakfast burrito before our hike. Instead, it was your boss giving me bad news.

Just a couple of weeks before, we traveled on what would be our final outing together, a trip to Fish Lake and the Remount Station nearby, mostly to enjoy the vine maple's bright red glow against black lava. You told me you had just paid the final installment on a surgery that fixed your heart a couple of years earlier. Did it fix your heart? The answer only seemed to be as definite as "prolly."

Our friendship was born of convenience. You were hired at the newspaper where I worked. Each week you got out in the woods and wrote about it. I was working part-time, so you figured I could join you once in awhile. I agreed.

About 80 percent of what I saw on those trips was your backside. You led, I followed. You hiked hard. You stopped only to take in the scenery and take a few photographs for the story. You befriended any hikers on the trail and got their story. Initially, I'd pack extra water and an extra sandwich because I could figure you'd forget. A major regret now is that we never got a photo of us together on the trail. Not one. So now, when I hike with someone, I get that shot right away.

You were a purist. You insisted on riding your mountain bike for the entire ride, even up the steepest trails. I'd be walking mine, breathing hard, and you'd be bouncing alongside in alpine gear, going along at the same speed I was walking. It was the principle of the thing.

We were always on the lookout for wildlife, but never saw any. Your voice was big. For instance, your laugh carried clear to the other end of the newsroom. Speaking of the newsroom — it misses you. It's too quiet. We all miss your bright smile and your eternally upbeat attitude, your penchant for "prolly" and that big sound that was Jim Witty.

I was pretty good at navigation. That's why you dubbed me "Map Guy." I'd always bring a map and GPS. Unfortunately, it was a ruse. I have never been a navigator. You figured that out on several outings, like when we were riding mountain bikes from Mt. Bachelor to Lava Lake. We missed the turn and ended up riding Century Drive for 8 miles.

Your heart, Jim Witty, just wore out. You used it a lot. You partitioned it out to your family, a million friends and everyone you met. You handed it over — a giver that gave it all. Thanks for my portion.

How would you write those last few minutes on that cold morning in mid November, 2008? Would it be a conversation with The Man? Would He have asked you if you were ready to go on the outing of a lifetime? Would your answer be "Prolly?"

THE END OF THE ROLL

by Mark Quon

I found an old photogragh of Jim and me from a rafting trip down the Trinity river. It was the last photo on the roll (remember rolls?) and unfortunately Jim's image was cut off.

Fading away.

Just like in the photo, Jim's life was cut short.

But what a roll.

Many people who had met Jim briefly said they felt like they'd known him for years. I met Jim in 1973.

So the way I figure it, I've known him for centuries.

I was fortunate to spend his last five years on Earth with him here in Bend. We corresponded daily, played music and hiked regularly and occasionally went on middle-aged trips together.

And I almost always brought him bad luck while fishing.

I associate Bend and Central Oregon with Jim. So much so, that I now feel awkward being here without him. Like the feeling you get when you're inside someone else's house, waiting for them to come home.

A week after his death he appeared in a dream and asked me what had happened.

"Jim, you had a heart attack."

"Oh," he responded quietly.

Now he understands.

I've received plenty of "messages" from Jim since, despite the fact that I'm the type of person who would literally need to see his ghost standing in front of me before I believed.

I want to believe that Jim is trying to tell me he is at peace.

He lives on in the juniper and sage, Deschutes River, Cascades and Badlands.

You get the picture.

So this feeling of awkwardness is slowly passing. I'm realizing that I'm NOT sitting around in Jim's house waiting for him to come home.

Because he never really left.

A SPECIAL THANKS

from the Book Team

When we began working on the production of this book, not quite a year ago, we did not realize that we would have the privilege of being so inspired by the enduring qualities of friendship. Mark Quon, Jim's lifelong friend, worked tirelessly on this project - guiding the process and coordinating and encouraging our efforts.

We wanted our tribute to Jim's memory to be something the Central Oregon outdoor community would find useful and something Jim would have been proud of. We began to realize that the value of this book would come as much from the simple enjoyment of reading it as it would from discovering and visiting the places it describes. But what we did not realize was that the work also would bring our family and friends even closer together, something that would have pleased Jim greatly.

In the effort to turn this project into reality, Mark has been our leader, spending hundreds of hours of his valuable time and talent creating this book. He skillfully transformed our good intentions, good ideas and enthusiasm into page and picture reality. Mark showed a remarkable ability to take the ideas and opinions of seven strong-minded adults and meld them into a coherent whole. His strengths as a leader include guiding us with tact, good humor, and sensitivity, all the while realizing that we are bound together by both love and loss. Mark's contributions and sacrifices have been pure, selfless expressions of the significance and power of friendship. We will always be grateful.

The rest of the book team,
Lori Witty
Edna Witty
Joan Witty
John Witty
Deedee (Witty) Sihvonen
Alan Sihvonen
Linda Quon

ACKNOWLEDGMENTS

Gifts from the following donors helped make publication of this book possible. The Witty family is forever grateful to all who donated funds, in-kind gifts, time and resources.

Juniper Sponsor
John & Vivian Nosler

Sage Sponsor
Bend Education Association
Bend-La Pine Teacher's Union
Stuart & Arlene Brenner
Deschutes County Historical Society
Kathy & Craig Emerson
Bob & Louise Markland
Alex Morley
Peck Family Enterprises
Kathy Poncy

Lava Sponsor
Camp Sherman Store
Greg & Laurie Colvin
Nancy & Dennis Dempsey
Michael Haluska
Alan & Lillian Jones
Jo & Bryce Powell
Bob & Zannie Saw
David & Inez Shapiro
High Desert Education Service District
Peter Pedone
Pine Mountain Posse

In-Kind Donations
Book Mart
Breedlove Guitars
The Bulletin
Greg Burke
Gary Calicott
Cascade Cottons
Dudley's Bookshop
The Fly Fisher's Place
Forever Moments: Wendi King
Tim Gallivan

Grandma's Booty
Great Outdoor Clothing Co.
Dean Guernsey
Jenny Harada
Helen Holder
Hot Box Betty
Chris Huffine
ICE
Scott Johnson
Local Joe's
McMenamin's
The Open Book
Pavé Jewelers
Pine Tavern
Bryce Powell
Powell's Sweet Shop
Mike Putnam / Pacific Crest Stock
Linda & Mark Quon
REI
The Riverhouse
Bob Sant
Joe Schulte
Showcase Hats & Apparel
Laura Sihvonen
Silver Moon Brewing
Silverado
Bob Speik
Linda Spring
Alan D. St. John
Frankie Shepard Stapleton
Rick Steber
The Summit Saloon & Stage
Traditional Mountaineering
Vanilla Urban Threads
Volcano Vineyards
Wildflowers of Central Oregon
John & Joan Witty
Lori Witty

ACKNOWLEDGMENTS

Support
Ben & Cecille Anderson
Donell & Ed Arvin
Gary Asher
The Bulletin Staff
Greg Colvin
Devon Comstock
Denise & John Costa
Greg & Karen Cross
Dr. Kathleen Doty
Suzanne Doty
Brent Fenty
Eric Flowers
Kirsten Goldstein
Dean Guernsey
Ritama Haaga
Kelly Haluska
Brian Hanson
High Desert Museum
Helen Holder
Peter Howse
Matt Hyman
Ann Ingham
Dave Jasper
Julie Johnson
Ellen Jones
Mary Keating
Abby Martinez
Gretchen Lawrence
Gary Lewis
Map Guy
Maverick Publications
Michael McClure
Kelly Cannon-Miller
Alex Morley
Bill & Dorothy Olson
Jen Overton
The Quons
Tyler Reichert
Chris Sabo
Bob Sant
Denise Sevigny
Deedee (Witty) Sihvonen & Alan Sihvonen
Silver Moon Brewing Staff
The Source Staff
Bob Speik
Linda Spring
Frankie Stapleton
Rick Steber
Walt Sullins
Shawn Swisher
Ellen Waterston
Danny Witty
Edna Witty
John & Joan Witty
Keven Witty
Lexie Witty
Lori Witty

We apologize for any ommissions to our support list. There were so many people who offered their moral support during the production of this book. Many thanks!

Readers
The Witty family would like to deeply thank all of Jim's loyal readers for their kind words and support.

Map Guy
Who is he anyway?
    Jim mentions his good friend and frequent Outing companion "Map Guy" in many of his articles. There has been lots of speculation about the identity of Map Guy. Jim got a kick out of keeping his identity a secret.
    Map Guy had become an endearing companion — Jim's sidekick. If Jim was *Don Quixote*, then Map Guy was *Sancho Panza*. He was the butt of many jokes and Jim's comic foil. He took his ribbing and kept on ticking.
    There are a handful of people who know Map Guy's identity, and to those people we ask that they **hold on to that secret.**
    That's what Jim would have wanted.

ACKNOWLEDGMENTS

Gretchen Lawrence
Illustrator

    The illustrations featured in *Meet Me In The Badlands* are from the talented hands of Gretchen Lawrence, who creates her art from her home and studio in Mackay, Idaho. Gretchen returned to Mackay after schooling in Montana with a Bachelors Degree in Art from Boise State University in 1998.

    Gretchen expresses herself in all mixed media but is especially drawn to watercolor, pen and ink, and pencil. She also enjoys traditional crafts - sewing, quilting and restoring antique dolls. When she's not cutting firewood for winter or creating art, she finds time for gardening, fishing, antiquing and decorating. We much appreciate her willingness to lend her artistic talents to the production of *Meet Me In The Badlands*. Gretchen can be reached at gcl@atcnet.net.

Photographers
A special thank you to these photographers for donating their beautiful photos:

Greg Burke
Gary Calicott
Tim Gallivan
Scott Johnson
Mike Putnam / Pacific Crest Stock
Alan D. St. John

CONTACT INFORMATION

Bend-Fort Rock Ranger District of the Deschutes National Forest 541-383-4000
Bend Metro Park & Recreation District Office 541-389-7275
Bureau of Land Management 541-416-6700
Camp Sherman Store 541-595-6711
Cove Palisades State Park 541-546-3412
Crooked River National Grassland 541-475-9272
Deschutes River Conservancy 541-382-4077
  • Upper Deschutes Watershed Council 541-382-6103
Fort Rock (Oregon State Parks Information Center) 800-551-6949
Friends of the Oregon Badlands Wilderness
  • Web site ...... www.meetup.com/www-FriendsofOregonBadlandsWilderness-org
High Desert District, Oregon State Parks 541-388-6055
High Desert Museum 541-382-4754
  • Web site .... www.highdesertmuseum.com
John Day Fossil Beds 541-987-2333
John Day River (Central Oregon Visitors Center) 541-296-9778
John Day River (Dalles Dam) 541-506-7819
Lower Deschutes River Boater Pass
  • Web site .... www.boaterpass.com
McKenzie Ranger Station, Willamette National Forest 541-822-3381
Nature Conservancy 503-802-8100
Newberry National Volcanic Monument
  • Lava Lands Visitors Center 541-593-2421
Ochoco National Forest 541-416-6500
Oregon Department of Forestry 503-945-7200
Oregon Natural Desert Association (ONDA) 541-330-2638
Oregon Parks and Recreation Department State Parks 800-551-6949
  • Reservations 800-452-5687
  • General Information 503-986-0707
  • Web site .... www.Park.Info@state.or.us
Paulina Lake Lodge 541-536-2240
  • East Lake Resort & RV Park 541-536-2230
Sisters Ranger District of the Deschutes National Forest 541-549-7700
Sunriver Marina 541-593-3492
U.S. Forest Service 800-832-1355
Don and Linda Wallace: Upland Bird Hunting Packages: 541-419-3923
Willamette National Forest 541-225-6300

INDEX

A Sand County Almanac, 5
Abbey, Edward, 26, 27, 31, 33, 183, 185
Alder Creek Canoe & Kayak, 261
Ana Reservoir, 49
Ana River, 48, 50
Antelope Flat Reservoir, 241, 242
Antelope, 244, 245
Applegate, Lindsay and Elizabeth, 247
Arnold Ice Cave, 45, 46
Arvin, Donell, 273, 281
Arvin, Ed, 281
Aspen Hall, 164
Badland's Dry Canyon, 24, 25
Badland's Rock, 35
Badlands WSA, 4, 11, 13, 14, 20, 22, 23, 24, 25, 35, 39, 34, 38, 39, 253, 255, 264, 267
Bald Eagles, 136, 171, 225
Barber, Rex, 198
Bass, 242, 247
Basin and Range, 50
Belknap Crater, 147
Bell, Thomas, 188
Bend-Fort Rock Ranger District of the Deschutes National Forest, 283
Bend Glacier, 98
Bend Metro Park and Recreation District, 164, 283
Benham Falls, 102, 103, 111, 158, 258, 259, 267, 268
Benson Lake, 148
Berrin, Larry, 38, 39, 61, 121, 255
Bessie Butte, 67
Big Cultus Lake, 80
Big Eddy, 111
Big Lake, 152
Big Obsidian Flow Trail, 70
Big Summit District, 203
Big Summit Prairie, 209, 210
Bingham Prairie, 212
Birding, 38, 40, 41, 42, 114, 135, 171, 189, 199, 216, 219, 224
Birds of Oregon Field Guide, 42
Birds of Oregon, 225
Birds of the High Desert, 38, 39

Birds of the Inland Northwest and Northern Rockies, 78
Birdwatching, See Birding
Bishop, Ellen Morris, 202
Black Butte, 135, 243
Black Crater, 148
Blow Lake, 119
Blue Bed, 239
Blue Pool, 160
Boating, 246
Boating, non-motorized, 122, 171, 199, 260
Boone, Daniel, 6
Booth Lake, 177
Borden Beck Wildlife Preserve, 237
Bowman Dam, 184, 242, 253
Bowman Museum, 206
Boyd Cave, 45
Brenner, Arlene, 280
Brenner, Stuart, 120, 280
Bridge 99, 135, 136: See also Lower Bridge
Broken Top, 33, 83, 96, 97, 133
Brothers Stage Stop, 18, 27
Brothers, 18, 19, 20, 27, 28, 33, 71
Brown Trout, 69
Brown, Bill, 19
Bull Trout, 136
Bulletin, The, 3, 6, 13, 57, 77, 273, 274, 278, 280, 281
Bureau of Land Management, 14, 30, 31, 37, 209, 283
Burke, Greg, 11, 22, 215, 280, 282
Burma Road, 226
Butte Trail, 100
Buzzard Rock, 32
C.O.D. Trail, 89, 90
Cabin Lake, 16, 40, 41, 42, 54
Caddis Fly, 50
Calicott, Gary, 103, 170, 259, 280, 282
Camp Polk Cemetery, 141
Camp Polk Meadow, 142
Camp Sherman General Store and Deli, 167, 169, 283
Camp Sherman, 135, 167, 168, 169

INDEX

Camping, 40, 53, 64, 112, 171, 172, 199, 205, 208, 219, 238, 241, 246, 266
Camping, horse, 141
Candle Creek, 135, 136
Canoeing, 110, 221
Canyon Wren, 139
Canyoneering, 229
Castle Crest Trail, 130
Caves, 14, 33, 45, 46, 47, 52, 60, 62, 68
Cemeteries, 140
Central Oregon Bentonite Company, 28
Central Oregon Map, 8, 9
Central Oregon Place Names: Crook County, 200
Central Oregon Trail Alliance, 88, 205
Chance, Paul, 229, 230
Chickahominy Reservoir, 33
Chimney Rock, 184
China Hat Butte, 53, 54
China Hat Road, 45
China Hat, 46, 55
Chitwood, Larry, 66
Christmas Valley, 52
Chukar, 71
Civilian Conservation Corps, 19, 145, 162
Clarno Palisades, 244
Clarno Unit, 243, 244
Classic Central Oregon, 251
Clear Lake Campground, 160
Clear Lake, 159, 169
Cleetwood Cove, 130
Cline Falls, 102, 237
Cole Loop Trail, 205, 207
Colson, Joellen, 263
Columbia River Basin, 246
Columbia River, 246, 247, 248
Columbia Southern Canal, 173
Colvin, Greg, 280, 281
Colvin, Laurie, 280
Comstock, Debbie, 281
Confederated Tribes of Warm Springs, 187, 219
Corbet, Mark, 56
Corral Loop, 204
Costa, Denise, 6, 281
Costa, John, 6, 273, 281

Country Mall, 2, 92
Cove Palisades State Park, 189
Cow Cave, 60
Cowboy Dinner Tree, 50
Coyote Butte, 67
Crack in the Ground, 52
Crane Prairie Reservoir, 80, 114, 115
Crater Lake Lodge, 130
Crater Lake National Park Pumice Desert, 129
Crater Lake National Park, 128, 129
Crater Rim Trail, 66
Cresent Moon, 86
Crooked River, 184, 185, 189, 190, 221, 223, 226, 228, 253, 254; See also North Fork Crooked River
Crooked River Canyon, 183, 184, 225
Crooked River Gorge, 197, 198
Crooked River High Bridge, 198
Crooked River National Grasslands, 141, 193, 194, 196, 205, 283
Crooked River Ranch, 186, 188, 217
Cross, Karen, 84, 281
Cross-country Skiing, See Nordic Skiing
Crow, Jason, 28
Curley, Paul, 96, 97
Davis Lake, 80
Day, John, 247
Dayville, 244
Dee Wright Observatory, 148, 161, 162
Deep Creek Campground, 208, 210
Derrick Cave, 33
Deschutes Basin Land Trust, 142
Deschutes Brewery & Public House, 191
Deschutes National Forest, 17, 42, 47, 56, 66, 67, 95, 100, 104, 124, 148, 162, 163, 172, 174, 179
Deschutes River Canyon, 229
Deschutes River Conservancy, 187, 237, 283
Deschutes River Trail, 103, 111, 168, 258, 268
Deschutes River, 102, 111, 216, 258, 268; See also Upper, Lower and Middle Deschutes River
Deschutes, 214
Desert Solitaire, 27
Detroit Lake, 158

INDEX

Devils Garden, The, 33
Devils Lake, 80
Dillon Falls, 111, 268
Donald M. Kerr Birds of Prey Center, 126
Doris Lake, 119
Doty, Dr. Kathleen, 281
Doty, Suzanne, 281
Dry Canyon, 137, 138
Drake Park, 168
Dry River Trail, 39
Dutchman Flat, 100, 108, 109, 116
Eagle, 224, 225
East Lake, 6, 70
Edwards, Leta, 59
Egertson, Chris, 25
Elk Lake, 79, 80, 108, 109
Entrada Lodge, 89, 90
Fall Color, 143, 164, 168
Fall Creek, 80
Fall River Fish Hatchery, 81
Fall River, 77, 78
Farewell Bend Park, 260, 268
Fenty, Brent, 39, 281
Field Guide to Birds of North America, 41
Fish Lake Guard Station, 145
Fish Lake Remount Depot, 145
Fish Lake Remount Station, 143
Fish Lake, 143, 144, 145
Fishing Central Oregon and Beyond, 115
Fishing Central Oregon, 50
Fishing, 48, 77, 114, 120, 122, 135, 152, 157, 168, 171, 186, 199, 216, 219, 232, 235, 241, 246, 253, 266
Fishing, Youth, 164
Fitzhenry, Thad, 225
Flagline Trail, 100
Flatiron Rock, 13
Flowers, Eric, 281
Fly Fisher's Place, 166
Folley Waters, 187
Forest Service Campground, 64, 172
Fort Rock (State Park), 16, 40, 42, 51, 52, 53, 59, 60, 283
Fort Rock Valley, 33
Fossil, 244
Four Wheelers, 16, 17
Frederick Butte, 18, 19, 20, 72
Freemont Meadow, 174
Fricke, Kevin, 268
Fuzztail Butte, 32
Gallimaufry, The, 167
Gallivan, Tim, 75, 122, 243, 280, 282
Geneva, 140
Geo-cacheing, 96, 221, 229, 230
Gerry Mountain WSA, 29, 30, 31
Giordano, Pete, 262
Giovanni's Mountain Pizza, 158
Glass Buttes, 33
Golden Eagle, 174, 189, 217, 224, 225
Golden, Brett, 237
Golden-mantled Ground Squirrels, 161
Goldstein, Kirsten, 85, 281
Goodrich, Bob, 59
Goody's, 91, 92
Gottberg Anderson, John, 69, 281
Grand Slam Trail, 90
Grandview Cemetery, 140
Gray Butte, 205, 206
Great Basin, 14, 25, 38, 49, 50, 257
Great Blue Heron, 217, 220
Great Horned Owl, 39, 42
Green Drake Hatch, 136
Green Lakes, 80, 82, 83, 124
Grizzly Mountain, 205
Guernsey, Dean, 36, 68, 94, 280, 282
Guide to Fly Fishing Central and Southeastern Oregon, 50
Hackleman Creek, 144
Haluska, Kelly, 125, 256, 273, 281
Haluska, Mike, 256
Halvorson, Ron, 37
Hampton, 33
Hancock Field Station, 245
Hand Lake Trailhead, 148
Hart Mountain, 243
Hatfield, Doc and Connie, 27
Hawaii Tribune Herald, 94
Hawaii, 61, 62, 93, 94, 273

INDEX

Hayrick Butte, 153
Haystack Butte, 194, 195
Haystack Reservoir, 191, 192
Heath, Corey, 16
Heart Attack, 5, 278
High Desert, 14, 15, 16, 19, 20, 21, 22, 26, 27, 32, 36, 37, 38, 39, 40, 46, 49, 52, 54, 57, 71, 117, 125, 126, 142, 172, 192, 194, 216, 256, 257, 263, 267
High Desert District, Oregon State Parks, 283
High Desert Museum, 38, 46, 121, 125, 126, 127, 255, 257, 281, 283
Hiking Oregon's Geology, 202
Hiking, 13, 18, 21, 24, 29, 34, 36, 38, 43, 48, 61, 64, 69, 77, 79, 82, 96, 102, 110, 112, 114, 118, 120, 135, 137, 143, 146, 149, 152, 157, 161, 164, 171, 173, 176, 178, 183, 186, 189, 191, 199, 201, 216, 221, 224, 226, 229, 253, 256, 264, 266
Hill, Geoff, 50
Hindman, Samuel and Jane, 141
Hoagland, Edward, 72
Hoffman Island Trail, 61, 63
Holder, Helen, 130, 280, 281
Hole in the Ground, 52
Hole of Inaccessibility Cache, The, 230
Holt, John, 223
Horse Butte, 57, 58, 67
Horse Ridge, 16, 20, 22, 33, 264, 265
Hosmer Lake, 80
Houston, Ryan, 155
Howse, Peter, 189, 281
Hughes, Dave, 214
Hunting, 71
Hutchens, Lisa, 20
Ice Skating, 91
In-Kind, 280
Independent Mine, 209, 210
Indian Canyon, 244
Indian Park Campground, 220
Ingham, Ann, 272, 274, 276, 281
IPASS, 234
Irish Lake, 105, 106
Jackman, E.R., 36

Jasper, Dave, 57, 281
John Day Dam, 246, 247, 248
John Day Fossil Beds National Monument, 243
John Day Fossil Beds, 243, 283
John Day River, 245, 246, 247, 248, 283
Johnson, Julie, 281
Johnson, Scott, 66, 70, 201, 280, 282
Jones, Ellen, 81, 227, 281
Joslin, Les, 97, 118, 144
Journey Home, The, 183
Judy, John, 214, 232
Juniper Butte, 194, 195
Juniper Rim Ranch, 72
Juniper, 21, 23, 53, 55
Juniper, tallest, 53, 55
Kalapana, 94
Kaufman, Kenn, 41
Kenny, Judith Keyes, 247
Kerr, Andy, 17
Kerr, Donald M., 125, 127
Kilauea Volcano, 94
Kimberly, 247
Kissing the Trail, 159, 160
Kliewer, Pat, 142
KO Butte, 33
Kocher, Marge, 96, 97
Koosah Falls, 160
La Pine, 51
Lafollett, Capt. Charles, 141
Laidlaw Oddfellows Tumalo Cemetery, 142
Laing, John, 244
Lake Billy Chinook, 135, 136, 140, 142, 169, 187, 189, 190, 191, 217, 220, 224, 229, 231, 237, 253, 254
Lake County, 40
Lake Millican, 25
Lake Simtustus, 219, 220
Lapat, Mike, 109
Last Chance Ridge, 19
Lava Butte, 57, 58, 259, 266
Lava Camp Lake Trailhead, 156, 178
Lava Cast Forest, 61, 62
Lava Island Falls, 111
Lava Lake, 80

INDEX

Lava Lands National Monument, 58, 283
Lava Lands Visitor Center, 95, 258, 266, 283
Lava River Cave, 45, 46
Lava River Interpretive Trail, 162
Lawrence, Gretchen, 42, 50, 60, 86, 98, 139, 156, 185, 200, 201, 206, 214, 220, 230, 233, 240, 281, 282
Lazinka Sawmill, 127
Le Page Park, 246, 247, 248
Leeches, 107
Lemish Lake, 105
Lent, Steve, 200, 206
Leopold, Aldo, 5
Lewis, G. Brad, 95
Lewis, Gary, 281
Lion in the Water, 247
Little Crater Trail, 66
Little Cultus Lake, 80, 105
Little Lava Lake, 80
Little Three Creek Lake, 172
Loggerhead Shrike, 42
Lost Forest, 52
Lost Lake Trail, 66
Lower Bridge, 135, 235, 237
Lower Deschutes River, 215, 219, 232, 234, 283
Lucky Lake, 118, 119
Lupine Trail, 86
Mack's Canyon, 214
MacPherson, Bill, 188
Madras, 219
Mahogany Butte, 33
Mallory, Andrew, 108
Mallory, George, 108
Map Guy, 53, 55, 60, 87, 89, 91, 99, 100, 105, 116, 118, 119, 143, 149, 178, 221, 253, 272, 277, 281
Map Guy, Mrs., 116, 117, 221, 253
Map, Central Oregon, 8, 9
Marks, Charity Ann, 145
Marlett, Bill, 22, 31
Martinez, Abby, 281
Maury Mountains, 241, 242
Maxwell, Lori, 165
McClure, Michael, 159, 216, 218, 281

McClure, Willie, 159
McCoin, Julius and Sarah, 206
McKenzie Highway, 146, 168
McKenzie Pass, 146, 148, 161, 162, 169
McKenzie River Trail, 159
McKenzie River, 143
McKenzie River Station, 283
McPhee, John, 50
Meadow Camp, 103
Meadow Picnic Area, 110, 268
Meissner Shelter, 86
Metolius Recreation Association, 169
Metolius River, 135, 167, 168
Mi Casa, 244
Middle Deschutes River, 187, 216, 235, 237
Mike Putnam, 133, 280, 281
Mill City, 157, 158
Mill Creek Wilderness, 202, 211, 212
Mill Creek, 211
Millican Trail, 156
Millican, 15, 16, 18, 33
Mirror Pond, 262
Misery Ridge, 226, 227
Mitchell, 20, 243
Monkey Face, 227
Moore, Andrew, 13
Morley, Alex, 143, 280, 281
Motorcycles, 16
Mount Bachelor, 79, 117, 121, 122, 194
Mount Jefferson Wilderness, 176
Mount Mazama, 52, 65, 128
Mount Washington Wilderness, 152
Mountain Biking, 64, 87, 112, 159, 164, 205, 226, 264
Mountain Man Trading Post, 166
Mrazek Trail, 174
National Speleological Society, 46
National Wild and Scenic River, 219
National Wilderness Preservation System, 14
Newberry Crater, 62, 64, 65
Newberry National Volcanic Monument, 43, 44, 61, 66, 67, 68, 69, 93, 94, 95, 258, 259, 283
Newhard, Joy, 229
Nordic Club, 204

INDEX

Nordic Skiing, 203, 263
North American Pronghorn Foundation, 20
North Fork Crooked River, 208, 209
North Fork John Day River, 247
North Matthieu Lake, 179
North Santiam River, 157, 158
North Santiam State Park, 157, 158
North Waldo Campground, 113
Northwest Trees, 150
O'Donnell, Linda and Jody, 265
Obernolte Trailhead, 23
Obsidian Flow Trail, 66
Ochoco Chapter of the Oregon Nordic Club, 204
Ochoco Mountains, 203, 212
Ochoco National Forest, 199, 203, 208, 283
Ogden, Peter Skene, 198
Olallie Campground, 143
Olallie Creek, 143
Old McKenzie Highway, 169
Old Mill District, The, 260
Old Santiam Wagon Road, 144
Ollerton, Micha, 263
Omnibus Public Lands Management Act, 14, 23, 35, 39, 255
On the Loose, 26
Oregon Badlands Wilderness, 14, 23, 35, 39, 255,
Oregon Department of Fish and Wildlife, 49, 171, 200
Oregon Department of Forestry, 21, 283
Oregon Desert, The, 36
Oregon Desert Guide, 17
Oregon Geographic Names, 172
Oregon Museum of Science and Industry, 245
Oregon Natural Desert Association, 31, 283
Oregon Scenic Waterway, 247
Oregon State Parks, 190, 283
Oregon Trunk Railroad Bridge, 198
Oregon's Outback National Scenic Byway, 51
Osprey Point, 114
Osprey, 114, 136, 153, 171
Otter, 126, 257
Ottenfeld, Bruce, 165
Overton, Jen, 274, 281

Pacific Crest Stock, 133, 282
Pacific Crest Trail Association, 179
Pacific Crest Trail, 106, 146, 147, 156; See also PCT
Painted Hills Unit, 243, 244
Paisley, 51
Paradise Campground, 160
Park, Ed, 126
Parrilla Grill, 175
Patjens Lakes Trailhead, 152
Patjens Lakes, 152, 153
Paulina Creek, 69, 70
Paulina Falls, 43, 69
Paulina Lake, 64, 65, 66, 69, 70
Paulina Lake Lodge, 283
Paulina Peak, 66, 70
Paulina Prairie Cemetery, 142
Paulina Springs Book Company, 167
Pauls, Brady, 198
PCT, 106, 147, 179; See also Pacific Crest Trail
Peck Family Enterprises, 280
Pelton Park, 220
Pelton Wildlife Overlook, 220
Pelton-Round Butte Dam, 187, 217, 219, 220
Peninsula Plateau, 190
Peter Skene Ogden State Wayside, 197
Peter Skene Ogden Trail, 66
Phantom Ship, 129
Phil's Trail, 89, 90
Philippi Park, 248
Photographers, 282
Pictographs, 25, 39
Pine Mountain Sports, 116
Pine Mountain, 15, 16, 27, 33, 37
Porcupine, 125
Portland General Electric, 142, 217, 219
Post, 28, 242
Powell, Bryce, 280
Powell, Jo, 280
Powell's Sweet Shop, 280
Prescott, Mike and Carolee, 159
Prescott, Monte, 159
President Obama, 14, 23, 35, 39, 255
Preston, Richard, 150

INDEX

Priday Beds, 239
Prineville Reservoir, 184, 221, 223, 242, 253, 254
Prineville, 28, 203, 208, 211
Pronghorn (Antelope), 18, 20
Putnam, Mike, 133, 282
Quartz Mountain, 33
Quinn, Billy, 115
Quon, Linda, 2, 84, 87, 253, 268, 274, 275, 279, 280, 281
Quon, Mark, 2, 4, 72, 137, 173, 175, 178, 191, 193, 216, 247, 253, 271, 273, 274, 275, 278, 279, 280
Quon, Owen, 262, 274, 275
Quon, Presley, 107, 274, 275
Ramberg, Anders, 102
Ray Atkeson Memorial Trail, 80, 122
Reese Cemetery, 142
Rex T. Barber Veterans Memorial Bridge, 197
Richardson, Johnnie and Norma, 238
Richardson's Recreational Ranch, 238, 240
Rim Drive, 128, 129
River Otter, 126
Riverfest, 235, 237
Robbin's Homestead Cabin, 127
Rock Climbing, 224, 226
Rockhounding, 238
Round Lake Christian Camp, 176
Round Lake, 176, 177
Round Mountain Trail, 200, 203, 204, 210
Rufus, 247
Russell, Terry and Renny, 26
Sabo, Chris, 162, 281
Sage Grouse, 17
Sage Hen Valley, 33
Sahalie Falls, 160
San Gabriel River, 235, 236
Sand Spring, 33
Sanderson, Bill, 158
Sandver, Donna, 171, 172
Sandver, Jerry, 172
Saporito, Fred, 89
Satellite Personal Tracker (SPOT), 7
Saw, Bob & Zannie, 280
Schelz, Mare and Hayden, 260

Schubert, John, 173
Scott Lake, 147, 148
Scott Pass, 155
Scotts Pass Trailhead, 155
Senoj Lake, 118, 119
Service Creek, 247
Shadow Bay Campground and Islet, 113
Shadow Bay, 113
Sheep Rock Unit, 243, 244
Shevlin Park, 164, 173, 174
Shevlin Pond, 164, 165
Shifting Sand Dunes, 52
Shopping, 166
Shoreline Trail, 112, 113
Sierra Club, 26
Sihvonen, Alan, 2, 274, 279, 281
Sihvonen, Deedee, 2, 3, 274, 275, 279, 281
Silica Trail, 66
Silver Lake, 50
Simtustus, Pipsher, 220
Sisters Coffee Company, 166
Sisters, 166
Sisters Ranger District, 283
Skeleton Cave, 45, 46
Skeleton Rock, 221
Skull Hollow, 205, 206
Smith Rock State Park, 181, 206, 224, 226, 227, 228
Smith, John, 227
Smokey's Gate, 230
Snake River, 32, 243
Snavely, Brook, 50
Sno-Cap, 149, 167
Snomobiling, 108
Snowboarding, 117
Snowshoeing, 84, 85, 116, 117, 203
Soda Creek Trail, 80, 82
Soda Creek, 82, 83
Soggy Sneakers: A Paddler's Guide to Oregon's Rivers, 262
Soldier's Cap, 19
South Matthieu Lake, 178, 179
South Pyramid Creek Trail, 149, 150, 151
South Pyramid Creek, 149

INDEX

South Waldo Lake Shelter, 113
Sparks Lake, 80, 122, 123, 124, 175
Sparks, Lige, 124
Spawning Beds, 233
Speik, Bob, 35, 84, 87, 96, 97, 108, 173, 174, 175, 229, 230, 231, 253, 264, 280, 281
Spelunking, 45, 46
Sponsors, 280
Square Lake, 176, 177
Squaw Creek, 167, 229, 230
St. John, Alan D., 181, 280, 282
Steber, Rick, 3, 4, 5, 280, 281
Steelhead Falls, 186, 187, 216, 217
Steelhead, 157, 214
Stegner, Wallace, 119
Steins Pillar, 201, 202
Stinking Water Pass, 32
Sullins, Walt, 103, 273, 281
Summer Lake Wildlife Area, 50
Summer Lake, 49
Sunday Drive, 15, 18, 26, 29, 32, 36, 48, 51, 53, 55, 67, 69, 79, 93, 105, 140, 143, 157, 166, 168, 183, 194, 197, 201, 219, 224, 243, 256, 266
Sundown Canyon, 186
Sunriver Lodge, 92
Sunriver Marina, 261, 283
Sunriver Village Mall, 91, 92
Sunriver, 81, 103
Support, 281
Suttle Lake, 167
Swamp Wells, 67, 68
Swampy Lakes Sno-park, 100
Swede Ridge Shelter, 100
Swisher, Shawn, 281
Tam McArthur Rim, 172
Tam-a-lau Trail, 189, 190
Tamolitch Falls, 159
Tangent Loop, 86
Tastee Treet, 208
Taylor Lake, 106
Teel, Harry, 50
Tekiela, Stan, 42, 225
Telemark Skiing, 117
Tenas Lake, 148
Ten-Mile Sno-park, 43, 70
Tenino Indians, 247
Terrebonne, 195
Tetherow Crossing, 237
Three Creek Lake, 171, 172
Three Pyramids Trailhead, 150
Three Sisters Wilderness, 82, 118, 119, 155
Three Sisters, 98, 133
Thundereggs, 238, 239, 240
Tinniswood, Bill, 49, 50
Tired Horse Reservoir, 32
Todd Lake Trail, 83
Todd Lake, 79, 84, 96, 120, 121
Trail of Molten Land, The, 258
Trout, 49, 50, 65, 69, 70, 78, 81, 82, 102, 104, 106, 107, 111, 112, 114, 115, 121, 124, 125, 126, 136, 137, 139, 144, 153, 154, 155, 157, 164, 165, 169, 171, 177, 199, 200, 210, 217, 218, 219, 220, 232, 233, 235, 236, 237, 241, 242, 254
Trout Creek Swamp, 154
Trout Creek Wetland Restoration Project, 155
Trout Creek, 232
Tumalo Creek Trail, 173, 174
Tumalo Creek, 164, 173, 257
Tumalo Falls, 257, 268
Tumalo Langlauf Club, 264
Tumalo Mountain, 116
Tumalo State Park, 102, 237, 267
Turkey Vulture, 185
Twin Pillars Trailhead, 212
Twin Pillars, 212
Umatilla Plateau, 243
Uncle Sam's Cabins, 144
University of Southern California, (USC), 274, 275
Upper Deschutes Basin, 142
Upper Deschutes River, 102, 110, 189
Upper Deschutes Watershed Council, 154, 283
U.S. Forest Service, 42, 144, 154, 155, 173, 283
Vermont Birds: An Introduction to a Familiar Species, 38
Vidae Falls, 130
Village Green, 167

INDEX

Virginia Meissner Sno-park, 85, 101, 263, 264
Vista Butte Sno-park, 99, 100
Vista Butte, 100
Waldo Lake Wilderness, 113
Waldo Lake, 112, 113
Wallace, Don and Linda, 19, 72, 283
Wallace, Lonnie, 72
Walton Lake, 199, 204
Walton Sno-park, 204
Walton, Izaak, 200
Wanoga Sno-park, 108
Warm Springs, 219, 232
Waterfalls, 43, 44, 66, 70, 110, 130
Water Skiing, 152
Waterin' Hole Tavern, 51, 59
Weasel Butte, 32, 67
Weaver, Lola, 28
Wednesdays Trail, 86
Western Big-eared Bat, 46
Wild Trees, The, 150
Whistler Point, 212
White Rock Campground, 212
White, Roger, 136, 167, 169
Whychus Creek, 142
Wickiup Reservoir, 80
Wild and Scenic River, 69
Wildcat Campground, 212
Wilderness Concept and the Three Sisters Wilderness, The, 98, 119
Wilderness Study Area, 13, 20, 23, 25, 29, 30, 31, 34, 35, 39, 225, 264, 267
Will, Kyle, 84
Williamette National Forest, 152, 283
Wind Cave, 45, 46
Wing, Raven, 50
Winopee Lake Trail, 119
Wise, Ted, 107
Witty, Daniel or Danny, 3, 91, 92, 105, 107, 125, 210, 212, 273, 281
Witty, Edna, 2, 274, 275, 279, 281
Witty, Jim, 2, 3, 4, 5, 6, 7, 271, 272, 273, 274, 275, 276, 277, 278, 279
Witty, Joan, 2, 274, 279, 280, 281
Witty, John, 2, 3, 7, 71, 272, 274, 276, 279, 280, 281
Witty, Keven, 3, 254, 273, 274, 275, 281
Witty, Lexie, 274, 281
Witty, Lori, 2, 5, 165, 271, 273, 279, 280, 281
Witty, Vince, 275
Wizard Island, 128, 130
Wright, Dee, 162
Wright, Kathy, 46
Zilly, John, 159